A WORLD OF CURRIES

A World of
CURRIES

AN INTERNATIONAL COOKBOOK

Ruth Philpott Collins

AVENEL BOOKS • NEW YORK

0-517-120097
Copyright © MCMLXVII by Ruth Philpott Collins
Library Of Congress Catalog Card Number: 67-28077
All rights reserved.
This edition is published by Avenel Books
a division of Crown Publishers, Inc.
by arrangement with Funk & Wagnalls
a   b   c   d   e   f   g   h
Manufactured in the United States Of America

CONTENTS

FOREWORD

ONE OF the earliest cookbooks we know of (*Kheme Sharma*) was compiled in the fifth century A.D. by a Brahmin named Sheta Karma who had gathered his material from the Vedas, Upanishads, and other sacred books of the Hindus. In it he told how the temple priests experimented for long years with native herbs and spices, finally evolving a dish worthy of offering to their gods, and one which would benefit their people—CURRY.

Curry, from the Tamil word *kari*, means simply meat or food, but meat blended in a manner to provide man with nutriment for his body, appeal to his senses of taste and smell, and aesthetic qualities to satisfy his artistic nature.

The Hindu prayer book, the Bhagavad Gita, deals with the three classes of man's food: the nutritive which gives health, longevity, clear intellect; the strong, salted foods which increase the passions and rouse fighting blood; and the stale impure ones which lead to the deterioration of the body and to death. These sacred texts also stress the importance of the preparation of the curry dishes, and indeed this preparation has over the centuries become a fine art.

Today curry still remains literally a dish for the gods throughout all India. The devout Hindu still places the first portion of his meal, prepared with ritualistic prayer, at the foot of the tulasi tree in his courtyard, where the gods, in the form of birds or beggars, may partake of it. On feast days he carries a flower-decked tray to the temple where the great stone Siva shares it with a priest or a sacred bull.

Curry forms the one main meal of the day for the vast majority of those millions of India's Hindus and Pakistan's Moslems. Its use has spread through Burma, Malaysia, and around the East Coast up as far as Hong Kong. It is always the most popular item on the *tiffin* (big breakfast or luncheon) menu on Orient-bound liners.

The *pukka sahibs*, those long-time European residents of India, have figures to prove that only those foreigners who eat this hot dish daily can withstand the debilitating climate for any length of time.

And those little hole-in-the-wall curry houses down in India Dock Road in London, or those hiding by the waterfronts in New York and San Francisco—places not listed in elegant food magazines—are always crowded with old-timers reminiscing amid the pungent odors of curry spices.

In the following pages I share with my readers some of the many recipes I gathered during the years I spent in the Orient. Many were secret recipes which had been treasured in families for generations; others were obtained from *mem-sahibs*, the wives of army officers and tea planters, who had struggled long with native cooks; and some were given to me by missionaries who had run big hospitals, using what was available in nearby villages to acquire a rich supply of tasty dishes. A few were wheedled from chefs of world-famous hotels or ocean-going steamships.

Many of the recipes, however, are those which I had to evolve for myself after returning to America, where I found it impossible to obtain authentic spices or other ingredients that went into the making of a *pukka* curry. By much experimentation, by trial and error, I was finally able to produce in my American kitchen dishes acceptable to nostalgic exiles from the Orient as well as to the adventurous novices at home. I believe them to be fair samples of the world's most exotic and flavorful food—curry.

RUTH PHILPOTT COLLINS

A WORLD OF CURRIES

Chapter 1

HOW TO SERVE CURRY

IN THIS DAY of fast travel, tastes in food are fast becoming changed. The American tourist or businessman who only a few hours before was eating an intriguing curry high over the Himalayas is more than likely to say to his wife that next weekend, "Let's have one of those curries for the crowd instead of a barbecue." And he may call for a curry the next time he goes into that downtown hotel.

Servicemen who have been in the Far East have acquired a taste for Eastern foods. They will not be satisfied nor deceived when a bilious yellow sauce hiding a few shrimps or bits of warmed-over meat is offered them as curry. More than likely, these amateur cooks will take it on themselves to show how to prepare a curry. They know well that the proper ingredients and the proper service, dishes, garnishes, and accompaniments do much to enhance the meal and make a suitable background for the yarns of their adventures.

Today importers are well aware of this trend in eating and have stocked their shelves with many Indian foods.

Rice is the first ingredient to think of. The instant rice now on all market shelves serves well for hurry-up occasions, but the ordinary rice is more nourishing for everyday use. The whole-grain brown rice is preferred by Indians, but it is less appetizing in appearance than the showy white polished rice. Rice should be freshly cooked to be at its best. Leftovers will not do for making curries.

As to spices and curry powders, if a shop specializing in spices is available, the adventurous cook may buy and blend her own powder, but in most shops the spices are seldom fresh enough to give the desired result. Many American women enthusiasts are now growing their own herbs and spices except for those which grow in the Tropics. A good imported commercial curry powder, which is made and bottled in India, is usually the safest to use.

Apart from the cooking, much of the appeal of a curry meal depends on the way it is served. In the big cities of India today many of the educated people have adopted European ways of dining at the table, using china and cutlery, but the vast majority still cling to the authentic native customs—a reed mat spread out on the clean-swept floor of the courtyard, with plantain leaves for plates. The one big mound of fluffy cooked rice is surrounded by numerous small bowls filled with all sorts of flavorful surprises. The tray will be garlanded with fragrant petals of frangipani, rose, and marigold in a profusion of beauty once deemed an oriental fable, but in fact, just a real curry dinner. The bowls may be gold and gem-studded if the host happens to be a rajah, or they may be brass or even clay, but the contents will be just as intriguing. I have counted as many as twenty of these mystery bowls at a feast-day table of an ordinary village offical.

For everyday use for the small family, a Lazy Susan is invaluable, with the tempting bowls of sauces and relishes whirling around on it. For a proper buffet setting for a party, first arrange a huge mound of snowy cooked rice, fretted with nuts, puffed raisins, and flower petals. Place the small bowls of curried meat and sauces of different kinds about this. Arrange petals of fresh flowers and fresh mint or watercress leaves in and around them. For a unique touch, do as the native houseboys still do so often— outline words in rose petals at one end of the table, such as "welcome" or the name of an honored guest. Here is an opportunity for the hostess to make use of those little bowls or souvenir dishes so long hidden on the shelf; fill them with relishes and chutneys. This is a chance too to bring out mother's crystal finger bowls; add a flower petal or a sliver of lemon to the water. Desserts, confections, and relishes should all be put on the buffet together, for the Indian eats his sweet along with his curry if he so pleases. Here the host should make use of the fine assortment of tropical or semitropical fruits now so widely offered in our markets—oranges, fresh figs, mangoes, papayas, bananas.

Sweet Turkish coffee is usually served at the end of a formal meal and ground aniseed is passed after that, usually in some dainty silver box; the guest takes just a pinch between finger and thumb and puts it on the tip of his tongue.

In America most diners eat daintily, taking up a dab of sauce along with a little rice. Others, usually the old-timers, mix everything together—and this is quite permissible—and eat with relish. The Westernized Indian in the cities eats with utensils and on dishes as do the Europeans, but the orthodox man of the village, even the well-to-do, eats daintily with his right hand, using thumb and finger to mold tiny balls of rice; he dips the rice ball into the bowl of sauce and flips it deftly into his mouth. He then uses the inevitable little brass finger bowl. If you are not eating with the fingers, use a large spoon such as a dessert spoon, and a fork if needed. Knives are never used. The old-timer on an Orient liner can be spotted at once by the way he serves, mixes, and eats his curry with a spoon.

Curry meat sauces sometimes improve by being cooked a day ahead of time and being reheated. However, dry curries, such as *pulaos* and *birianas*, made with fish, vegetables, or meats, must be cooked fresh always and cannot be reheated. This is one of the secrets of serving a curry meal—everything must be freshly prepared.

Chapter 2

SPICES FOR CURRY

IN THE BIG CITIES of India today, with their modern Westernized supermarkets, many people are now using commercial brands of bottled curry powders, but in the villages, where ninety per cent of the population still lives, the housewife rises as of old at dawn, lights her tiny oil flame before her household god, and prays for guidance in choosing the fare for the day. She hastens then to the bazaar to purchase fresh fruits and vegetables. Returning, she sits for long hours on a mat in the courtyard, herbs piled before her in colorful little mounds on a plantain leaf, grinding the ingredients for the curry powder on a stone which has probably been used for generations. And at dusk, from that big black pot which has been steaming over a twig fire all day, comes forth a dish which is fit not only for the gods but for her own family.

There are nine basic spices used in the ritual curry powder, but every country, every state, every housewife, finally evolves her own special blend. Therefore there is no monotony in this dish. It can be suited to climate and temperaments. People living in the cold North within sight of the Himalaya snows prefer bland curries; those languishing in equatorial sun like fiery ones which spur their jaded appetites. The rajahs, men who do the fighting and hunting, demand salty pungent mixtures. The saintly yogi, meditating on the supernatural, controls his diet (but does not fast) by eating curries of nut and vegetable which dull the passions. The noncaste people known as the Harijans (beloved of God), suffering their lowly estate because of sins committed in some former birth, get along with a ball of cold rice daubed with a curry made from three spices or roots.

To blend good curry powder such as is used in the richer homes in the East, there are some rules which must be followed.

First, all spices must be fresh. The taste in this dish which annoys so many Westerners comes from using stale old curry powder. There are few worthwhile canned or bottled brands to be found on the shelves of the American supermarket. One should mix and blend one's own from fresh spices. When not available locally, the spices should be ordered from a reputable high-grade import house.

Second, all spices used in blending your own curry powder should be purchased whole. If the spice is the kind which comes in a pod or husk, like the cardamom, this should be left whole for grinding. The Indian cook skillfully winnows the chaff as she works and considers that more nutriment of the spice is thus preserved. It cannot be emphasized too often that the cook *must protect her eyes* when grinding these spices, whether using an old-type stone or an electrical grinder. Certain curries, too, call for inclusion of spices unground, such as a cinnamon stick, a finger of ginger, whole peppercorns or cloves, etc.

Third, all curry powder must be cooked before adding it to other ingredients. This is perhaps the most important rule for the American housewife experimenting with curried dishes, and the one most disregarded. This rule applies whether you are merely adding a pinch of raw curry powder at the last minute to the mulligatawny soup, or mixing it with cream cheese for a canapé or hors-d'oeuvre mixture. The raw taste could antagonize your guests forever against any curried dish. In every use the curry powder should be fried well in a small amount of heated fat.

The proper fat is also an important choice for the cook. *Ghee,* which is clarified butter made from buffalo milk, is used most often. Ordinary clarified butter will do, or plain butter although it is more apt to burn because of the milky particles still in it. Any vegetable oil can be used in place of butter or *ghee* except margarine, which scorches too easily and therefore is not recommended. Indians use mustard oil mostly with fish curries. Peanut oil and coconut oil offered in many commercial brands are growing in favor in India. Meat drippings can add to the flavor of a curry dish, but pork fats are taboo.

In general we think of spices as parts of tropical plants, but there are some herbs which grow in temperate zones which are used either in making curry powders or are added when cooking a curried dish. These are the chief spices and herbs used.

ALLSPICE is the berry of the allspice tree (*Pimenta dioica*). It is known also as the Jamaica Pepper. The berry is a small hard black seed resembling a peppercorn and is often mistaken for a member of that family. It is, in fact, a distinct species found only in the West Indies, Central America, and Brazil. The berry has the blended flavor of cloves, nutmeg, and cinnamon and is used largely for flavorings, especially for pickles, soups, stews, vegetables, and cakes. The Indians use it in many of their curry powders. Allspice berries are available whole or ground.

ANISEED is the small dried seed of anise, a plant very similar to parsley or Queen Anne's Lace (*Pimpinella anisum*). It has a strong licorice flavor. In the West it is used for flavorings and liqueurs, etc.; in India, for making small cakes used in festivals. A spoonful of ground aniseed is usually passed in polite circles after a heavy curry. Each diner takes a pinch, puts it on the tip of his tongue to aid digestion. Aniseeds are available whole or ground.

BAY LEAVES, from a species of laurel tree (*Laurus nobilis*), are often added, fresh or dried, as they are in America to stews or curries and generally removed before a dish is served. They have a pungent aromatic flavor and they should be used with a cautious hand. This is a Mediterranean tree so these leaves are considered herbs rather than spices. They are available fresh, dried, and ground.

CARAWAY SEED is used all over the world for flavorings of pastries, breads, soups, pickles, etc. The perennial herb (*Carum carvi*) is similar to anise in appearance. Imported largely from Lebanon, it is one of the more important additions to curry powders. Usually one finds the whole seeds, but occasionally ground seed is available also. It may also be grown from seed in the home garden.

CARDAMOM is often called the Seed of Paradise in the East because of its delicate flavor and aroma as well as its exhilarating effect on the user. This spice is the fruit of an East Indian herb (*Elettaria cardamomum*) and is a small pod slightly larger than a pea with a papery husk. Inside are many brown seeds. The Indian cook discards the husk as she grinds the spice, but if the pods are used for a recipe that is to be cooked for any length of time, the husk will dissolve. Cardamoms are available as pods or ground. It too is served after a meal, along with betel nut or aniseed, in place of the Western after-dinner cigarette.

CASSIA BUDS are the dried unripe flower buds of a certain cinnamon tree, sometime call Chinese cinnamon (*C. cassia*). The buds taste much like ground cinnamon. This spice blends well with stewed fruits, pastries, fancy drinks and, because of its delightful aroma, with potpourris which so delight women of East and West.

CINNAMON is the aromatic bark of any of several kinds of lauraceous trees (genus *Cinnamomum*). The Chinese variety is known as cassia bark. This is probably the most popular of all spices used in Western cooking, for it is used in the baking of pastries, pies, puddings, and pickles of many kinds. Sticks, which are pieces of rolled-up bark, are added whole to spiced drinks and wines, also to the tasty dry curries of India. While most packaged cinnamon has a standard length of 2 inches, good shops will stock longer pieces. It is also available ground.

CLOVES are the dried unopened flower buds of a tropical tree (*Eugenia caryophyllata*) belonging to the myrtle family. This pungent aromatic spice is much used in the Orient to disinfect sick rooms and is used today in Western deodorants. A most powerful little spice—one clove too many will spoil the curry powder; but used with care, it improves pickles, sauces, and puddings. From it is obtained too a valuable oil which goes into perfumes and medicines. The tree is a native of the Moluccas but now is cultivated all over the Tropics. American cooks favor it for apple pies and baked hams. Whole cloves and ground cloves are offered.

CORIANDER SEEDS have a sweet lemon flavor and are used largely to flavor puddings, cakes, etc., or to season meats such as sausage. This spice, the ripened dried fruit of an herb (*Coriandrum sativum*), has only lately become known to Americans, but has been popular in the East, and in Morocco particularly, for over 7,000 years. The Mexicans use it to flavor their soups. Indians add it to their curry powder as it is believed that it prevents flatulence. The seeds are available whole and ground. The fresh leaves of the herb are also used as an ingredient in curries and in Mexican food, and as a garnish.

CUMINSEED is an aromatic seed which comes from a dwarf plant (*Cuminum cyminum*) native to Egypt and Syria. It was used as a tithe or tax as far back as the days of Christ. Today it is in demand by bakers all over the world for breads, cookies, pies, and other baked goods. In the Middle Ages European students were supposed to have eaten it to give themselves the wan complexions believed to go with much learning. These are available whole or ground.

FENNEL is an herb (*Foeniculum vulgare*) belonging to the carrot family. Fennel seeds are very popular in Europe where cooks sprinkle the top of breads and pastries with them. The tiny seeds shaped like watermelons have a sweet aroma and taste like aniseed. They are an excellent addition to fish sauces. The Brahmin priests claim that fennel in curry powder, or a pinch of ground fennel held on the tip of the tongue, will ward off evil. Fresh seeds, dried seeds, and ground fennel are sold in many shops.

FENUGREEK (*Trigonella fœnumgræcum*), Greek hay, is a plant of the pea family. The seeds have a flavor similar to that of maple sugar. It is used not only in curry powders, but in increasing amounts in sweets, especially in the jelly beans so popular with children of the West.

GINGER comes from a fragrant tropical plant (*Zingiber officinale*) with lovely blossoms which are much used for garlands and food decorations. The part used as a spice is the root.

This spice is available in many forms. The fresh root, which is called *green gingerroot,* can be purchased in a sort of clump called a "hand" in Spanish or Oriental markets and it is also available sliced in cans. When a piece of the "hand" is separated it is called a "finger." The term "green" refers to age, not to color. When using the green gingerroot, soak the root in hot water for 1 hour or more, till the skin will peel off easily. Then scrape or peel it. It can be added in a chunk to cooked dishes or pared paper-thin for use in fresh salads or as a garnish. Since the spice is so pungent, its odor and fiery properties cling to one's fingers which should always be well washed after using. Eyes, too, should be protected.

Dried gingerroot has shriveled to twisted knobby pieces, as hard as can be. This can be bought in the spice shop or in the bazaar and can be ground at home, but it is hard to grind.

Ground ginger comes bottled or canned. The hands or fingers of the root as they come from the grower have to be washed well, then the skin is scraped or peeled off. At this stage it is known as "white ginger" and is often bleached by chemical means or in the sun to make it even lighter in shade. This is then ground into the product most familiar to us. Ground ginger is used as a condiment and in many medicines, especially those needed for flatulence. Mixed with butter, it makes a fine basting for fowl or meat. It is one of the most important spices used for curry blending. When extra fire is needed for a curried dish, add a pinch of ginger rather than adding more hot peppers. Protect the eyes when using the ground spice, especially.

Candied or *Crystallized gingerroot* is a popular sweet used widely in the East as a confection and also an ingredient for many of their curry dishes. Also, great stone jars of preserved ginger-root (see p. 211) are lined up in the storerooms of every well-run Eastern home. It can be kept for many months. Altogether, ginger is one of the most widely used spices in the world.

MACE is an aromatic spice which comes from the fibrous covering of the nutmeg. It is used ground as a flavoring for sweets, and adds a unique orange tint to pickles, rarebits, and cocktails. The Indians add it to their curries. Mace is available ground and looks and smells similar to nutmeg. It is also available in the shreds of the husk or aril; these are called "blades of mace."

MINT, an herb native to Asia, is used all through the East. There are more than 30 species of this plant (*Mentha*) and many are used in cooking. Mint is mentioned in Greek mythology. The Romans decked their banquet halls with it and carried it to England where to this day it is included in all herb dishes. It is a favorite accompaniment to roast leg of lamb and a universal favorite for cold drinks, jellies, and sauces. The Hindu adds it in paste form to many of his curries. Mint grows anywhere in the temperate zone, so the best way to have the leaves or sprigs fresh is to grow it yourself. It is also available dried and ground.

MUSTARD SEEDS come from a low-growing plant (*Brassica*) which spreads profusely in both tropical and temperate zones. Seeds are used whole in the making of pickles and curry powders. When ground and mixed with liquid, it serves as the hot condiment so beloved by the Englishman; a milder form serves for the French. There are several varieties of this plant. The seeds are available whole; when ground it is called dry mustard.

NUTMEG is the large seed of a peachlike evergreen tree (*Myristica fragrans*) which is a native of the Moluccas. It is used as a flavoring for puddings and pies, and its aromatic qualities add a popular fillip to many fancy drinks. A sprinkle of nutmeg on boiled cauliflower or spinach works wonders, and it adds an indefinable bouquet when added to piecrust or soups. Indians use this spice in curries, and in other preparations as well. It is the seed's outer husk which is called mace. The seeds are dried after gathering and they become very hard. Nutmegs are available whole; when ground, it is called grated nutmeg.

PEPPERS (*Capsicum*) are the fruits of a large plant genus originally growing in tropical America. There are many species, each having a distinctive flavor; the sizes and shapes and colors vary incredibly—some are mild and sweet and others hot; they can be green, yellow, red, almost white, almost black.

Chili peppers, called chili in our text, grow in subtropical and tropical regions. The pods are small and these little chilies, green or red, can be used fresh. However, they are more familiar to us dried; the pods, membranes, and seeds are ground together to make a fiery seasoning. *Chili powder* however, is not exactly the same as ground chilies; the powder is usually a combination of hot and milder chilies and sometimes has other herbs ground with them. In Mexico chili powder is a blend of the ground chilies and a touch of orégano and garlic. Some blends add allspice, cloves, and even black pepper. It is chili powder which is used in *chili con carne.* It is the unmixed ground chilies which the Indians use.

Paprika is the favorite spice of the Hungarians and it is made by grinding the dried pods of a sweet mild pepper. There are sharper varieties of this spice made by grinding some of the seeds and membranes with the pods, but they are seldom available in America.

Cayenne peppers are the most pungent. The spice called *cayenne* is made from grinding the dried seeds and the brilliant red pods together to make a very fine and very hot powder.

Tabasco is a small hot pepper grown in warm climates which is the chief ingredient of a hot sauce of that name and of other hot sauces.

After Columbus discovered this plant genus in the Americas, the pepper was carried to India by the Portuguese and has been used as a curry ingredient ever since.

PEPPER (*Piper nigrum*) is a climbing shrub native to India. The fruits of this plant, called *peppercorns,* make the most popular spice in the world. For black peppercorns, the spike of berries is picked when unripe and put in the sun to dry. When fully dry, the berries are pulled off, graded, and packed. For white peppercorns the berries are riper before being picked and they are soaked or slightly fermented before packing. Both kinds are available whole, and these are called peppercorns, or cracked, or finely ground. They keep their flavor best when stored whole and ground just before using. White pepper is milder than black.

POPPY SEED is a fruit of an annual plant (*Papaver somniferum*) of a genus with over a hundred varieties, wild or cultivated, which grow the world over. Prized for its flamboyant blossoms in infinite shades of red, white, pink, and gold, the plant is also of great commercial value for the milk (latex) from its stem which goes into potent and often dangerous medicines. The seeds are contained in long ropelike pods, as many as 25,000 in one pod, but it takes some 900,000 of these to weigh a pound. The dried seeds, which are used whole or ground, have a nutlike flavor and a crunchy texture. They are used extensively for flavoring, toppings for pastries and breads, for seasoning cabbage and other vegetables, for salads, etc. They are a favorite addition to the curry powder blend.

SAFFRON, the rarest and most exotic of all spices, is the stigma of the lowly yellow crocus blossom (*Crocus savitus*). It has been valued since Biblical times. Nero is said to have had his parade routes saffron-sprinkled for its perfume. Since only one ounce will give that vivid golden nonfading tint to a voluminous robe, the yogis, sanyasis, and Buddhist monks had long since adopted it as their own. All over the world it is in great demand not only for dyes but for flavorings for confections, pastries, etc. In the East it is most highly prized for the curry powders. Since it takes some 75,000 stigmas to produce one pound of saffron and one ounce sells for over ten dollars, it is usually reserved for festive or sacred feast dishes. Turmeric is used often as a substitute but is easily detected by the connoisseur or the trained palate. Saffron comes in cake form, as dried stigmas, or ground and bottled. Use it with caution as one pinch stains badly.

SESAME is a world-famous seed because of Ali Baba and the famous command "Open Sesame!" It is used in the popular Turkish confection known as halvah. Coming from tall beanlike pods, from North Africa, South America, etc., with a pleasing nut flavor, the seeds can sometimes be used in place of almonds. In France the seeds are used for sprinkling on top of vegetables. In the Far East they are often blended in curry powders. The seeds are almost white, but their flavor is accentuated by toasting. They are also pressed to make sesame oil.

TURMERIC is an East Indian plant (*Curcuma longa*) belonging to the ginger family. As with ginger, the part used is the root, but turmeric has a more brilliant color and a much sweeter and more delicate flavor than ginger. It is used often in India as a substitute for saffron, to give color and flavor to everyday curries. In the West it is used to give color and crispness to pickles but must be used with caution as a pinch too much gives bitterness. The Indian mixes turmeric with mint leaves and pounds them to make a paste which they claim will remove the scars left by smallpox. The root can sometimes be found in specialty shops, but this spice is generally available ground.

In addition to these spices and herbs, there are other leaves, fresh and dried, and other barks which are sometimes added to curry powders. The aromatic mild petals of flowers such as the rose, violet, or rose geranium are often used in delicate sweets or salads to accompany curries.

The proper blending of curry powder, like that of the rest of the ingredients for the dish, requires time, experiment and patience, but this gives the creative cook the satisfaction of finding exactly what is best for her and therefore truly individual. Other cooks, pressed for time, may utilize one of the good curry powders from an import house and be assured of satisfactory results. All the ingredients used in these recipes are obtainable at import stores, especially those handling Indian foods.

Grind the spices together in a mortar, sprinkling with vinegar and water while mixing to keep down the fine dust; this is done to protect the eyes. If using an electric grinder, it, too, should be kept covered when in use.

CURRY POWDER I—RITUAL OR BASIC BLEND

4 ozs. ground turmeric
4 ozs. coriander seeds
4 ozs. cuminseeds
3 ozs. dried gingerroot
2 peppercorns

1 cardamom pod
1 dried red chili
1 oz. saffron
½ oz. mustard seeds

CURRY POWDER II

8 ozs. ground turmeric
8 ozs. coriander seeds
8 ozs. cuminseeds
4 ozs. dried gingerroot
4 peppercorns
2 ozs. cardamom pods

2 ozs. fennel seeds
2 ozs. dried red chilies
2 ozs. blades of mace
1 oz. whole cloves
1 oz. mustard seeds
1 oz. poppy seeds

CURRY POWDER III

2 tsps. coriander seeds
½ tsp. cuminseeds
¼ tsp. caraway seeds
1 tsp. peppercorns
1 tsp. poppy seeds

2 tsps. mustard seeds
¼ tsp. ground turmeric
6 whole cloves
1 cinnamon stick, 2 inches
10 dried chilies

Use 2 teaspoons of this blend of powder to each pound of meat.

CURRY POWDER IV

2 tsps. mustard seeds	1 cinnamon stick, 2 inches
2 tsps. peppercorns	1½ tsps. cardamom pods
1 tsp. cuminseeds	¼ Tb. ground chilies
1½ tsps. poppy seeds	6 whole cloves
1½ tsps. coriander seeds	1 Tb. dried mint

Use 2 teaspoons of this blend to each pound of meat.

CURRY POWDER V—FIERY SOUTH INDIA BLEND

1-inch piece of green gingerroot	2 tsps. peppercorns
30 dried red chilies	1 tsp. ground turmeric
4 dried green chilies	2 tsps. poppy seeds
10 cardamom pods	2 tsps. mustard seeds
10 whole cloves	1½ lbs. coriander seeds
4 cinnamon sticks, each 2 inches	4 bay leaves
2 tsps. cuminseeds	2½ Tb. dried mint leaves

Peel the green gingerroot, cut into small pieces, and soak in water till soft; then grind into a paste before adding to the other spices. This recipe came from the chef of a small freighter plying the Malay Coast, and the powder was prepared in large quantities for a crew which ate curry twice daily.

CURRY POWDER VI

3 Tbs. ground cinnamon	1½ Tbs. ground cardamom
2 Tbs. ground coriander	1½ Tbs. garlic salt
2 Tbs. ground turmeric	1½ Tbs. ground poppy seeds
2½ Tbs. ground cuminseed	2 Tbs. ground dried chilies
1 Tb. ground fenugreek	2 Tbs. ground black pepper
1½ Tbs. dry mustard	1 Tb. ground ginger

Sprinkle often with lime juice or vinegar while blending these spices. This powder may be sealed tightly and stored for many months, but it will not give the same rich-flavored dish as does the one using freshly ground spices.

Chapter 3

CURRY SAUCES

TIMES are changing from the era when each day's food was prepared on that day and anything uneaten on the day was discarded. The modern young Western-educated Indian housewife with a refrigerator is adopting many dishes formerly used only by the white *sahibs*. She is discovering that bottled or canned curry pastes and sauces found now on supermarket shelves can turn that cold cooked meat or vegetable into an excellent curry.

The American housewife who prepares good curry paste and bottles it to keep on her pantry shelf will find it invaluable when making a hurry-up casserole, stew, soufflé, or canapés.

Because coconuts, coconut juice and coconut milk are such basic ingredients in the sauces, it may be well to examine what each consists of.

Coconut

Coconut is used in curried dishes to a tremendous extent. What is used most often is not the meat of the nut or the natural juice, but an extract of the meat or pulp which is called *coconut milk* and is a chief ingredient in curry sauces. The coconut palm produces many useful products. From the nut alone we get fresh pulp and juice, the dried meat known as copra, and coconut oil, and the leaves, fibers, and wood are the source of many other benefits to man.

An Indian boy who sprints up a tall palm to cut down a coconut cleaves it open with one blow from a hatchet. The exasperated American housewife who tries to crack that same hard-shelled nut when she buys one at the supermarket often finds herself chasing it around the kitchen with a hammer or some other dangerous tool. The simplest manner is to grasp the three-eyed end firmly in the left hand, then give some sharp glancing blows on the opposite end, tapping all the way around. One good blow then will open the nut. Hold the nut over a bowl to catch the liquid if you want to use it. Scrape the pulp from the hard shell with a spoon or scoop. It can be eaten just as it is, or it can be shredded or grated, or pulverized in an electric blender, to use in recipes.

Coconut Juice

This natural juice of the fruit is called by various names; sometimes it is called coconut milk, which causes confusion as to what is meant in recipes. Coconut liquid is used for fancy drinks in America but it is not often used by the Indian. The liquid of unripe coconuts is used in the Tropics more often.

Coconut Milk

An average coconut as it appears in the American market will yield 3 to 4 cups of grated pulp. This will make 1 or more cups of coconut milk, depending on the amount of liquid used. The less liquid, the richer the extract. Pour 2 cups liquid, milk or water, over 1 cup grated pulp; the milk or water may be hot or cold. Allow it to steep for 15 minutes to several hours. Then strain the whole mixture through a cloth-lined sieve or several layers of cheesecloth into a bowl. Gently squeeze the cloth to extract as much liquid as possible. There will be at least 1 cup of rich coconut milk. Usually the dried pulp is discarded, but it may be used in recipes or as a garnish.

Coconut milk can be made from dried coconut too, although the milk will not be as rich. To do this, pour 2 cups liquid over 1 cup dried coconut and bring the mixture very slowly to a simmer. When the mixture becomes bubbly, take off the heat and strain, as above. There will be at least 1 cup of coconut milk.

There will be many variations of this basic method in the recipes which follow—different proportions of liquid to pulp, different times for steeping, and sometimes the whole mixture, liquid and pulp, will be used together. When recipes call for coconut milk, follow this basic method; as you cook more curried dishes experiment to find the time and proportions best suited to you.

BASIC WHITE SAUCE ❀ ❀ *about 1 cup*

1 Tb. butter
1 Tb. flour
1 cup milk

1 bay leaf
½ tsp. salt
⅛ tsp. ground white pepper

Heat the butter in the top part of a double boiler; when the butter bubbles, stir in the flour. Simmer for a moment, till mixture is smooth. Add the milk, bay leaf, salt, and pepper. Stir well, then simmer for 10 minutes or more, till the sauce is smooth and thick. Remove the bay leaf before using. This sauce may be used in recipes for meat, fish, or vegetable dishes.

CURRY SAUCE I ❀ ❀ ❀ *about 4 cups*

1 fresh coconut, grated, or 1 cup dried coconut
4 cups milk
2 large onions, chopped fine
4 Tbs. vegetable oil or butter
2 tsps. curry powder or 1 tsp. canned curry paste

2 Tbs. flour
1 garlic clove, mashed
1-inch piece of green gingerroot, sliced very thin, or 1 tsp. ground ginger
½ tsp. salt

Put the coconut and milk in the top part of a double boiler and let the mixture simmer over boiling water for 30 minutes. In the meantime brown the onions lightly in the heated oil in a skillet; remove onions. Fry the curry powder and flour together till dark brown. Stir in the mashed garlic and let simmer for 3 minutes. Add this mixture with onions and gingerroot to the milk and let simmer gently for another 30 minutes, stirring often till sauce is smooth. Strain. Add salt to taste, taking care not to add too much since the mineral content of some of the curry spices tends to intensify the seasoning.

Seal the sauce in a sterilized jar and keep for future use. It improves by standing. When reheated, add a little cream to thin it. An excellent sauce for warmed-over meat, fowl, vegetable, or hard-cooked eggs.

CURRY SAUCE II   ❋   ❋   ❋   *about 3 cups*

1 cup shredded dried coconut
Milk (about 2½ cups)
2 Tbs. butter or vegetable oil
1 onion, minced
1 Tb. curry powder
2 Tbs. flour

1½ cups meat gravy
1 tsp. tomato catsup
1 tsp. sugar
1 tsp. vinegar
½ tsp. salt

Soak the coconut in milk to cover (about 1 cup) for 1 hour. Heat the butter and brown the onion in it; remove onion. Fry the curry powder and flour together, letting them simmer for 3 minutes. Put 1½ cups milk in the top part of a double boiler and add the browned onion, fried curry powder, the coconut and the milk in which it is soaking, the gravy, catsup, and sugar. Let simmer gently over boiling water for 30 minutes, stirring often to make a smooth sauce. Add the vinegar for the last 5 minutes. Add salt to taste when the sauce is done. The sauce may be strained, or the coconut may be left in. Seal in hot sterilized jars.

NOTE If using canned curry paste instead of curry powder, do not fry it first, but add directly to the ingredients in the double boiler.

CURRY SAUCE III   ❋   ❋   *about 1½ cups*

1 cup minced onion
4 Tbs. mustard oil
2 Tbs. curry powder
2 Tbs. flour
⅛ tsp. ground cayenne pepper

1 cup tomato juice
1 cup diced unpeeled sour apple
¼ cup diced celery
½ tsp. salt

Brown the onion lightly in the heated oil and remove onion. Mix the curry powder, flour, and cayenne and fry in remaining oil till dark brown. Simmer for 3 minutes, adding a drop or two of water if needed to keep paste from sticking. Add the tomato juice with the browned onion, the apple, celery, and salt. Simmer for 30 minutes, or till apple and celery are soft. Stir constantly. Add more tomato juice if needed, to keep at the same amount. When sauce is cooked, press it through a sieve and seal in hot sterilized bottles. This sauce should be as thick as mayonnaise. It can be used like mayonnaise as it is, or it can be made more liquid by adding milk or cream. If a more fiery dish is liked, add a pinch of ground ginger.

PLANTER'S CURRY PASTE   ❋   *about 4 cups*

4 large onions, chopped fine
2 unpeeled large tart apples, chopped fine
½ cup olive oil or butter
2 Tbs. curry powder
2 Tbs. flour
4 cups milk
½ lb. cooked lean ham, diced fine

2 sprigs of fresh thyme or ½ tsp. ground thyme
2 bay leaves
4 peppercorns
1 blade of mace
1 tsp. sugar
Salt

Brown the onions and apples lightly in the heated oil and remove them. Mix the curry powder and flour and fry in remaining oil till dark brown. Simmer for 3 minutes, or till mixture is smooth and bubbling. Put milk in the top part of a double boiler and add the onions, apples, fried curry and any oil remaining, the ham, herbs, spices, and sugar. Cook over boiling water for 30 minutes, or till sauce is thick and smooth. Add the salt last, to taste. If a more fiery sauce is liked, add a pinch of ground ginger. Press through a sieve. Seal the sauce in hot sterilized jars for future use. This improves by standing. Use thick as a mayonnaise, or thinner as a sauce, with milk added, to be heated quickly and briefly with cold meats, vegetables, etc.

KORMA

1 cup yogurt or curd (see p. 30)
1 Tb. minced green pepper
1-inch piece of green gingerroot, sliced thin, or ½ tsp. ground ginger
1 tsp. ground cinnamon
1 tsp. ground turmeric
½ tsp. freshly ground black pepper
2 tsps. poppy seeds
2 tsps. ground almonds
1 tsp. salt, or less

Mix all ingredients in the top part of a double boiler and simmer over boiling water for 1 hour, or till the mixture loses the raw spice taste. Seal the mixture in a sterilized jar. It will keep for many weeks to be used in *pulao* mixtures.

HAWAIIAN CURRIED SAUCE   ❋   *about 2½ cups*

1 fresh coconut
3 cups milk
3 Tbs. olive oil
1 medium-sized onion, chopped fine
1 garlic clove (optional)
1 Tb. curry powder, or less
3 Tbs. flour
1-inch piece of gingerroot or ½ tsp. ground ginger
1 tsp. salt

Grate the pulp of the coconut and soak it for 1 hour in the milk which has been heated but not brought to a boil. Press the coconut and milk through a sieve until all liquid is extracted. Set aside the liquid. The dried pulp may be discarded, though often it is used for other dishes. Heat the oil and brown the onion lightly in it; remove the onion from skillet. Mash the garlic into the onion. In oil remaining in skillet fry the mixed curry powder and flour till they are dark brown and form a smooth paste. Stir in the coconut milk, onion mixture, ginger-root, and salt to taste. Simmer till a smooth sauce is formed. Lift out the gingerroot and discard it. This sauce is served as a relish with curried vegetable or meat dishes. The amount of ginger can be varied to the taste.

Chapter 4

RICE AND DAL

Rice

THE GREAT PADDY FIELDS of India are found mainly in its southern and eastern parts; thus it follows that rice is the staple diet there. That called Patna rice, grown in the Patna district which is on the Ganges plain, is considered by many the choicest rice of all the varieties grown. But all through the East, and indeed in Europe and the United States, rice is now being used almost as extensively as wheat. Rice is native to India, but today it grows all over the world wherever the climate will permit. There are many varieties of this grain to be found in the bazaar or on supermarket shelves—polished, unpolished, brown; long- or short- or round-grained; green rice fresh in from the harvest, and rice that has been maturing for years in clay-walled storerooms. In addition, rice packaged with all sorts of seasonings can be found in the United States, as well as precooked rice and enriched rice. Wild rice is a plant of another family altogether, a native North American grass. Each has its own characteristic and each demands its own type of cooking.

Indians claim that rice must be at least five years old to be digestible. The husk rice bought in the native bazaar and winnowed at home is probably the most nutritious; modern packaged varieties, especially the tempting instant rice, have naturally lost much of their mineral content.

There are different ways of cooking rice in each country. In India the jog-trotting coolie eats a soggy cold ball of it unrolled from a bit of plantain leaf. It comes to the rajah's table, a snowy

(22)

mound on a great brass tray, festooned with flowers and nuts in a manner reminding one of the Arabian Nights.

In India and other parts of the East flour is made by grinding rice on the old family stone. This flour is often used in place of the whole grain, but it demands well-aged grains taken from the carefully guarded storeroom at the end of the courtyard. Such rice must be first soaked in water, then dried in the sun before pounding. It is soaked again in water before use as flour.

BOILED RICE   ❋   ❋   ❋   *4 to 8 servings*

Wash well 1 pound (2 cups) uncooked rice in cold water. Add to 6 cups boiling water with 1 teaspoon salt. Boil for about 20 minutes, or till a kernel can be pressed soft between thumb and finger. Turn the rice into a sieve and pour cold water over it. Cover the sieve with a towel and let it stand in the oven at very low heat (250°F. or less) till the rice is dry and fluffy. To ensure whiteness and lightness, add the juice of 1 lemon to the rice during the last 3 to 5 minutes of cooking.

VILLAGE BOILED RICE   ❋   *4 to 8 servings*

Wash 2 cups uncooked rice well and drain thoroughly. Put it in a large pot with 4 cups cold water and 1 teaspoon salt. Bring to a boil over moderate heat. At the moment the water starts to boil, cover the pot with a damp cloth and put on the lid as well. This will ensure that no steam escapes. Turn the heat very low and leave simmering for 20 minutes without removing any covering. By that time the rice will be cooked, each grain puffed and separate.

HOP LING'S RICE

A long-time resident of the Far East claims that only the Chinese know how to cook rice properly. This recipe comes from a cook named Hop Ling.

"Wash the rice thoroughly. Drain it and dribble it through the fingers slowly into a pan of fast-boiling water. Boil at a gallop

10 minutes or until the grains are just tender. Dash in a cup of cold water to stop the boiling. Drain rice through a sieve and put in a dry pan. Cover with a linen cloth and let stand at very low heat or in the oven with the door open till the rice is quite dry. Shake the pan occasionally."

FRIED RICE   ❋   ❋   ❋   ❋   *4 to 8 servings*

1 lb. (2 cups) uncooked rice	5 cups boiling water
2 tsps. salt	4 Tbs. butter or vegetable oil

Wash and drain the rice. Mix well with the salt till the grains appear glazed. Cover with the boiling water. Bring to a boil again and simmer for about 30 minutes, till all the water is absorbed. Heat the butter to bubbling, add rice, and fry to a light brown. Dry in an uncovered pan in a very slow oven (250°F. or less) for about 10 minutes, till the grains are dry and fluffy.

SAFFRON RICE   ❋   ❋   ❋   *4 to 8 servings*

1 lb. (2 cups) uncooked rice	1 tsp. ground saffron
4 cups chicken broth	1 tsp. salt

Put the rice in the cold broth with the saffron and salt. Bring to a boil and simmer over very low heat, without uncovering the pan, for 30 minutes. All liquid should be absorbed when the rice is cooked.

PARSEE RICE   ❋   ❋   ❋   *4 to 8 servings*

4 Tbs. butter or vegetable oil	4 peppercorns
2 onions, minced	1 cinnamon stick, 4 inches
1 lb. (2 cups) uncooked rice	2 tsps. sugar
4 cardamom pods	1 tsp. salt
6 whole cloves	4 cups boiling water

Heat the butter and fry the onions lightly in it. Stir in the rice and cook till it bubbles up, about 3 minutes. Add the cardamoms, cloves, peppercorns, cinnamon, sugar, and salt. Pour in the boiling water. Cover and simmer for about 30 minutes, or till the rice is soft and all liquid absorbed.

GOLDEN RICE   ❊   ❊   ❊   *4 to 8 servings*

2 Tbs. butter or vegetable oil
1 tsp. ground turmeric or saffron
1 lb. (2 cups) uncooked rice
4 cups chicken broth
½ tsp. salt

½ cup browned slivered almonds
1 Tb. minced chives
1 Tb. minced watercress
Fried onion rings

Melt the butter and fry the turmeric or saffron for 3 minutes.
Stir this into the rice and add chicken broth and salt. Bring to
a boil, cover, and let simmer over low heat for 30 minutes, or
till all liquid is absorbed and the rice grains are dry and fluffy.
Sprinkle nuts, chives, watercress, and onion rings on top.

COPRA KAMA (Coconut Rice)   ❊   *6 to 8 servings*

2 cups milk
2 cups water
1 cup shredded coconut
1 tsp. salt

1 small onion, minced
2 Tbs. vegetable oil or butter
1 Tb. curry powder
2 cups uncooked rice

Mix the milk, water, and coconut in a kettle. Add the salt and
bring to a boil. Remove from the heat and let stand for 15 minutes. Strain off the liquid and discard the coconut pulp. Brown
the onion lightly in the heated oil and remove onion. In remaining oil fry the curry powder to dark brown. Add the uncooked rice and stir till it is slightly browned. Add the coconut
milk and onion. Cook over very low heat, stirring often, for 30
minutes, or till all the liquid is absorbed and the rice is dry and
fluffy. This is the standard curry used with vegetable dishes.

BURMESE COCONUT RICE   ❊   *6 to 10 servings*

4 cups milk
2 cups shredded coconut
3 cups uncooked rice
3 onions, minced

2 Tbs. peanut oil
½ tsp. salt
Extra coconut milk (1 to 2 cups)

Bring the milk to a boil and add the shredded coconut. Remove
from the heat at once and let stand, covered, for 1 hour. Mix

the uncooked rice and onions and fry together in the heated oil for about 3 minutes. Add this mixture to the milk and coconut and add the salt. Mix well and bring to a boil. Reduce heat, cover, and let simmer over low heat for 30 minutes, or till rice has absorbed all the liquid. If mixture becomes too dry before rice is soft, add a little of the extra coconut milk; heat it before adding, but do not let it boil.

SIMPLE TOMATO PULAO
(See also Chapter 11)   ✳   *6 to 8 servings*

3 Tbs. vegetable oil or butter
1 tsp. curry powder
2 cups uncooked rice

4 cups tomato juice
3 cups broth, any kind
½ tsp. salt, or more

Heat the oil in an ovenproof pot and fry the curry powder in it till dark brown. Stir in the rice and cook till it bubbles up. Add the tomato juice, broth, and salt. Bring to a boil, then set the pot in a moderate oven (350°F.) and bake for 1 hour, or till all liquid is absorbed and the rice is dry and fluffy. Serve with vegetable curries and sweet chutneys.

Dal

Dal (*dhal* or *dhall*) is a word used loosely in India to refer to any dried legume such as peas, beans, lentils, or other similar Indian plants. It also refers to certain preparations of the dried lentil which are used alone or as a side dish or in the preparation of curries, and to the flour made from dried peas or lentils. Ordinary *dal*, which is just a boiled-down lentil mash, is often dried and sold in the native bazaar in cake form. This usually has to be soaked for 1 to 6 hours before using.

Dal resembles American undiluted canned pea or bean soup. This simple dish takes the place of a curry sauce to serve with rice for many of India's people, and often it is the main meal of the day. In this case a small portion of soaked *dal* is boiled with rice in salted water and the meal is then ready for serving. Sometimes fried onions and spices are added to boiled *dal* with saffron or turmeric sprinkled on top, to make a tastier dish. *Dal* is occasionally boiled with other cereals, or combined with mangoes or other fruits, or fried crisp in vegetable oils. Soaked and boiled *dal* may be spiced and wrapped in cabbage leaves for a main dish. It is soaked and added to sauces, fritters, cake batter, and is even the basis for a dessert pudding (see p. 223).

Dal is used also as a thickening for curry dishes. When *dal* is a thickening, soak it in water to cover for 1 hour or more, until it becomes soft enough to mix readily with other ingredients. An Indian cook would use the dried lentil cake from the bazaar for the recipes in this book; she would break or cut off the needed amount and soak it before using. An American cook may substitute the same amount of condensed undiluted pea or bean soup; the soup is not as hard as the lentil cake, but it does need to be softened and mixed in well or it will remain in lumps instead of blending smoothly with other ingredients to thicken the mixture.

Like dried peas or beans, *dal* may be soaked and boiled and used as a vegetable dish, a thick soup, or a sauce. As a sauce preparation it is an accompaniment to curry dinners. It is served as a sauce, or it can be eaten as a kind of dip; in that case the diner eats it by dipping pieces of Indian bread into it. A recipe for this kind of *dal* follows.

DAL FOR SERVING WITH CURRY ❋ *4 to 6 servings*

1 cup dried split peas
1 onion, minced

2 Tbs. butter or vegetable oil
3 cups cold water

Soak the dried peas in cold water overnight. In the morning drain and let stand to dry. Fry the onion in the butter and mix in with the peas. Add the 3 cups water and let it come to a boil. Turn heat very low, cover, and let the peas simmer for about 30 minutes, or till they are soft enough to mash. Salt is not added to the *dal* as the curried food with which it is served is usually highly seasoned.

INDIAN KEDGEREE   ❄   ❄   ❄   *4 servings*

There is no fish in Indian kedgeree. Instead rice and *dal* are cooked together with curry spices.

1 cup dal (see p. 26)
3 cups water or broth
¼ cup mustard oil or butter
2 onions, chopped fine

1 tsp. ground cardamom
1 tsp. ground cloves
1 cup uncooked rice
1 tsp. salt

Put the *dal* and 1 cup of the water in a saucepan and simmer for 15 minutes, stirring occasionally to keep *dal* from sticking; set aside. Heat the oil and brown the onions lightly in it; remove onions. Fry the spices in the same oil, then return onions and add remaining 2 cups water, the *dal* and water in which it simmered, the uncooked rice, and salt. Cover and simmer till all liquid is absorbed and the rice is dry and fluffy. Serve with curry sauces (see Chap. 3), or plain with chutney.

NOTE   This simple dish can be varied by adding or substituting other spices; for instance cuminseeds, cinnamon stick, and ground turmeric, or by using the browned onions as a garnish instead of cooking them with the rice and *dal*.

Chapter 5

MILK, YOGURT, AND CHEESE

THERE IS AS yet little refrigeration in the Far East, especially for the masses of people. Since milk forms the main part of their diet, some way had to be contrived to preserve it in a hot climate. Much of the milk is used in the form of curd, which is soured and thickened milk. Most popular, however, is yogurt which is now regarded everywhere as a health food. Yogurt was once an imported food in India, but now it is used extensively by Indian villagers. Yogurt is similar to curd, but in this case the milk has bacterial cultures added to sour and thicken the mixture and this gives it a characteristic flavor unlike that of curd. The commercial sour cream available in the United States is made from cream by somewhat the same methods, using bacterial cultures, but it has quite a different taste, even though the texture is similar.

Cheese making is very like the process used for these simpler milk products; however, the thickened milk that is to become cheese is drained longer, dried, and compressed. Often other flavors are added, and of course hard cheeses are stored for long periods to ripen.

The milk of sacred cows, goats, water buffaloes—each has a distinctive flavor and a special place and value in diet and religion in India. For recipes for drinks made from milk and milk products, see Chapter 19.

CURD (*Dahi*)

Bring 2 cups fresh milk to a boil and take off the heat. While still warm, add 1 tablespoon vinegar or the juice of 1 lime. Let the mixture stand, covered, in a warm room for 24 hours. It will then have turned to a thick cream. Use in curry sauces, or eat it as it is, plain or with spices and fruits. Drain through a muslin bag to obtain a drier curd to use as a more solid sweet. Curd is often used in place of yogurt in recipes.

BUTTERMILK CURD

Heat fresh buttermilk over very low heat, keeping it below 100°F. until it becomes quite thick. When thickened, drain it through a muslin bag suspended over a bowl for 4 to 6 hours. Squeeze the bag till the curd is quite dry. Mix the curd with sauces or mayonnaise; or mix with chopped chives, watercress, or curry and serve as a relish. Serve like cottage cheese with Indian bread.

DRIED MILK

Drying is another means of preserving milk. We are now familiar with dried skim milk in powdered form, but it is never made at home. In India the whole milk is dried by evaporation and is regularly made at home, since it is a necessary ingredient for various dishes, but especially for a favorite confection, *barfi*, a sort of fudge mixture.

To make dried milk, simmer whole milk for 2 hours, or till most of it has evaporated and skim remains on top. This skim is called dried milk. Milk is of varying richness in India; that of the buffalo and goat is usually much richer than cow's milk. Also most of it is watered by the vendor. As a result, the housewife usually boils down a large quantity, 2 to 3 pints, to get ½ cup dried milk for her *barfi*.

YOGURT

Put 4 cups of milk, either whole or skimmed, in a heatproof glass bowl. Put over very low heat and bring just to blood heat, or to the point when a skin crinkles across the surface. Remove from the heat and stir in 1 tablespoon of commercial yogurt, bought in the bazaar or a shop, mixed with 1 tablespoon of fresh milk. Stir well and cover the bowl. Place it in a very low oven (115°F.) for 2 to 5 hours. Remove, cool, and chill. Chilling stops the further growth of bacteria.

YOGURT MAYONNAISE   ❋   *about 1½ cups*

½ cup whole-wheat bread
  crumbs
¼ cup yogurt
4 garlic cloves, mashed

2 egg yolks
1 cup olive oil
3 Tbs. lemon juice
¼ tsp. salt

Soak the bread crumbs in the yogurt for 10 minutes. Add the mashed garlic and mix well. Add the egg yolks and beat well with an egg beater. Continue to beat while adding the oil drop by drop. Add lemon juice and salt last. Chill before using.

ACORN SQUASH WITH YOGURT   ❋   *4 servings*

2 acorn squash, unpeeled
½ cup whole-wheat crumbs
1 carrot, grated
½ tsp. salt
½ cup chopped mushrooms

1 onion, minced
1 celery stalk, minced
½ cup yogurt
⅛ tsp. ground saffron

Split the acorn squash and clean out the seeds. Make a mixture of the whole-wheat crumbs, carrot, salt, mushrooms, onion, celery, and yogurt. Fill the squash halves with the mixture. Place them in a baking pan with a little water around the bottom. Bake in a moderate oven (350°F.) for 40 minutes, or till squash pulp is tender when pricked. Sprinkle the saffron on top just before taking from the oven.

YOGURT SPICED CABBAGE   ❋   *4 servings*

1 small red cabbage, shredded
2 Tbs. vegetable oil or butter
2 cups chopped raw apple
⅛ tsp. ground saffron

⅛ tsp. ground allspice
1 tsp. salt
1 cup yogurt or sour cream

Fry the cabbage gently in the heated oil until beginning to wilt. Add apple, spices, and salt and simmer for 20 minutes or more, until the cabbage and apple are tender. Add the yogurt just before taking from the heat.

YOGURT ONIONS   ❅   ❅   ❅   *6 servings*

2 cups milk
2½ Tbs. butter
6 onions, minced
1 cup yogurt
3 egg yolks, well beaten
½ tsp. salt

⅛ tsp. freshly ground black pepper
⅛ tsp. ground saffron
1 Tb. wheat germ
2 Tbs. grated American cheese

Put milk, butter, and onions in a saucepan and cook for 20 minutes, or till onions are tender. Drain the onions and put in a buttered baking dish. Bake in a moderate oven (350°F.) for 20 minutes. Mix the yogurt, egg yolks, salt, and spices. Pour over the onions. Sprinkle the wheat germ and cheese on top. Bake for 15 minutes longer, or till egg mixture is set and top nicely browned.

YOGURT-STUFFED POTATOES   ❅   ❅   *2 to 4 servings*

2 large baking potatoes
1 cup cottage cheese
2 Tbs. yogurt

2 Tbs. chopped parsley
2 Tbs. chopped chives
½ tsp. salt

Bake the potatoes in their skins. Scoop out contents and mash well. Add all other ingredients and toss lightly to keep mixture fluffy. Pile lightly into the potato shells and bake in a very hot oven (450°F.) for 10 minutes.

YOGURT POTATO PANCAKES   ❅   ❅   ❅   *4 servings*

2 Tbs. yogurt
1 egg, beaten
1 small onion, grated
Vegetable oil (about ¾ cup)

2 Tbs. rice flour
½ tsp. salt
2 cups grated raw potatoes

Mix yogurt, egg, onion, 3 tablespoons of the oil, the flour, and salt. Fold in the grated potatoes and mix until the batter is just blended. Pour just enough oil to cook each batch of pancakes onto the griddle. Heat the oil, pour out batter by spoonfuls, and cook till just brown on both sides.

YOGURT SOY CAKES ❄ ❄   *4 to 6 servings*

2 cups soybeans, cooked and
 mashed
½ tsp. salt
½ cup wheat germ

2 Tbs. yogurt
2 eggs, well beaten
Vegetable oil

Mix mashed soybeans, salt, wheat germ, yogurt, and eggs to make a pancake batter. Fry on both sides on a hot griddle, adding just enough oil to cook each batch of pancakes.

VEGETABLE YOGURT
MOLD ❄   *4 to 6 servings*

Grate enough carrot and pineapple to make about ¾ cup shreds of each, about 2 carrots and a quarter of a small pineapple. Soften 1 envelope of unflavored gelatin in 2 tablespoons of water, then dissolve it in 1 cup water over low heat. Stir till it is dissolved, then cool and chill. When gelatin is syrupy and beginning to set, stir in 1 cup yogurt and the grated carrot and pineapple. Chill again until firm.

YOGURT OMELET ❄ ❄ ❄   *4 servings*

5 Tbs. dal (see p. 26)
1 onion, minced
⅛ tsp. freshly ground black pepper
½ tsp. salt

4 cardamom pods, ground
¼ tsp. coriander seeds, ground
6 eggs, well beaten
½ cup yogurt
6 Tbs. butter

Mix the *dal* with the onion, seasonings, and spices. Beat in the well-beaten eggs and stir in the yogurt. Heat the butter in a heavy skillet and pour in the egg mixture. Cook gently till the omelet has set. Fold over once and serve hot.

YOGURT FISH BAKE ❊ ❊ *4 servings*

1 egg, well beaten
3 cups hot mashed potatoes
1½ cups yogurt
2 cups flaked cold cooked fish
1 green chili, minced

1 onion, minced
1 Tb. minced watercress or parsley
½ tsp. salt
½ cup chopped chives, or less

Add the beaten egg to the mashed potatoes. Put half of the potato mixture in a greased casserole. Mix the yogurt with the fish, green chili, onion, watercress, and salt. Spread this mixture over the layer of potatoes. Spread the rest of the potatoes on top. Bake in a moderate oven (350°F.) for 15 minutes, or till top is nicely browned. Sprinkle chives over the top before taking to table.

VILLAGE CHEESE

The coagulant for this cheese can be bought in the bazaar or in a drug store (See page 35). Add 1 teaspoon of coagulant to 1 cup of fresh milk just as the milk has come to a boil. Remove milk from the heat and stir till it curdles. Let this mixture drip through a muslin bag overnight, or until quite dry. Remove the dry curd from the bag, salt it lightly, and put under a heavy weight for 24 hours. It is then ready for use.

INDIAN PEA CHEESE

6 Tbs. vegetable oil
4 onions, chopped fine
2½ tsps. ground turmeric
2 lbs. fresh green peas, shelled

1 Tb. minced green chilies
1 Tb. minced fresh mint leaves
4 cups cottage cheese
½ tsp. salt

Heat the oil in a heavy kettle and brown the onions lightly; remove onions. In remaining oil fry the turmeric dark brown. Return onions to the kettle and add the peas, green chilies, and mint. Cover and let simmer for 15 minutes, or till peas are tender. Add a drop or two of water if the mixture becomes too dry before peas are tender. Add the cottage cheese and salt during the last 5 minutes; allow just enough time to heat cheese well. Mixture should be quite dry when taken from heat. Cool and let stand for a few hours before serving.

GANDHI'S GOAT'S-MILK CHEESE

Mahatma Gandhi lived mainly on goat's-milk cheese for many years. He had huge quantities of it made for his ashrams, using 20 quarts of milk at a time to make his 4-pound cheeses. The cheese, however, is simply made by anyone and it will keep for some weeks. A coagulant called rennet, which was well known to all our pioneer grandparents and which can still be bought at any druggist's, is used to make a curd from the whole fresh milk. Instructions are given on the rennet packages.

Bring milk just to a boil, then remove from the heat and add the rennet. As soon as the curd forms, drain the mixture through muslin or a fine sieve. Let it stand for several days at room temperature, then season it with ground spices of your choice— sesame seeds, saffron, coriander seeds, celery seeds, ginger, chilies, or other spices. The cheese is then molded into small balls and put to ripen in a cool, dry, dark place for 6 weeks. Turn the cheeses every day and scrape off any mold that forms on the outside.

NOTE   Goat's milk has long been recognized as being the most nutritive of all milks. Health clinics in the Far East dealing with undernourished children are making special use of the fat globules found in goat's milk for the desperately needy cases. Honey and nutmeg are often added to the milk to disguise the taste to which many object at first.

Chapter 6

CURRIED SOUPS

EVERY COUNTRY has its favorite soups. The English have their oxtail and pea soups and the Scotch their barley broth. The Russians pride themselves on their borsch, the French on their *petite marmite*, and Americans clamor for their chowders. But from the time the big Orient liner leaves the Liverpool docks, the call is for mulligatawny, that famous old stand-by known to every British Tommy for the last century and to every European who lived or still lives out in the district of India.

A famous French chef once said that soup is the real base of a meal. The trouble with good soup, the Englishman replies, is that it takes away the appetite for the rest of the meal. And the Scot responds, why should any man ask for more than a bowl of broth?

In any case, whatever the viewpoint or prejudice, good soup in any land requires good fresh vegetables, meat with the bones left in, and long slow cooking over low heat.

Mulligatawny

In India few *mem-sahibs* ever asked what went into that big black pot out in the cookhouse. All the house mistress knew was that it was delightful mulligatawny that came to the table in the big old-fashioned soup plates. The houseboy knew the proper way to serve it, bringing on the soup first, then passing the hot boiled rice separately to let the diner spoon out a portion to drop into his own soup. A newcomer might add just a polite bit, but the old-timer, knowing that the soup was the whole meal, dealt himself a goodly portion.

CHICKEN MULLIGATAWNY I ✻ 6 servings

1 stewing chicken (4 lbs.)
8 cups cold water
2 tsps. salt
8 Tbs. butter
1 onion, minced
1 Tb. curry powder
1 Tb. flour
1 tsp. sugar
2 unpeeled tart apples, diced

2 green peppers, chopped
½ cup chopped celery
2 carrots, chopped fine
2 whole cloves
1 tsp. ground mace
½ tsp. freshly ground black pepper
1 cup tomato pulp

Cut the fowl into pieces and put it in a heavy kettle with the water and 1 teaspoon salt. Simmer for 3 to 4 hours, or till meat is tender but still firm. Remove the chicken from the kettle, take meat from the bones, and return the bones to the cooking liquid. Cut the chicken into small pieces and set aside. Cook the broth and bones until broth measures about one third less. Discard bones and reserve 4 cups of the broth in the kettle. Heat the butter in a skillet and brown the chicken pieces; remove chicken and brown the onion; remove onion. Fry the mixed curry powder and flour in the same pan. Add the sugar and simmer till a smooth paste is formed. Add to the reserved broth with remaining salt, the apples, green peppers, celery, carrots, cloves, mace, and black pepper. Simmer the soup for 30 minutes, or till vegetables are soft. Force broth and vegetables through a sieve. Return the puréed mixture to the kettle and add the chicken, browned onion, and tomato pulp. Simmer for 10 minutes longer. Serve hot boiled rice in a separate dish.

CHICKEN MULLIGATAWNY II ✻ 4 servings

½ cup dried lentils or ¼ cup dal (see p. 26)
1 stewing chicken (4 lbs.)
8 cups water
2 tsps. salt

3 onions, chopped fine
4 Tbs. butter
1 Tb. curry powder
2 bay leaves
1 cup coconut milk (see p. 16)

Soak lentils in water to cover overnight, or soak *dal* for at least 1 hour. Cut the fowl into pieces and put them in a heavy kettle with the water and 1 teaspoon salt. Let simmer for at least 2 hours, till meat is tender but still firm. Remove chicken from kettle, take meat from the bones, and return bones to the kettle. Cook down the liquid till it measures about 4 cups. Discard bones.

Brown the onions lightly in the heated butter in a separate pan; remove onions. In remaining butter fry the curry powder to a dark brown. Add the curry mixture and onions to the reserved broth and add bay leaves, coconut milk, soaked lentils or *dal*, and remaining salt. Simmer for about 20 minutes, till the soup is a thick rich broth. This may be strained, or the ingredients may be left in as desired. Add the chicken which has been cut into small pieces. Simmer for 5 more minutes, then serve with hot boiled rice in a separate dish.

CURRIED GINGER SOUP   ❋   ❋   *6 servings*

1 plump stewing chicken (5 lbs.)
1 lemon, halved
8 cups cold water
2 tsps. salt
2 large onions
2 leeks, chopped fine
4 peppercorns
1 bay leaf
¼ cup peanut oil
4 tsps. ground ginger
1 cup bean sprouts or bamboo shoots
1 parsley sprig, minced
4 Tbs. chopped watercress
4 hard-cooked eggs, sliced

Wash the fowl and dry it. Rub it inside and out with the lemon pieces. Put it in a large heavy kettle and cover with the cold water. Add the salt. Chop one of the onions and add to the kettle along with the leeks, peppercorns, and bay leaf. Bring to a fast boil, then turn heat low and simmer for about 4 hours, till the chicken is tender. Strain off the liquid and set aside. Remove the bones from the fowl and chop the meat fine.

In a skillet heat the peanut oil. Chop the second onion and fry it lightly in the oil; remove onion from the pan. In oil remaining, brown the ginger and let it bubble up for a moment. Put the strained liquid back into the kettle, and add the chicken pieces and the oil and ginger. Add the sprouts, parsley, and watercress. Simmer for 10 minutes longer. There should be 6 cups of soup when it is done. Serve the soup hot, with hot boiled rice in a separate dish, and egg slices for each diner to add to his own soup plate.

MUTTON MULLIGATAWNY   ❋   *6 servings*

2 lbs. neck of mutton with bones
8 cups water
Salt
2 Tbs. butter or vegetable oil
2 onions, chopped fine

2 tsps. curry powder
5 Tbs. dal (see p. 26)
3 Tbs. ground almonds
Lemon slices

Put the mutton in a heavy kettle with the water and 1 teaspoon salt. Simmer for 4 hours or more, till the meat drops from the bones. Add more water, if necessary, to keep the meat covered as it cooks. Lift out the meat and remove the bones. Simmer down the liquid till it measures 6 cups; set aside. Heat the butter in a separate pan and brown the onions lightly in it; remove onions. In remaining butter fry the curry powder to dark brown. Add this curry mixture and the browned onions to the reserved broth. Add the *dal* and salt to taste and simmer for 15 minutes. Add the mutton to the soup and simmer for 5 minutes longer. Serve hot, with ground almonds sprinkled on the surface. The lemon slices are a useful garnish, for a drop of lemon counteracts the strong muttony flavor. Serve rice separately.

LENTIL MULLIGATAWNY   ❋   *4 servings*

2 cups dried lentils
4 cups water
Salt
4 Tbs. butter

1 onion, chopped fine
2 tsps. curry powder
1 garlic clove, mashed
1 tsp. lemon juice

Wash the lentils and soak in water to cover overnight. In the morning drain off soaking water and cover with 4 cups fresh water. Add 1 teaspoon salt and simmer the lentils for about 30 minutes, till they are soft. Heat the butter and brown the onion lightly in it; remove onion. In remaining butter fry the curry powder to dark brown. Stir in the garlic and simmer for 3 minutes. Add this curry mixture to the soup. Add the onion and salt to taste. Simmer all together until well blended and smooth. There should be about 4 cups when ready for serving; if not enough add a little water. Squeeze in the lemon juice at the last moment. Serve hot, with hot boiled rice in a separate dish.

ALMOND LAMB
MULLIGATAWNY   ❋   ❋   ❋   *6 servings*

¼ cup mustard or sesame oil
4 lbs. lamb stew meat with bones
2 onions, chopped fine
1 tsp. mustard seeds
1½ tsps. coriander seeds
2 whole cloves
8 cups water
1 tsp. salt

1-inch piece of green gingerroot,
  shaved fine
2 bay leaves
5 Tbs. dal (see p. 26)
1 cup coconut milk (see p. 16)
4 Tbs. ground almonds
Lemon wedges

Heat the oil in a large heavy kettle and brown the meat quickly; remove meat. Brown the onions lightly in the remaining oil and remove onions. Grind the mustard and coriander seeds together and fry the mixture in the oil left in the kettle. Return the onions and add the cloves, water, salt, gingerroot, bay leaves, and browned meat. Simmer for 3 to 4 hours, or till the meat is tender and dropping from the bones.

Meanwhile soak the *dal* in water to cover for 1 hour or longer, till it has become a paste. Lift out meat and bones and strain the liquid and measure it. If more than 6 cups, simmer until it is reduced to 6 cups. If less, add enough water to make up the amount. Remove the meat from the bones and add the meat to the soup with the softened *dal*. Simmer for 15 minutes, then add the coconut milk and almonds and simmer for 5 more minutes. Serve hot, with hot boiled rice separate. Serve lemon wedges with each portion; the diner adds lemon juice as he wishes.

HAWAIIAN RICE SOUP   ❊   ❊   *4 servings*

½ cup uncooked brown rice
1 garlic clove, mashed
⅛ tsp. ground turmeric
⅛ tsp. ground chilies
1 tsp. peanut oil
1 can (10½ ozs.) mushroom
soup, undiluted

4 cups water
1 green pepper, chopped fine
3 tomatoes, chopped fine
1 tsp. salt

Simmer the rice, garlic, turmeric, and ground chilies in the heated oil till it bubbles up. Add the mushroom soup and water and mix well. Add the green pepper, tomatoes, and salt; add more salt if necessary. Cover and let simmer for 30 minutes, or till the rice is tender. As the rice absorbs the liquid, add more water or soup so that there will be 4 cups of soup when it is done. Serve hot.

PRAWN SOUP   ❊   ❊   ❊   ❊   *4 servings*

¼ cup mustard oil or butter
1 onion, minced
1 tsp. curry powder
1 lb. shelled raw prawns

4 cups water
1 tsp. salt
1 cup coconut milk (see p. 16)

Heat the oil and brown the onion lightly in it; remove onion from skillet. In remaining oil fry the curry powder to dark brown. Add the shelled raw prawns and simmer for 3 minutes. Return the browned onion to the pan and add water and salt. Cover and let simmer for 15 minutes or less, till prawns are tender. Add the coconut milk and simmer for 5 minutes longer.

Cold Curried Soups

Cold soups have always been popular in hot lands. They are rapidly gaining favor today with Westerners, especially since our modern refrigeration makes preparation so easy. Soup is prepared in the same way, the curry powder being cooked beforehand to avoid any raw curry taste in the cold soup. The unfailing rule is: curry powder must first be fried in fat before being added to any dish, hot or cold.

CURRIED APPLE SOUP ❋ ❋ *6 servings*

2 tart apples
2 tsps. curry powder
2 Tbs. butter or vegetable oil
6 cups chicken broth

1 tsp. salt
½ cup apple juice
1 cup heavy cream
Ground ginger

Pare the apples, reserving a few curls of peeling for garnish. Mince the peel and keep it in water mixed with a little lemon juice until it is needed. Fry the curry powder in the butter till it is dark brown. Stir in 1 cup of the broth and cook till the mixture is smooth. Add remaining broth and the salt. Mince the apples and drop at once into the broth; if they are left in the air they will discolor. Cover and let simmer gently for 20 minutes, or till apples are soft. Add the apple juice and blend well. Chill the soup for several hours. Add chilled cream just before serving. Sprinkle a little ginger on the soup, if desired, and garnish with the minced apple peel.

CURRIED COCONUT SOUP ❋ *4 servings*

1 coconut
1 cup fresh milk
3 cups chicken broth
1 onion, minced
1 tsp. peanut oil or butter

2 egg yolks, beaten
1 tsp. salt
½ cup heavy cream
Mango slices

Crack open the coconut, scrape out the pulp, and grate it. There should be about 3½ cups. Scald the milk and let the grated coconut stand in it for 1 hour. Then press out the liquid through a fine sieve. Discard the dried pulp. Add the coconut milk to the chicken broth in a heavy kettle. Brown the onion lightly in the peanut oil and add it to the broth. Mix a little of the broth with the beaten egg yolks, then add egg mixture to the kettle. Add salt to taste. Simmer the soup for 10 minutes, stirring constantly, till it is smooth and thickened a little. Let it cool. Add chilled cream to the soup just before serving if it needs thinning, but it may be served just as it is. Serve slices of chilled fresh mango with the soup.

BUTTERMILK FRUIT SOUP   ❊   *4 servings*

1 cup orange juice
¼ tsp. grated orange rind

¼ cup sugar
3 cups buttermilk

Chill all the ingredients separately. At serving time combine them and serve at once. Lemon juice, pomegranate juice, or any fruit flavoring may be added instead of orange juice. Serve with Indian breads.

CURRIED BROCCOLI SOUP   ❊   *4 servings*

1 bunch of broccoli (about 2 lbs.)
Salt
4 cups chicken broth
4 Tbs. butter or vegetable oil
1 onion, chopped fine
2 tsps. curry powder

⅛ tsp. ground cayenne pepper
1 Tb. cornstarch or instant potato
½ cup heavy cream
½ cup finely chopped fresh watercress

Trim the broccoli and cut it into pieces. Cover it with boiling water with 1 teaspoon salt added and cook it for about 15 minutes, till it is tender. Drain, mash, and add to the chicken broth in a heavy kettle. Heat the butter in a separate pan and brown the onion lightly. Add onion to the broth. In butter remaining in the pan fry the mixed curry powder and cayenne to a dark brown. Stir in the cornstarch and cook till a smooth paste is formed. Add a little broth to this, mix well, and then return all to the kettle. Let simmer for 5 minutes, then press all through a sieve. Add more salt to taste if needed. Chill well. Add the chilled cream just before serving. Sprinkle with chopped watercress. This is an attractive green soup which goes well with a light luncheon.

COLD DAL SOUP   ✳ ✳ ✳   *6 servings*

2 cups dried lentils or peas or 1
   cup dal (see p. 26)
6 cups beef broth
1 ham bone
1 celery stalk, minced
4 Tbs. butter or vegetable oil

2 onions, minced
4 tsps. curry powder
½ tsp. cuminseeds, crushed
½ cup yogurt or sour cream
1 tsp. salt
Light cream

Soak the lentils or *dal* in water for 2 hours or longer, then drain. Cover with fresh cold water in a heavy kettle, simmer for 15 minutes, then drain again. Add broth to lentils and bring to a boil once more. Add the ham bone and celery. Heat the butter and brown the onions in it; remove onions to the soup kettle. In oil remaining in the pan fry the curry powder and cuminseeds to dark brown. Add a soup ladle of the lentil soup to the curry and simmer till a smooth paste is formed. Add this mixture to the soup kettle. Simmer for 30 minutes, or till about 4 cups of liquid remain. Lift out the ham bone; if there is any meat clinging to it, reserve it for other recipes. Force the soup through a sieve or purée in a food mill or blender. Let it cool. Add the yogurt and salt and chill well before serving. If the soup is too thick, add well-chilled light cream till it reaches the right consistency. Scatter minced watercress or mint leaves on the surface when serving.

CURRIED POTATO SOUP   ✳ ✳   *4 servings*

2 large potatoes
2 cups boiling water
Salt
4 Tbs. butter
4 onions, chopped fine
1 tsp. curry powder
2 Tbs. cornstarch

3 cups milk
⅛ tsp. celery salt
⅛ tsp. freshly ground black pepper
1 cup light cream
1 cup chopped watercress

Peel the potatoes and cut them into chunks. Pour the boiling water over them and add ½ teaspoon salt. Cook till soft enough to put through a sieve; there should be 1 cup of sieved potato. Heat the butter in a heavy skillet and brown the onions lightly;

remove onions. In the remaining butter fry the curry powder till brown. Stir in the cornstarch and cook for 3 minutes, till a smooth paste is formed. Put the milk in the top part of a double boiler and heat over boiling water till hot. Add the curry mixture to the milk with the sieved potato, celery salt, black pepper, and extra salt to taste if needed. Simmer this mixture for about 15 minutes, till it thickens slightly. Cool until very cold. Add the chilled cream just before serving; add only enough to give a good consistency; the soup should not be too thin. Sprinkle each serving with some chopped watercress.

Chapter 7

MEAT CURRIES

BECAUSE OF religious taboos the use of meat, and even eggs which contain the germ of life, is restricted among devout Hindus.

The Brahmin priests who drew up the rules of diet in the fifth century A.D. were astute men, influenced not only by their belief in transmigration, but by the fact that meat deteriorated with terrifying rapidity in their torrid climate. Hence they simply forbade all use of it except by certain fighting castes.

Meat is still eaten, however, by the millions of Moslems (excepting pork), the great mass of noncastes, and, till just recently, the many foreign service men. There is always an adequate supply, though it may be of inferior quality, to be found in the native bazaar, but it should always be well washed in permanganate of potash before going into the curry pot.

Today, however, with modern refrigeration and new canned and frozen meats in Westernized supermarkets, even the orthodox Hindus in the big city are forgetting their taboos.

Curries are prepared in a variety of ways, even as in the West. Meats are served as stews, roasts, casseroles, hamburgers, barbecues, etc. The main difference lies in the fact that in India curry spices are used in each dish. And there are no leftovers. Sometimes meats or vegetables are parboiled or soaked in spiced tenderizer and preservative mixture.

There are too many dishes to be listed here but curries fall into a few main classes, the names denoting the method of cooking.

SAUCE OR STEW where meat and/or vegetables are cooked with as little liquid as possible over low heat for a long time. Rice is served separately.

BIRIANA, a Moslem dish in which meat and rice are cooked together, garnished with a profusion of nuts, flower petals, raisins, etc.

PULAO, Pellaw, Pilaf, etc., a dry curry in which raw rice and meat are cooked with whole spices which are left in; all liquid is absorbed in the cooking.

KABAB, Kebab, Kebob, etc. Portions of meat or meat mixtures are threaded on swords or skewers and broiled over an open fire; during the broiling they are basted often with hot curried sauces. Besides these there are many variations of curried dishes such as BALLS, MASHES, MINCED CUTLETS, KORMAS, BUFFATHS. There are puffed spiced pies, chops stuffed with pistachio nuts, etc., young lambs roasted whole and coated with silver or gold tissue, and a multitude of fantastic dishes which, to the Westerner, seem to belong to the Thousand and One Nights feasts.

Each district in India, or farther East, clings to its own favorite blend of curry spices as well as its own method of cooking. So much so that any old-timer—the name by which the *pukka sahibs* of former days were known—could tell at first mouthful of curry from whence his cook hailed. Climate and availability of ingredients no doubt account for the partiality the various communities have towards their own special curries. Hence in Ceylon, where vegetation is lush and the beaches fretted with those dried fish, their curry demands dried fish, potatoes, eggplant, *dal*. Malabar uses vinegar to drown that strong mutton taste, adding coconut and potato. Madras likes tomatoes and coconut milk. Prawn curry is found on all coasts. Closer to the Equator, too, the curries tend to become more fiery, as though intent on pepping up jaded spirits. Flaming kababs are favored up in the cold clean regions of the great snow mountains.

The Thousand and One Nights feasts are still celebrated in India but more and more rarely. Western eating habits and Western foods are being adopted more and more in the Far East, just as the intriguing dishes of other lands are being accepted by Americans.

This book deals only with simple curries—typical dishes from each class—and ones which the American housewife can make successfully.

Beef Curries

STANDARD BEEF CURRY
(Western Style)   ❋   *6 servings*

Any kind of beef may be used for this curry but round steak is most satisfactory. The fat or suet from the meat can be used for frying in place of butter, margarine or *ghee*.

4 Tbs. butter
1 large onion, chopped fine
2 lbs. beef, cut into 1-inch cubes, all fat trimmed off
1 Tb. curry powder
1 medium-sized potato, chopped fine

1 tart apple, diced fine
1 cup water, or more if needed
1 cup peas, fresh or canned
1 tsp. salt, or more

Melt the butter in a heavy iron skillet and brown the onion only lightly, then remove onion. In remaining butter brown the meat well and remove it. Fry the curry powder till dark brown, then return the onion and meat and add all the other ingredients except peas and salt. Meat should be barely covered with water. After simmering over very low heat for 2 to 4 hours, or till very tender, there should be only a small amount of very rich gravy. Add fresh peas 20 minutes before the curry is finished, canned peas 5 minutes before. Add salt to taste with the peas.

NOTE Apples and potatoes are never used in Indian curries in India but are popular with the American housewife.

FRENCH BEEF CURRY   ❋   ❋   *4 servings*

Curries of Pondichéry, the former French province in India, are famous. Cooking is always done in a heavy iron skillet, and the native cook uses only a wooden spoon, claiming that metal spoils the flavor of any curry.

2 large onions, diced
4 Tbs. butter
1 lb. chuck or round steak, cut into small cubes
1 tsp. ground ginger
1 tsp. ground turmeric
1 tsp. ground allspice
½ tsp. chili powder
4 cardamom pods
½ tsp. black peppercorns, freshly ground

4 whole cloves
2 garlic cloves, mashed
1 tsp. mild curry paste
1 large sweet red pepper, chopped
2 fresh tomatoes, chopped
¼ green pepper, chopped
1 tsp. salt
1 cup water, or more if needed

Fry the onions in the heated butter till they are pale brown; remove onions from pan. Brown the meat in butter remaining in the pan and remove it. Brown the spices and garlic till dark, then return the onions and meat and add all other ingredients. Cover and let simmer over low heat for 2 to 4 hours, or till meat is tender. The gravy should be rich and thick when done.

MOSLEM BEEF KORMAH ❀ ❀ *6 servings*

4 onions, chopped fine
¾ cup butter
2 lbs. beef, cut into small pieces
1 tsp. coriander seeds
5 cardamom pods, ground
⅛ tsp. ground saffron
1 tsp. chili powder

4 whole cloves
1 garlic clove, mashed
2 cups water or broth
1 tsp. salt
1 cup dal (see p. 26)
1 tsp. vinegar or lemon juice

Brown the onions lightly in the heated butter and remove onions from the pan. Brown the meat well and remove it. Mix the spices and fry till dark brown, but do not scorch. Return onions and meat to pan. Add the garlic, water, salt, and *dal*. Simmer for 2 to 4 hours, till meat is very tender. Add the vinegar or lemon juice just before the curry is served. Very little but very rich gravy remains.

MAHRATTA BEEF CURRY   ❋   6 to 8 servings

1 Tb. butter or ghee
4 large onions, chopped fine
2 lbs. beef, cut into 1-inch cubes
2 tsps. curry powder
1 tsp. ground aniseed
2 cups water or broth
½ cup grated fresh coconut or 2 Tbs. dried coconut

1 fresh red chili, chopped fine
1-inch piece of green gingerroot, sliced thin, or 1 tsp. ground ginger
1 tsp. salt
Juice of 1 lemon

Melt the butter in a heavy skillet and brown the onions lightly; remove onions. Fry the meat till well browned and remove it. Mix the curry spices and fry in remaining butter till deep brown; then return meat and onions to the pan and cover with the water. Add coconut, chili, and ginger, and simmer for 3 to 4 hours, or till meat is very well done. Add salt last. Lemon juice is added just before serving. When done, this curry should be almost dry with the scant bit of gravy rich and thick. This mixture is spooned out on top of servings of hot boiled rice; pickles and chutneys are served along with it.

BEEF CURRY WITH CURD   ❋   4 servings

2 cups 1-inch cubes of fresh beef
2 onions, 1 sliced very thin, 1 minced
3 green chilies, cut into thin strips
1 cup curd (see p. 30)

6 garlic cloves, mashed
4 Tbs. butter
1 tsp. curry powder
1 cup water, or more
Salt
1 cinnamon stick, 2 inches

Put the meat in a bowl and cover with the sliced onion, green chilies, curd, and garlic. Let stand while browning the minced onion in the hot butter. Remove onion, then brown the curry powder. Put this fried curry mixture, browned onions, and the meat mixture in a heavy saucepan and cover scantily with water; add salt to taste and the cinnamon stick. Simmer till meat is tender, 2 to 4 hours.

NOTE Curd is used in many curry dishes. Dried lentils, peas, or beans are often added to these curd dishes, with a generous spoonful of hot mango chutney to add flavor.

TEA PLANTER'S CURRY
(Nilgiri Hills)   ❋   *4 servings*

This is the basic stand-by curry dish used on the tea plantations. Any meat, game, fowl, etc., may be used. The broth may be made from a packaged extract or concentrate, or from a commercial brand of soup.

4 Tbs. butter
1 small onion, chopped
3 or 4 coriander seeds
6 peppercorns
¼ tsp. ground turmeric
1 dried chili
1 garlic clove, mashed

2 cups beef broth
1 small tart apple, diced
1 cabbage heart, shredded
2 cups diced cold cooked meat
1 tsp. salt
Juice of 1 lemon

Heat the butter and fry the onion lightly; remove onion. Pound all the spices well in a mortar to pulverize, then fry till dark brown in the butter left in the pan. Cook for about 3 minutes. Add the garlic, fried onion, broth, apple and cabbage and let simmer till all are soft, about 30 minutes. Add the cold meat and salt to taste. Cook for 15 minutes longer, then add the lemon juice just before taking from the heat. Serve this sauce with hot boiled rice and chutneys.

TEXAS CURRY   ❋   ❋   ❋   ❋   *4 servings*

1 small onion chopped fine
4 Tbs. butter
1 Tb. curry powder
1 Tb. flour
¼ tsp. dry mustard
2 cups beef broth

2 cups minced cold cooked meat
Salt
3 Tbs. heavy cream
Pinch of ground ginger, if
   needed

Brown the onion in the hot butter and remove onion from pan. Mix the curry powder with the flour and mustard. Fry in remaining butter till dark brown and smooth. Simmer for about 8 minutes, adding a little water if needed to keep from scorching. Return onion to pan and add the broth and meat. Simmer for 20 minutes. Add salt to taste. Add cream to the sauce for the last 5 minutes. The sauce should be thick but scant. Serve with fluffy boiled rice and Major Grey's mango chutney.

NOTE Cayenne or chilies are never added to make a curry hotter. A pinch of ground ginger is the answer.

VEGETABLE MEAT CURRY
(Buffath)   ❋   *4 servings*

1 onion, minced
4 Tbs. butter
½ lb. fresh or cooked meat, chopped fine
1 tsp. curry powder
1 cup chopped radishes

1 cup chopped potato
1 cup chopped celery
1 cup chopped carrot
1 cup water
1 tsp. salt

Brown the onion lightly in the hot butter and remove onion. Brown the meat and remove it. Fry the curry powder till dark brown, then add all other ingredients. If necessary, add more water to cover the mixture. Simmer till vegetables and meat are done, about 1 hour if cooked meat is used, 2 to 4 hours if fresh meat is used. There should be very little gravy in this mixture when served, but it must be rich. Spoon on top of hot boiled rice and serve slices of lemon with it.

HAMBURGER EGGPLANT CURRY   ❋   *4 servings*

4 Tbs. butter
1 onion, chopped fine
1 cup ground beef
1 tsp. curry powder

1 tsp. chopped parsley
3 tomatoes, chopped fine
1 tsp. salt
1 large eggplant

Heat the butter in a heavy skillet. Brown the onion and remove it. Brown the meat in the remaining butter and remove it. Fry the curry powder till dark brown, then mix with it the onion, meat, parsley and tomatoes. Add salt to taste. In the meantime pare the eggplant very carefully, place it in a deep kettle, and cover it with boiling water. Simmer eggplant till it is tender but still firm, about 20 minutes. Lift from the water with great care, then cut off the top. Spoon out the center seeds and fill the cavity with the beef mixture. Replace eggplant top and fasten with food picks. Bake in a moderate oven (350°F.) for 20 minutes. Melted butter dripped over the eggplant while baking adds to richness. Serve with hot boiled rice, ringed with fresh parsley and lemon wedges.

CURRIED GREEN PEPPERS ❋ *6 servings*

¼ cup uncooked rice
Salt
2 cups water
6 large green peppers
1 onion, chopped fine
2 Tbs. butter

2 cups ground beef
2 Tbs. curry powder
4 Tbs. milk
½ tsp. ground black pepper
2 cups tomato juice

Wash the rice and cook it with ¼ teaspoon salt in the water till it is just beginning to soften, about 15 minutes. Drain, rinse in cold water, and set aside. Remove the tops from the green peppers and scoop out the seeds. Prepare the filling. Brown the onion in the hot butter in a heavy skillet and remove onion. Brown the ground beef in remaining butter and remove it. Fry the curry powder till dark brown. Add the browned onion and beef, the milk, drained rice, pepper, and salt to taste; mix well. Fill the pepper shells with the mixture, taking care not to cram filling down too tight. Set peppers close to each other in a baking dish and dribble the tomato juice over them. Bake in a moderate oven (350°F.) for 1 hour.

NOTE Cooked meat may be used for this filling; in that case, the baking period may be only 20 minutes.

CURRIED MEATBALLS I   ❈   ❈   *4 servings*

1 green pepper, chopped fine
1 onion, chopped fine
1 lb. meat, ground (beef or lamb)
2½ Tbs. yogurt

1½ tsps. salt
2 Tbs. chopped watercress leaves
1 tsp. curry powder
4 Tbs. butter or oil

Mix the first 7 ingredients and shape into small balls the size of cherries. Heat the butter in a heavy skillet and fry the balls till nicely browned. Serve with hot boiled rice or as accompaniments to *pulao* dishes.

CURRIED MEATBALLS II   ❈   *4 servings*

1 lb. cooked meat, ground
1 egg, slightly beaten
1 large onion, minced
1 green chili, minced
4 Tbs. butter or oil
1 tsp. ground ginger
1 tsp. ground turmeric

1 tsp. ground cuminseed
2 tsps. ground coriander
¼ tsp. ground chilies
1 tsp. curry powder
½ cup hot water
Salt

Mix meat and egg and form into small balls the size of chestnuts. Mix the onion and green chili and brown in the heated butter; then remove. Fry all the spices in remaining butter till dark brown. Return the browned onion and chili to the pan. Put in the meatballs. Fry till nicely browned, then add the hot water. Let simmer for a few minutes till a nice thick gravy is formed. Add salt to taste. Serve with hot boiled rice.

CALCUTTA MEATBALLS   ❈   *8 servings*

2 lbs. ground beef
3 Tbs. bread crumbs
2 Tbs. minced onion
2 tsps. salt
¼ tsp. chili powder
½ tsp. ground turmeric

1 garlic clove, mashed
⅛ tsp. ground black pepper
1 egg, beaten slightly
4 Tbs. butter or mustard oil
4 Tbs. water

SAUCE

2 cups finely chopped cabbage	2 cups boiling water
4 onions, chopped fine	1 tsp. salt
4 pimientos, chopped fine	¼ tsp. ground black pepper
2 Tbs. mashed potato	4 Tbs. yogurt or sour cream

Mix the beef, bread crumbs, onion, salt, chili powder, turmeric, garlic, pepper, and egg together. Shape into small balls and brown in the hot butter in a heavy skillet. Add the water and simmer, covered, for 30 minutes. Meanwhile make the sauce.

Put the cabbage, onions, pimientoes, and mashed potato in the boiling water. Simmer for 15 minutes, or till a smooth sauce is formed. Add seasoning last with the yogurt or sour cream. Pour this over the curried meatballs.

NOTE Sauces in the North of India are much blander than in the South. This sauce can be made without the yogurt, using only the vegetable liquid as gravy.

MEM-SAHIB'S CURRIED MEATBALLS ❊ ❊ 8 servings

1 Tb. butter	½ tsp. ground cloves
2 Tbs. vegetable oil	1 garlic clove, mashed
1 onion, minced	2 lbs. ground beef
½ tsp. ground cinnamon	Salt
1 tsp. ground ginger	2 cups beef broth, or more
1 tsp. ground coriander	1 Tb. tomato purée

Blend butter and oil and heat. Pour off half of the melted mixture and set aside to fry the meatballs. In the other half, in the pan, brown the onion lightly and remove onion. Mix the spices with the mashed garlic and fry till dark brown in fat in pan. Mix in onion and beef and fry till slightly done. Add salt to taste. Cool mixture and shape into small balls. Add reserved fat to pan and brown meatballs. Add broth and purée and simmer meatballs for 1 hour, or till cooked. Serve meatballs with hot boiled rice and chutney.

CURRIED FORCEMEAT BALLS
(Kofta-Ka-Kari)

8 to 10 servings

2½ Tbs. minced onion
½ cup butter or mustard oil
2 lbs. meat, fish or fowl, finely ground
1 tsp. chili powder
2½ tsps. mixed herb seasoning
1 tsp. ground turmeric

½ tsp. ground ginger
½ tsp. ground black pepper
1 garlic clove, mashed
2 cups water or broth
2 tsps. salt
1 egg, lightly beaten
1 cup bread crumbs

Brown the onion lightly in half of the butter and remove onion from pan. Brown the meat in butter remaining and remove it. Mix the spices well and fry to a dark brown shade. Return onion and meat to the pan with cooked spices. Add garlic, water and salt and simmer gently for 2 hours, or till meat is tender and quite dry. Remove from pan, let cool, and shape into small balls.

Dip the balls into the beaten egg and roll in the bread crumbs. Add remaining butter to the pan and fry the meatballs lightly. Or place the balls in a baking dish, add a little water or broth, and brown in the oven. These *koftas* are served with hot fluffy rice and various chutneys.

Veal Curries

Veal is used for curries in the same manner as beef but since it is of much more delicate taste the Indian cook adds lemon or tamarind juice to pep up the flavor. The American housewife has adopted the tart apple for this.

VEAL CURRY I ❅ ❅ ❅ ❅   *4 servings*

4 Tbs. butter or vegetable oil
1 onion, minced
1 Tb. curry powder, or less
2 Tbs. flour or mashed potato
1½ cups beef broth or gravy

½ tart apple, chopped fine
1 tsp. salt
2 cups cooked veal, cut into small pieces
Juice of ½ lemon

Heat the butter in a heavy skillet and brown the onion; then remove onion. In remaining butter fry the curry powder and flour; let the mixture simmer for 3 minutes, or till it is smooth and dark brown. Return the onion to the pan with the broth, apple, and salt. Simmer for 20 minutes, or till apple is cooked. Add the veal and simmer for another 15 minutes. Add lemon juice just before removing from heat. Serve with plain boiled rice and tart chutneys.

VEAL CURRY II ❋ ❋ ❋ ❋ *6 servings*

1 large onion, chopped fine
4 Tbs. butter or vegetable oil
2 lbs. fresh veal, cut into 1-inch cubes
1 Tb. curry powder, or less, or 1 Tb. curry paste
1 garlic clove, mashed

2 cups water or broth
1 tart green apple, chopped fine
½ cup raw potato, grated, or ¼ cup mashed potato
1 tsp. salt
Juice of 1 lemon

Brown the onion in the heated butter and remove onion. Brown the veal well in butter remaining in the pan, then remove veal. Fry the curry powder with the garlic in the same pan. Add more butter if needed. Let simmer for a few minutes till dark brown. Return onion and meat. Add the water, apple, potato, and salt. Simmer till meat is tender, for 2 to 3 hours. The gravy should be rich but scant at the end. If it needs thickening, more potato may be added. Add lemon juice and mix in well just before curry is taken from the heat. Hot boiled rice and relishes are served with this.

JAMAICAN CURRIED VEAL ❋ *6 to 8 servings*

½ cup butter or oil
2 onions, chopped fine
2½ lbs. fresh veal, diced
2 Tbs. curry powder
2 cups broth or water
1 tsp. salt
¼ tsp. ground black pepper
½ tsp. ground ginger

1 dash of Pepper Pot or Tabasco
1 Tb. tomato chili sauce
½ cup dark molasses
2 apples, chopped fine
1 cup diced celery
2 egg yolks, well beaten
½ cup cold water

Heat the butter, brown the onions lightly, and remove them from the pan. Brown the meat and remove it. Fry the curry powder till dark brown, then return onions and meat to the pan. Add broth, salt, pepper, ginger, Pepper Pot, chili sauce, molasses, apples, and celery. Let simmer till meat is very tender, about 30 minutes. Add more liquid if needed to keep meat from sticking, but the mixture should be thick when done. At the last minute mix the egg yolks with the cold water, add to the curry, and cook for another minute to thicken. Serve with lemon wedges, chutney, and hot boiled rice.

Lamb and Mutton Curries

Lamb is the most preferred meat for curries, not only in India but all over the world. What is called lamb in the Indian bazaars, however, is usually the meat of the half-starved goats which wander at will on the plain. The native cook, though, is a wizard and with certain herbs can tenderize the toughest cuts. His curry spices smother that strong mutton odor and flavor which are so objectionable to Westerners.

LAMB CURRY NORTH INDIA ❀ ❀ *6 servings*

2 onions, chopped fine
2 Tbs. butter or vegetable oil
1 lb. fresh lamb, cut into small pieces
2 tsps. curry powder
1 garlic clove, mashed

1 cup water or broth
2 tomatoes, chopped fine, or 1 cup canned tomatoes
1 tsp. salt
Juice of ½ lemon

Brown the onions lightly in the butter and remove them from the skillet. Brown the lamb in remaining butter and remove. Fry the curry powder till dark brown, then add to it all other ingredients except the lemon juice. Simmer for 2 to 4 hours, or till meat is very tender. Add the lemon juice just before serving. The curry should not resemble a stew with plentiful gravy, but rather be like a thick rich sauce, just moist enough to bind together that ball of boiled rice which the Indian molds in his fingers. Tasty mango pickles and chutneys are served with this curry.

NOTE Cold cooked lean lamb may be used in this curry. In that case, cooking time will be about 30 minutes.

CURRIED LAMB SHANKS I   ❊   *4 servings*

This curry is rapidly gaining favor in the Western world. Well-known restaurants are now making a speciality of it.

4 medium-sized lamb shanks	1 cup broth or water
4 Tbs. butter or lamb drippings	Salt
1 onion, chopped fine	4 Tbs. mashed potato, or 1 small
1 Tb. curry powder	raw potato, grated
1 garlic clove, mashed (optional)	1 cup sauterne

Trim the lamb shanks neatly but leave on any tender skin. Brown the shanks in the hot butter in a heavy skillet. Transfer browned shanks to a deep kettle. In the remaining butter in the skillet brown the onion and remove it. Next fry the curry powder to dark brown. Add the garlic if desired, then the browned onion and broth. Season with salt to taste. Stir in the potato and pour over the shanks. Cover and bake in a moderate oven (350°F.) for 2 to 3 hours, or till meat begins to fall easily from the bones. Add more hot liquid if the pan becomes too dry, enough to keep it at the original level. The sauterne is added for the last 20 minutes. The sauce should be rich and thick at the end. Pile the shanks on a platter and ring them around with hot fluffy rice, dribbling the curry sauce over them. Serve Major Grey's mango chutney, lemon wedges, and tomato slices with this.

CURRIED LAMB SHANKS II   ❊   *4 servings*

4 lamb shanks	1 cup dry sherry or sauterne
4 Tbs. vegetable oil or lamb drippings	½ tsp. salt
	½ tsp. garlic salt, or less
4 Tbs. flour	½ tsp. freshly ground black pepper
2 tsps. curry powder	per
1 cup water or lamb broth	1 onion, minced

Prepare the shanks by trimming off untidy ends. Use a heavy skillet with a tight-fitting lid. Heat the oil and brown the shanks slowly on all sides. Remove shanks from the pan and add the flour and curry powder to the oil in the pan. Simmer till a thick smooth paste forms, about 3 minutes. Add the water, wine, and seasonings and simmer for 10 minutes, or till a thick smooth sauce is formed. Put the shanks back in the kettle and sprinkle the minced onion over them. Baste with the liquid. Cover tightly and simmer for 1½ to 2 hours, or till meat is very tender. A little instant potato added to the liquid left in the pan after meat is removed will give a rich gravy. Hot boiled rice is served with this dish along with Major Grey's mango chutney.

SHUB DEG (MUTTON CURRY)   ❈   ❈   *6 servings*

2 lbs. mutton, cut very fine
4 Tbs. butter or vegetable oil
2 Tbs. curry powder
Vinegar
2 cups buttermilk or yogurt

½ cup finely chopped carrot
½ cup finely chopped pumpkin
½ cup finely chopped turnip
½ cup finely chopped onion
1 tsp. salt

Brown the meat well in the heated butter and remove meat from skillet. In remaining butter fry the curry powder to a dark shade, adding a drop or two of vinegar to make a smooth paste. Simmer for 3 minutes. Return meat to skillet and mix well. Cover with the buttermilk and let simmer at very low heat for 1 hour, or till meat is cooked, adding more liquid as needed. About 20 minutes before meat is soft, add the chopped vegetables. Let simmer till they are just tender but not mushy. Add salt at the last moment. This mixture should be quite dry when ready, with all the liquid absorbed. Formed into small balls, this curry is often served with just plain boiled rice or as an accompaniment to some other curry sauce (see Chap. 3).

NOTE In Calcutta dried lentils or peas which have been presoaked in water are often used instead of the fresh vegetables in this curry.

HAWAIIAN (MUTTON) LAULAUS ✳ ✳ *8 servings*

Mutton curry is a favorite dish among the Hawaiians and South Sea Islanders. This is one of the most popular recipes.

2½ lbs. mutton, ground or cut
  into small pieces
1 onion, minced
1 tsp. salt
½ tsp. ground black pepper
½ tsp. ground ginger

½ cup flour
½ cup butter or vegetable oil
4 large spinach leaves, well
  washed, for each laulau
2 cornhusks for each laulau

Season the meat with onion, salt, pepper, and ginger. Mix well and dredge with the flour. Fry lightly in the hot butter. Place a large tablespoon of the mixture on each spinach leaf and roll up. Place 4 spinach rolls on 2 cornhusks and roll up again, tieing with string to keep the shape. Place in a deep kettle and cover with boiling water. Simmer for 2 hours. Remove cornhusks before serving. A hot curry sauce is usually served with this (see Chap. 3) along with boiled rice, chopped coconut, and pickles.

HAWAIIAN CURRIED LAMB ✳ *6 servings*

4 Tbs. butter or lamb drippings
2 tsps. curry powder
1 Tb. flour
1 cup lamb gravy or broth
1 cup water
Salt
2 cups diced cooked lamb

½ cup diced cooked ham
2 onions, minced
3 Tbs. raisins
1 egg yolk, beaten
½ cup milk
4 cups hot cooked rice

Melt the butter in a heavy skillet and brown the curry powder well. Stir in the flour and simmer for a minute till mixture is smooth. Add the gravy and water and salt to taste. Put in the top part of a double boiler and add the meats, onions, and raisins. Simmer, covered, over boiling water for 1 hour. Stir often. At the last moment, right after taking from heat, stir in the beaten egg yolk and milk. Mix well and pour into the center of a molded ring of rice.

To make a rice ring, lightly grease the mold and pack tightly with boiled rice. Set the mold in a pan of hot water in a slow oven and unmold at the last moment. Serve with bananas and sweet mango pickle.

CURRIED SHOULDER OF LAMB ❋ *4 servings*

1½ lbs. shoulder of lamb with bones left in
Salt
1 bay leaf
4 Tbs. butter or lamb drippings
2 large onions, chopped fine
2 tsps. curry powder
2 Tbs. flour or instant potato

1 garlic clove (optional)
4 small potatoes, diced fine
4 large carrots, diced very fine
1 cup diced pumpkin or yellow squash
1 cup sauterne (optional) or juice of 1 lemon

Place the shoulder of lamb in a heavy kettle, cover with cold water, and add ½ teaspoon salt and the bay leaf. Bring to a boil, then simmer at low heat for 2 or more hours, or till meat falls easily from the bones. Remove the meat and discard the bones. Boil down the liquid till 1½ cups remain; strain and set aside. Melt the butter in a skillet and brown the onions; remove onions. Mix the curry powder and flour (if instant potato is used, reserve it to thicken sauce at end of cooking) and fry to a dark brown. Add garlic if desired. Add browned onions, meat, vegetables, and reserved 1½ cups stock; add salt to taste. Mix well and simmer for 30 minutes, or till the vegetables are soft but not mushy. The sauterne, if desired, should be added during the last 15 minutes. The mixture should be fairly dry when served, with most of the liquid absorbed. Serve with hot boiled rice and Major Grey's chutney.

CURRIED LAMB'S LIVER ❋ ❋ *8 servings*

2 cloves
2 dried red chilies
1-inch piece of green gingerroot
½ tsp. cardamom pods
2 tsps. coriander seeds
2 tsps. ground turmeric
½ tsp. ground cinnamon
3 garlic cloves

4 Tbs. lamb drippings or vegetable oil
2 onions, chopped fine
1 cup yogurt
1 cup water
1 tsp. salt
2 lbs. lamb's liver, diced

Grind all the spices and the garlic together in a mortar. Heat the drippings and brown the onions in it. Remove onions from the pan. In remaining fat brown the spices. Return browned onions to the pan and add the yogurt, water, and salt. Add meat last and simmer till it is tender, about 30 minutes. Serve with hot boiled rice or pile the mixture on Indian bread. Serve with mango pickle and relishes.

Curried Pork

For reasons of health, probably, the Koran bans pork to its Moslem followers all over the world. The use of even lard in army cookhouses has caused wars. Since the pig is the scavenger in all hot lands, most fastidious people of all nationalities avoid its meat. Hence in India only the outcaste class, the Harijans, "beloved of God" as Gandhi called them, make use of it.

Wild boar, belonging to this porcine class but feeding on the cleaner herbage of the jungle, is of course enjoyed as game by the Rajahs and the white *sahibs*, the *shikaris* (hunters).

Today, however, with new sanitary methods of raising pigs, and refrigeration more available, pork is appearing in abundance in the new Westernized supermarkets of the East, and in native bazaars as well. Since this meat demands long slow cooking, it lends itself well to curry dishes.

STANDARD PORK CURRY   ❋   *4 servings*

1 Tb. vegetable oil or ghee
1 onion, chopped fine
2 tsps. curry powder
¼ tsp. ground ginger
1 garlic clove, mashed (optional)

1 cup water or broth
1 tsp. salt
2 cups diced lean cooked pork
2 Tbs. mashed or instant potato
Juice of 1 lemon

Heat the oil and brown the onion in it; then brown the curry powder and ginger. Add the garlic and simmer for 3 minutes. Return onion to the pan and add the water, salt, and meat. Simmer for 30 minutes, or till meat is very tender. Add potato for the last few minutes to thicken the mixture. Cooked pork need not be browned first. Add lemon juice just before serving.

CURRIED PORK LOAF   ❋   ❋   *8 servings*

2 Tbs. butter or vegetable oil
1 large onion, chopped fine
2 tsps. curry powder
1 garlic clove, mashed (optional)
1 lb. lean fresh pork
1 lb. boiled smoked ham
½ cup vinegar

1 tsp. salt
1 tsp. freshly ground black pepper
1 egg white, beaten lightly
1 cup undiluted evaporated milk
4 slices of bacon
8 cups boiling water

Heat the butter and brown the onion lightly in it; remove onion from the pan. In remaining butter fry the curry powder till dark brown. Add the mashed garlic and simmer for 3 minutes, till smooth. Put the pork and ham through a food chopper, using the medium blade. Add the meats with the browned onion, the vinegar, seasonings, egg white, and evaporated milk to the fried curry in the pan. Simmer gently for 10 minutes, tossing lightly to keep from sticking. Add a few drops of vinegar if needed. Let mixture cool.

Place the slices of bacon on a square of cheesecloth and place on them the meat shaped lightly into a loaf. Roll up in the cloth and tie ends securely. Place on a trivet in a deep kettle filled with the boiling water. Simmer, covered, for 2 hours. Remove from the liquid and let stand till cool. Place in refrigerator and let stand overnight if possible. This loaf improves with standing and may be prepared 2 or more days before needed. Remove cloth before slicing very thin. Serve with Indian breads and Major Grey's chutney.

CURRIED PORK OF SOUTH INDIA ❈ *4 servings*

3 Tbs. minced onion
2 Tbs. butter or vegetable oil
1 tsp. ground ginger
2 Tbs. coriander seeds
1 tsp. mustard seeds
½ tsp. fenugreek seeds
2 tsps. ground turmeric
1 tsp. cuminseeds
1 tsp. freshly ground black pepper

1 tsp. chili powder
1 garlic clove, mashed
2 cups cold cooked lean ham
Liquid drained from 1 coconut
1 cup coconut milk (see p. 16)
1 cup broth
1 Tb. vinegar
1 Tb. tart jelly
Salt

Brown the onion lightly in the heated butter and remove onion from the pan. Pound all the spices together in a mortar or put through a grinding mill, then fry till dark brown in the butter left in the pan. Return the browned onion to the mixture and add garlic, meat, coconut liquids, broth, vinegar, and jelly. Add salt to taste. Simmer for about 1 hour, till meat is very tender. Game, wild fowl of any kind, or rich goose meat may be curried this way.

MEM-SAHIB'S PORK CURRY ❈ *4 servings*

1 onion, chopped fine
2 Tbs. vegetable oil
1 lb. cold cooked lean pork, diced
2 tsps. curry powder
½ tsp. ground ginger

2 Tbs. flour
1 garlic clove (optional)
2 cups broth
2 tart apples, diced
½ tsp. salt
Juice of 1 lemon

Brown the onion lightly in the oil and remove onion from the pan. Brown the cooked pork and remove from the pan. In remaining oil fry the curry powder, ginger, and flour till a smooth paste is formed. Simmer for 3 minutes, then stir in mashed garlic if desired. Add browned onion and meat, the broth, apples, and salt. Simmer for 30 minutes, or till sauce is cooked. This should be a thick sauce and not a thin gravy. Add lemon juice just before serving. Major Grey's chutney or sweet mango pickle and hot boiled rice are served with this.

CURRIED HAM SOUFFLÉ   ❋   *4 servings*

4 Tbs. butter or vegetable oil
1 small onion, chopped fine
½ tsp. curry powder
4 Tbs. flour
2 cups milk
2 cups finely ground cooked lean
  ham

½ cup soft bread crumbs
¼ tsp. salt
½ tsp. freshly ground black pepper
4 eggs, separated

Heat the butter and brown the onion lightly in it; remove onion from the pan. Fry the curry powder till dark brown. Stir in the flour and simmer for 3 minutes to a smooth paste. Stir in the milk and simmer till a smooth sauce is formed. Add the browned onion, ground ham, bread crumbs, salt, and pepper. Mix well. Beat egg yolks only slightly and blend, a little at a time, with the warm meat mixture. Place over heat again and cook quickly for 1 more minute. Remove from heat and let cool while beating the egg whites till they form peaks. Fold whites carefully into the cooled meat mixture and slide the whole mixture gently into a greased baking dish. Set in a shallow pan with 1 inch of hot water in it. Bake in a moderate oven (350°F.) for 1½ hours, or till light and slightly firm in the center. Serve at once with chutney and Indian breads.

South Indian Curries

Coconut is used in most South Indian curries. Tamarind, a sharp sweet fruit which grows on a magnificent tree in great profusion, is often used instead of lime or lemon as an antacid to the curry spices.

MALABAR MUTTON CURRY   ❈   *4 servings*

4 Tbs. butter or ghee
1 small onion, diced
1 lb. mutton or lamb, cut fine
1 Tb. curry powder
2 cups water or broth
1 raw potato, grated, or 2 Tbs.
  instant potato

1 tsp. salt
½ cup coconut milk (see p. 16)
¼ cup mild vinegar
Juice of ½ lemon

Heat the butter in a heavy skillet. Brown the onion in the butter and remove onion. Brown the meat well and remove it. Fry the curry powder to dark brown, then return the onion and meat. Add the water and grated potato (add instant potato last if used). Add salt to taste. Simmer for 2 hours, or till meat is very tender. Coconut milk and vinegar are added for the last 30 minutes. Lemon juice is added just before serving. Serve with hot boiled rice and chutneys.

MUTTON VEGETABLE
CURRY   ❈   ❈   *8 servings*

4 Tbs. butter or ghee
1 onion, chopped fine
2 lbs. mutton or lamb, cut into
  small pieces
1 Tb. curry powder
2 green chilies, chopped fine

1 cup chopped carrot
1 cup chopped turnip
2 cups broth or water
1 Tb. tamarind or lime juice
1 tsp. salt
1 cup yogurt

Heat the butter in a heavy skillet. Brown the onion lightly in the butter and remove onion. Brown the meat in the butter remaining in the skillet and remove it. Fry the curry powder to dark brown, then return onion and meat. Add the chopped vegetables, broth, and tamarind juice. Mix well and add salt. Cover and simmer for 2 hours, or till meat is very tender, adding more broth if needed. Yogurt is added for the last 30 minutes, but sauce should be rich and most of the liquid absorbed when done. Spoon this mixture on top of hot boiled rice.

MAHRATTA MUTTON
CURRY ❋ *6 to 8 servings*

1 Tb. ghee or vegetable oil
1 large onion, minced
2 lbs. mutton, cut into small
pieces
1 Tb. curry powder
1 tsp. ground aniseed

½ fresh coconut, grated
1 cup coconut milk (see p. 16)
1 cup water
1 tsp. salt
Juice of 1 lemon or 1 Tb. tamarind juice

Heat the *ghee* and brown the onion in it. Remove onion from pan. Brown the mutton and remove it. Fry the spices in the same pan till dark brown, then return the onion and meat to the pan, and add the grated coconut. Add the coconut milk, the water, and salt. Simmer for 2 hours, or till meat is very tender and liquid almost all absorbed. Add lemon juice just before serving.

FRITHATH CURRY ❋ ❋ ❋ *6 servings*

This is known as India's hottest curry and only the old-time *sahibs* enjoy it. Few Europeans can take more than a mouthful or two without calling for water. It is cooked without any water.

2 large onions, diced fine
4 Tbs. butter or vegetable oil
2 lbs. mutton, ground fine
1 tsp. caraway seeds
1 tsp. cuminseeds
1 tsp. ground turmeric
10 cardamom pods

10 whole cloves
10 dried red chilies
½ cup vinegar
1 tsp. salt
1 cup extra vinegar, if needed
1 Tb. curry powder
1 Tb. lemon or tamarind juice

Brown the onions lightly in the butter and remove them from the skillet. Fry the meat till well browned and remove it. Grind all the spices together in a mortar, sprinkling with vinegar to keep the harmful spice dust from the eyes. Fry the curry powder in the butter remaining in the skillet till dark brown. Mix onions and meat with the curry, add salt, and simmer over low heat till meat is done, adding more vinegar if needed to keep from sticking. Mixture should be quite dry when done. Add lemon or tamarind juice at last minute. This curry is served with hot boiled rice and very sweet pickles.

NOTE A very sweet dessert should be served with this curry.

SOUTH INDIA CURRY ❃ *4 to 6 servings*

2 onions, chopped fine
4 Tbs. butter
1½ lbs. chuck steak, cut into small cubes
1 tsp. each of ground cloves, cuminseed, coriander and turmeric
½ tsp. ground chilies
1 cup water, or more

4 cardamom pods
4 whole cloves
¼ tsp. mild curry paste
½ green pepper, seeded and chopped fine
1 large sweet red pepper, seeded and chopped fine
4 fresh tomatoes, chopped fine
1 tsp. salt

Brown the onions lightly in the heated butter and remove onions from the pan. Brown the meat well in remaining butter and remove it. Fry the ground spices till dark brown, but take care not to scorch. Return onions and meat to the pan and cover with water. Add cardamom pods and whole cloves. Add the curry paste and let simmer till the meat is very tender. Add the fresh peppers and tomatoes for the last 30 minutes and add salt to taste. There should be only a small amount of liquid left in this curry, but it should be thick and rich in flavor.

SOUTH INDIA CURRIED EGGPLANT ❃ ❃ *6 servings*

6 small round eggplants
Salt
1 onion, chopped fine
4 Tbs. butter
1 tsp. curry powder

2 cups minced cold cooked meat
1 Tb. tomato juice
3 Tbs. uncooked rice
1 Tb. minced mint leaves
6 cups chicken broth

Wash the eggplants well. Cut off and reserve the tops. Scoop out the pulp (there should be about 2 cups) and lightly sprinkle the insides of the eggplants with salt. Set aside. Chop the pulp well, salt heavily, and place in a colander; weight it with a plate.

After 1 hour squeeze out the pulp to remove the brine, also that brownish substance which is (erroneously) deemed poison by many. In the meantime brown the onion in the hot butter in a heavy skillet and remove onion. Brown the curry powder till dark brown. Add the browned onion, cold meat, tomato juice, uncooked rice, mint, and drained eggplant pulp. Add a little more salt if needed. Fill the eggplants carefully with this mixture. Fasten on tops with food picks. Stand the eggplants upright, wedged in a high narrow kettle; cover with the chicken broth. Let simmer over very low heat for 1 hour or more, or till eggplant is tender but firm. Curry sauces (see Chap. 3) are served with this dish.

Sikh Curries

Because they are a fighting caste the Sikhs, although orthodox Hindus, are allowed by ritual law to eat meat and eggs. They favor kababs which are so popular in the northern part of India. There are many variations of the kabab, but all are based on the basic idea, chunks of meat threaded on skewers (or in the case of the fighting men, on their swords) and broiled over the open flame. Fancier kababs thread many other savory tidbits between the pieces of meat, such as onion rings, green-pepper rings, wedges of fresh tomato or cucumber, etc.

SIMPLE BEEF KABABS ❊ ❊ *4 servings*

½ tsp. poppy seeds
1 tsp. cuminseeds
4 whole cloves
4 dried red chilies
1-inch piece of green gingerroot, minced

1 Tb. dal (see p. 26), soaked
Salt
2 cups minced beef
1 egg, slightly beaten

Grind spices, dried chilies, and gingerroot in a mortar till a paste is formed. Add to the *dal* which has been soaked in water to a paste consistency. Add salt to taste. Mix meat well with all ingredients. Use the egg to bind the mixture into small balls. Thread balls on skewers and broil over a flame or bake in an oven. A curry sauce is ofen served with these balls, but just as often they are eaten dry with Indian breads or boiled rice. Fresh cucumber slices, tomato wedges, mango pickle, etc., are served with these.

SIKH KABABS I ❄ ❄ ❄ ❄ 4 servings

1 lb. fresh meat, any kind
½ cup butter or vegetable oil
1 small onion, minced
1 garlic clove, mashed
½ tsp. coriander seeds
1 Tb. chili powder
1 tsp. ground ginger

1 tsp. ground turmeric
1 cup water or broth
1 tsp. salt
Few green-pepper slices
Few whole mushrooms
Few sweet-onion rings

Remove all bone and gristle from the meat but leave the piece whole. Crisscross the meat lightly with a knife, taking care not to cut through it. Prepare a marinade. Heat 4 tablespoons of the butter in a heavy skillet and brown the onion lightly; remove onion. Fry the garlic and all the spices in the same skillet. Return browned onion and add the water and salt. Simmer for 5 minutes. Put the meat in a deep bowl and pour the marinade over it. Let stand for 30 minutes, turning occasionally, till most of the curry marinade is worked into the meat.

Remove meat from the bowl and cut into inch-thick cubes. Replace in the mixture and turn cubes in remaining marinade for another hour. Remove and drain. Dip the cubes into the remaining butter, melted, and thread on skewers, interspersing with the pepper slices, mushrooms, and onions. Broil over a hot fire and serve with Indian bread (*chapati*).

SIKH KABABS II ❄ ❄ ❄ 8 servings

1 Tb. poppy seeds
½ tsp. ground cinnamon
½ tsp. ground cloves
½ tsp. ground cardamom
½ tsp. ground nutmeg

1 Tb. olive oil
1 large onion, minced
1 cup water
1 tsp. salt
2 lbs. lean meat

Make a marinade. Blend all the spices well together in a mortar. Heat the oil and fry the onion in it. Fry the spices to deep brown in the remaining oil. Add the water and salt and simmer for about 3 minutes. Cut the meat into strips 1 inch wide and 6 inches long. Place the strips in a deep bowl and pour the marinade over them. Let them soak for 1 hour or more. Thread on skewers, with fresh onion or other vegetables as desired. Broil over a hot flame and serve with Indian *chapati* or *paratho* (see Chap. 14).

CURRIED KABABS ❊ ❊ ❊ *8 servings*

3 strongly flavored onions, diced fine
4 Tbs. butter
1 Tb. curry powder
1 garlic clove, mashed
3 Tbs. beef broth or water
3 fresh tomatoes, chopped fine
½ cup beef broth or water
1 tsp. salt
2½ lbs. beef, cut into 1-inch cubes
Sweet-onion rings
Paper-thin slices of green ginger-root
Tomato slices

Brown the diced onions in the heated butter and remove onions from pan. Fry the curry powder till it is a dark brown shade. Return the onions to the pan and add the garlic and the 3 tablespoons of broth. Simmer for about 3 minutes, or till the mixture is quite dry. Add the chopped tomatoes, the ½ cup broth, and the salt, taking care not to add too much salt if broth is used. Let this mixture simmer for 30 minutes, then pour it over the raw beef cubes and let them marinate for 2 hours. Remove meat and thread on skewers, alternating with the slices of sweet onion, ginger, and tomato. Broil over a flame or bake in an oven till meat is cooked. These kababs are served with hot boiled rice or Indian breads (see Chap. 14). Small individual skewers are now available in American stores.

CUBED KABABS ❋ ❋ ❋ ❋ 4 servings

1 tsp. ground poppy seeds
1 tsp. ground ginger
2 tsps. coriander seeds
1 tsp. ground turmeric
¼ tsp. ground chilies
1 tsp. salt

1 tsp. onion juice
2 tsps. water
2 tsps. yogurt
1 lb. meat, cut into cubes
1 Tb. olive oil or butter

Blend all the spices in a mortar. Add the salt, onion juice, and water to form a paste. Squeeze this essence through a muslin bag or press through a sieve. Add yogurt to the liquid obtained. Soak the meat cubes in boiling water for 5 minutes. Drain, then marinate in the spice mixture for 30 minutes. Thread on skewers, roll in the oil, and broil gently till meat is cooked. A pan should be set below to catch the drippings, which are used to make a sauce for the kababs. Serve with Indian breads (see Chap. 14), and pickles.

LAMB KABABS ❋ ❋ ❋ ❋ 4 servings

1 lb. mutton or lamb
4 onions
2 Tbs. fresh green gingerroot
4 Tbs. butter or lamb drippings
1 Tb. curry powder

1 garlic clove (optional)
4 cups boiling water
1 tsp. salt
1 large tomato, chopped fine, or
1 cup drained canned tomatoes

Cut the meat into 1-inch cubes. Quarter 2 onions and slice the gingerroot paper-thin. Thread the meat cubes on skewers, interspersing with the onion quarters and gingerroot. Place in a baking pan and set aside. Chop the other 2 onions fine and brown them in the butter. Add the curry powder and fry till dark brown. Add garlic and boiling water, salt, and tomato. Simmer this mixture for 10 minutes, then pour it over the skewered meat. Cover the pan and bake in a moderate oven (350°F.) till kababs are quite dry and all the liquid absorbed, about 45 minutes. These may be eaten with hot boiled rice, or Indian breads such as *chapati* (see Chap. 14). Serve mango pickle and chutneys as relishes.

Hunter's Curries

Curried dishes rank high with hunters and bushmen. A dash of curry powder or a dab of curry paste can transform a can of beef, a bit of tough goat meat, or a wild bird into a most satisfying meal. All that is needed is a heavy iron pot and a few embers kept glowing for some hours. No cooking time is specified since it is known that the longer the cooking the better the curry.

Rabbit, the most tasteless of all game, is well adapted to curry cooking.

AUSTRALIAN CURRIED RABBIT ❋ ❋ 6 servings

1 rabbit, skinned
4 Tbs. vegetable oil
2 large onions, chopped fine
1 Tb. curry powder
1 tsp. flour

1 tsp. curry paste
2 cups canned beef or chicken broth
1 tart apple, minced
1 tsp. salt

Cut the rabbit into pieces, leaving the bones in for flavor. Heat the oil in a large kettle. Brown the onions in the heated oil and remove onions from kettle. Brown the rabbit pieces quickly and remove them. Fry the curry powder and flour till dark brown. Stir in the curry paste and simmer for a few minutes. Return the onions and rabbit to the pot. Add the broth and apple; season. Simmer till meat is tender, or till the dish is needed. Hot boiled rice goes well with this, or canned Indian breads, such as *popadams*, etc. Also a bottle of Major Grey's mango chutney.

CURRIED WILD HARE OF
NORTH INDIA ✿ *6 servings*

1 hare, skinned
1 cup buttermilk or yogurt
4 Tbs. vegetable oil
1 large onion, chopped fine
1 tsp. curry powder or 1 tsp. curry paste

1 cup canned condensed tomato soup
1 cup water
1 tsp. salt
1 Tb. lemon juice, vinegar, or wine

Disjoint the hare to make as many pieces as possible, leaving the bones in. Soak the pieces of hare in the buttermilk for at least 1 hour; add a little water if necessary to cover hare with liquid. Remove the hare and let drain. Brown the pieces in the heated oil and set aside. In remaining oil brown the onion lightly and remove it. Then fry the curry powder to dark brown and let simmer for 3 minutes, till a smooth paste is formed. (If curry paste is used instead, add it with the tomato soup.) Return onion and hare to curry mixture and add soup, water, and salt. Cover and let simmer for 4 hours or longer, till meat falls from the bones. Add the lemon juice just before taking from heat. The gravy should be scant but rich. Serve with hot boiled rice in a separate dish, or with Indian breads.

CURRIED DEER ✿ ✿ ✿ *50 servings*

6 cups finely chopped beef suet or 4 cups vegetable oil
12 lbs. fresh deer meat, cut into small pieces
12 Tbs. curry powder
12 garlic cloves, mashed

12 cups water or canned soup
5 Tbs. salt
2 Tbs. freshly ground black pepper
1 cup vinegar or lemon juice

Fry out the suet in a heavy kettle and in it brown the pieces of meat. In a little of the melted suet in a small pan fry the curry powder till dark brown. Mix in the mashed garlic and simmer for 3 minutes. Add to the meat in the kettle with the water, salt, and pepper. Cover the pot and simmer over very low heat for 6 or more hours, till meat is very tender. Add more water to keep meat covered if needed. About 30 minutes before curry is done add the vinegar or lemon juice. Let liquid simmer down till most of it is absorbed at the end. A large pot of rice, serving for 50, should be prepared to serve with the meat, or plain canned baked beans.

BARBECUED VENISON
CHOPS ❈ ❈ *6 servings*

6 venison chops
½ cup olive oil
1 tsp. curry powder
1 tsp. minced onion

½ cup spiced vinegar
½ cup bottled curry sauce
Salt

Arrange the chops on the barbecue broiler. Make the curry sauce. Heat the oil and fry the curry powder to dark brown. Add the minced onion and cook for 1 minute. Add the spiced vinegar, bottled curry sauce, and salt to taste. Mix well and bring to a boil. Simmer over low heat for 20 minutes. Brush the chops on both sides with the curry sauce. Broil the chops, and as they cook brush them again with sauce every 5 minutes. After 20 minutes turn the chops over and continue to broil them and brush with sauce until they are done.

SHIKAR (HUNTER'S) CURRY ❈ *2 servings*

4 Tbs. butter or vegetable oil
2 large onions, chopped fine
2 cups diced mutton
2 tsps. curry powder
2 tsps. curry paste
2 tsps. mango chutney or other hot preserves

Drop of cassareep (optional)
1 garlic clove, mashed (optional)
2 cups broth
1 tsp. salt
1 whole clove (optional)
Juice of ½ lemon

Use a heavy skillet to heat the butter. Brown the onions lightly and remove them. Brown the mutton well and remove it. Fry the curry powder till dark brown. Stir in the curry paste, chutney, and (if desired) the drop of cassareep. Using the same pan, stir in the browned onions and meat, the garlic, broth, and salt.

Drop in the clove and simmer the curry over low heat for 2 to 3 hours if meat is raw, or for only 30 minutes if cooked. Cook till nearly all liquid is absorbed. Add lemon juice the last minute.

NOTE Cassareep, the hottest known condiment, is extracted from the root of the bitter cassava or manioc. It is a basic ingredient of the famous Pepper Pot of the West Indies which is available in all import shops and which may be used instead of the raw extract. Caution must be taken though even with this, as one drop gives a fiery curry.

VELDT CURRIES

During the last century many thousands of East Indian laborers and tradesmen emigrated to South and East Africa. They were obliged to evolve their own curries, making use of every nourishing part of meat available.

½ lb. beef suet
1 onion, chopped fine
½ lb. beef, cut fine
1 lb. heart meat free of sinew
1 lb. liver
½ lb. sweetbreads, blanched (see p. 78)

1 lb. brains, membrane removed
2 Tbs. curry powder, or more
Salt
½ cup instant potato or flour

Fry out the suet in a heavy kettle and brown the onion well in it, then remove onion. Cut the meats into small pieces; set aside the brains. Brown well all the other meats. Fry the curry powder in a small amount of suet in a separate skillet and add to the meat in the kettle. Add salt to taste and water equal to three times the amount of meat. Cover and simmer for 5 to 6 hours, till liquid has become a thick gravy. About 30 minutes before the dish is finished, add the brains. Thicken in the last 15 minutes with the instant potato or flour which has first been mixed to a smooth paste with a little water. If a more fiery curry is desired, ground ginger should be added, but very cautiously. Serve with hot boiled rice and chutney.

CURRIED TRIPE   ❉ ❉ ❉   6 servings

Dickens's homely dishes of yesterday are the gourmet's delicacies of today. Heart, liver, sweetbreads, brains, and curried tripe are found on the sideboards of hunting lodges all over the world; or in chafing dishes for that Sunday-morning buffet awaiting the late risers; or for that weekend brunch in suburbia, or that patio supper. These curried dishes are not only relished by the guests but appreciated by the cooks, who can prepare them ahead of time. Curried tripe, for instance, is actually improved by standing overnight and being reheated in the morning.

2 lbs. tripe
4 Tbs. drippings or vegetable oil
2 large onions, diced
1 Tb. curry powder

1 tsp. curry paste
2 cups clear broth
Salt
1 tsp. flour or instant potato

Soak the tripe in salted water for 30 minutes, then drain and dry. Cut into 1-inch squares. Heat the drippings in a large heavy skillet. Brown the onions in the heated fat and remove onions from pan. In remaining fat fry the curry powder till dark brown, then stir in the curry paste. Add the broth and browned onion and the squares of tripe. Add salt last, taking care not to add too much, as there is salt in the curry paste. Simmer for 1 hour, or till tripe is very soft and breaks easily. Remove any scum which forms on the surface. Add the flour, or instant potato moistened into paste with a little water, for the last 5 minutes if needed. The tripe should be just moist and not swimming in gravy. Serve with hot crisp toast, rusks, or Indian breads.

CURRIED SWEETBREADS   ❉   4 servings

Sweetbreads are especially adaptable to currying and to service from the chafing dish. There are several varieties of sweetbreads but all must be blanched to be made firm and white before further use. Blanching is done thus: Soak sweetbreads in cold water for 1 hour or more to free them from blood. Put in a saucepan, cover with fresh cold water, and bring slowly to a boil. Simmer gently for 5 minutes, then let them cool in the same water; or remove and wash well in cold water. Press sweetbreads between plates to firm them, so they can be fried or cut into pieces for currying.

1 large onion diced
2 Tbs. butter or vegetable oil
1 tsp. curry powder
1 cup clear broth
1 pair calf's sweetbreads,

blanched and sliced
½ tsp. salt
½ cup heavy cream
1 tsp. instant potato or flour

Brown the onion in the heated butter, then remove onion from pan. Fry the curry powder in remaining butter, then return onion and add the broth and sweetbreads. Add the salt. Simmer gently for 30 minutes, or till the meat is cooked. Add the cream and thickening at the end to make this a thick rich dish. Serve with hot boiled rice or with Indian breads or dried toast.

CURRIED HEART　❊　❊　❊　*4 servings*

1 lamb or beef heart
½ cup drippings or butter
1 onion, minced
1 cup cold cooked lamb or veal, diced (optional)
1 tsp. curry powder

1 tsp. salt
¼ fresh green pepper, minced
¼ cup diced celery
1 cup uncooked rice
Extra broth or water

Prepare the heart by soaking first in warm water for 1 hour or more. Drain and dry, and trim off any cartilage or gristle. Cut out the muscular wall dividing the cavities. Boil down all these spare bits to make a broth. Add enough water to the broth to make 1 cup of liquid. Set aside heart and broth.

Heat the drippings in a heavy skillet and brown the onion lightly in it; remove onion from the pan. Brown the cooked meat if used; remove it. Fry the curry powder till brown, then return meat and onion to the pan. Add the reserved broth, the salt, green pepper, celery, and uncooked rice. Simmer for just a few minutes, till liquid is half absorbed. Stuff the heart with this forcemeat.

Cover the opening of the heart with aluminum foil and tie securely. Bake in a moderate oven (350°F.) for 1½ hours or more, or till heart meat is quite tender. Add broth or water as necessary to keep the meat moist and baste frequently as it cooks. Serve with chutney.

NOTE   The meat may be omitted from this stuffing and only the vegetable-rice mixture used.

CURRIED LAMB KIDNEYS   ❊   *3 servings*

Lamb kidneys are the gourmet's delight. These, like all other organ meats, require special preparation. First immerse the kidneys in boiling water for 2 minutes; then drain and dry them. Remove skin and white core with a sharp knife, taking care not to spoil the shape of the kidney. Then fry the kidneys in hot butter in which curry powder has been already browned. They must be served instantly, as they tend to toughen as they cool. Another method is to fry and serve them with a rich curry sauce, as in the recipe which follows.

12 lamb kidneys	1 cup broth or water
4 Tbs. lamb drippings or butter	½ tsp. salt
1 onion, minced	1 tsp. flour or instant potato
1 tsp. curry powder	

Blanch the kidneys as directed above. Prepare a rich curry sauce. Heat the drippings in a heavy skillet and brown the onion first, then the curry powder. Add the liquid, salt, and kidneys and simmer very gently for 30 minutes. Use flour or instant potato to thicken gravy if needed, but sauce should be rich and scant when dish is ready. Serve on rusks, dried toast, or Indian bread.

VILLAGE CURRIED OXTAIL   ❊   *6 servings*

1 oxtail, cut apart at the joints	2 onions, chopped fine
6 cups water	1 Tb. curry powder, or less
Salt	½ tsp. flour
1 tsp. dried thyme	½ garlic clove, mashed (optional)
3 bay leaves	
3 parsley sprigs	2 tart apples, diced fine
1 cup diced cooked lean ham	Juice of 1 lemon
4 Tbs. vegetable oil or butter	

In a heavy kettle put the oxtail, water, 1 teaspoon salt, the thyme, bay leaves, and parsley. Simmer for about 4 hours, or till meat is beginning to be tender. Add the cooked ham and cook for 10 minutes longer. Remove meats and arrange in a baking pan. Boil down liquid to 2 cups and strain; set aside.

Prepare the gravy. Heat the oil and brown the onions in it; remove onions from skillet. Fry the curry powder and flour together till dark brown. Add garlic and simmer for 3 minutes. Return onions to the pan and add apples and the reserved 2 cups broth. Simmer the mixture for 30 minutes, to a rich thick gravy. Add lemon juice last. Add more salt if needed. Pour over ox joints and heat in the oven for 30 minutes. Serve with hot boiled rice and chutneys.

KANGAROO OR OXTAIL
CURRY (Australia) ✳ *4 servings*

1 kangaroo tail or oxtail	½ tsp. ground black pepper
2 onions, chopped fine	1 tart apple, skin left on, diced
4 Tbs. butter or drippings	1½ cups beef broth
1 Tb. flour	1 tsp. salt
1 Tb. curry powder	Juice of 1 lemon

Wash the kangaroo tail well, split at the joints, and blanch. In the meantime brown the onions in the hot butter in a heavy skillet and remove onions. Mix the flour and curry powder and fry till dark brown in the butter remaining in pan. Add the browned onions, pepper, apple, and broth and let simmer for a few minutes, till smooth. Place the blanched joints in a deep kettle, cover with the broth mixture, and add salt to taste. Let simmer for 4 to 5 hours, or till meat begins to drop from bones. Add more liquid as needed. There should be only 1 or 2 cups of gravy left at the end and it should be rich and thick. Add lemon juice at the last minute before serving. Hot boiled rice is served separately, along with chutneys, etc.

NOTE Certain strong-smelling or -tasting vegetables or meats (such as livers, kidneys, dried beans, turnips, etc.) are improved in color and taste by blanching. To do this, cover the meat with cold water and bring slowly to a boil. Lift the meat from the water, discard the water, and then proceed with the recipe.

Chapter 8

POULTRY CURRIES

CHICKEN, as well as any fowl such as turkey, duck, pigeon, guinea hen, game birds, etc., is excellent for curry dishes. But here again each country, each province, has developed its own special blend of spices for its curry powder. In South India, for instance, where coconut is used so largely as an ingredient for curry, cuminseed and coriander seed are often omitted when blending the curry powder, as these two spices tend to drown the delicate flavor of the coconut.

The Moslems, too, in preparing their specialties, have set rules as to whether the rice and other ingredients are to be cooked together from the start, or rice added at some certain period; also which spices are to be blended for the various meats. Each of these curries has its own distinctive flavor, so pronounced that the Indian can tell at first taste of the curry from which part of the country the cook hails.

MALAY CURRIED CHICKEN ❋ *6 servings*

1 large stewing chicken (about 5 lbs.)
4 Tbs. butter or vegetable oil
1 onion, chopped fine
1 tsp. ground turmeric
4 cardamom pods, ground
1 garlic clove, mashed
2 cups coconut milk (see p. 16)
1 tsp. minced fresh red chilies
1 cinnamon stick, 2 inches
3 whole cloves
3 cucumbers, peeled and diced
1 tsp. salt

Put the chicken in a heavy kettle and cover with cold water. Bring to a boil and simmer gently till the meat falls from the bones. Discard bones and cut meat into small pieces and set aside. Boil down the broth till it measures 2 cups; set aside. Heat the butter and brown the onion lightly in it; remove onion from skillet. Fry the turmeric and cardamom in remaining butter till dark brown, then stir in the garlic. Simmer for 3 minutes. Put the coconut milk and reserved broth in a heavy kettle. Add the browned onion, curry mixture, red chilies, cinnamon stick, cloves, and cucumbers. Let simmer for 30 minutes. Add the chicken pieces and let simmer till the liquid is almost absorbed and only a thick rich sauce remains. Add salt at the last. Serve with hot boiled rice and chutney.

HYDERABAD CURRIED CHICKEN ❊ ❊ *6 servings*

1 large stewing chicken (about 5 lbs.), cut into pieces
Salt
2 Tbs. butter or vegetable oil
1 large onion, chopped fine
1 tsp. curry powder
2 tsps. curry paste
2 garlic cloves, mashed

2 cardamom pods
2 whole cloves
1 cinnamon stick, 2 inches
Pulp of ½ coconut, sliced very thin
1 large tomato, chopped
Juice of 1 lime

Stew the chicken gently in water with 1 teaspoon salt for 4 hours till meat drops easily from the bones. Discard bones and cut the meat into small pieces; set aside. Boil down the broth till it measures 2 cups; set aside. Heat the butter and brown the onion lightly in it; remove onion from skillet. In butter remaining fry the curry powder to a dark brown, then stir in the curry paste and garlic and simmer for 3 minutes, till a smooth paste is formed. Put reserved chicken broth, browned onion, fried curry mixture, whole spices, coconut slices, and tomato in a heavy kettle. Simmer for 20 minutes, or till the liquid has become only a thick sauce. Add the chicken for the last 10 minutes. Add the lime juice as curry is taken from the heat. Add salt to taste. Serve hot boiled rice separately with this curry, also chutneys and pickles.

NOTE When whole spices are used as above, they are left in the dish when it is served.

MOSLEM SPICED CHICKEN ❋ *6 servings*

2 large broiling chickens (2½ lbs. each), cut into pieces
6 Tbs. vegetable oil
1 Tb. chili powder
1 Tb. coriander seeds
⅛ tsp. ground saffron
1 tsp. sugar
½ tsp. freshly ground black pepper
1 garlic clove, mashed
1 cup yogurt or buttermilk
1 tsp. salt

Pierce the pieces of chicken all over with a fork. Heat half of the oil and fry the spices in it. Mix in the sugar, black pepper, garlic, and yogurt. Add salt to taste. Spoon this over the chicken pieces and let them marinate for 20 minutes, turning often. Put the remaining oil in a shallow heavy baking pan and arrange the chicken pieces in it in one layer. Broil the chicken, keeping it about 4 inches below the source of heat, for about 30 minutes. Turn often till done. Serve with saffron rice and chutney.

SOUTH INDIAN CHICKEN CURRY ❋ *6 servings*

4 Tbs. butter or vegetable oil
1 roasting chicken (4 lbs.), cut into pieces
1 small onion, minced
2 tsps. curry powder
⅛ tsp. ground turmeric or saffron
½ tsp. ground ginger (optional)
½ cup minced celery
1 Tb. instant potato or ½ small raw potato, grated
1 cup chicken broth
Salt

Heat the butter and brown the chicken pieces; remove chicken. Brown the onion lightly and remove it. Fry the curry powder and turmeric (add the ginger if fiery curry is liked) to dark brown. Add the browned onion, the celery, and potato to the curry mixture in the pan. Mix well and simmer for 5 minutes; then add the pieces of chicken, the broth, and salt to taste. Cover and let simmer for 2 hours, till meat is well done and sauce is rich and thick. If more thickening is needed add more potato. Rice is served separately, as well as Major Grey's chutney and other relishes.

CHICKEN KORMA ✻ ✻ ✻ *4 servings*

1 cup buttermilk or yogurt
4 garlic cloves, mashed
1 frying chicken (3 lbs.), disjointed
4 Tbs. butter or vegetable oil
2 onions, chopped fine

1 Tb. curry powder
½ tsp. ground ginger
1 Tb. ground almonds
2 whole cloves
1 tsp. salt

Mix the buttermilk and garlic and let the chicken stand in the mixture for 2 hours, turning occasionally. Keep at room temperature. Heat the butter and brown the onions lightly in it; remove onions from skillet. In remaining butter fry the mixed curry powder and ginger. Return the onions to the pan and add the almonds, cloves, salt, chicken pieces, and buttermilk. Cover and let simmer over low heat for 2 hours, or till meat is very tender. Serve with hot boiled rice and chutneys.

TANDOORI CHICKEN ✻ ✻ *4 servings*

The word *tandoor* means oven. The skewered chicken is cooked in a big clay pot, in the oven, which is heated red hot by glowing charcoal banked around it. This is a delectable dish but one which needs an experienced Indian cook. The Western cook will be more successful cooking the bird in a broiler.

1 small roasting chicken (2 lbs.),
whole
1 onion
1 garlic clove
1-inch piece of green gingerroot
or ½ tsp. ground ginger
1 tsp. ground cuminseed
1 tsp. ground coriander
½ tsp. chili powder

2 tsps. salt
4 Tbs. yogurt or buttermilk
1 Tb. vinegar
1 Tb. Worcestershire sauce
Juice of 1 lime or lemon
2 Tbs. butter or drippings
Sprinkle of mixed ground nutmeg, cinnamon, and coriander

Wash and dry the chicken. Prick deep holes in the flesh with a fork. Grind the onion, garlic, and green gingerroot to a paste. Add to it the cuminseed, coriander, chili powder, and salt; mix well. Beat the yogurt in a bowl and add the spiced paste, the vinegar, Worcestershire, and lime juice. Mix well again. Rub the mixture into the chicken and let it stand for 4 hours. Then roast the bird on a rotary spit for about 30 minutes, or till meat is done, basting constantly with a mixture of the melted butter and the nutmeg, cinnamon, and coriander. Serve with hot boiled rice or with Indian breads and chutneys.

MEM-SAHIB'S CHICKEN CURRY ❊ ❊ *6 servings*

This is a simply and quickly prepared chicken curry, calling only for ingredients found on the shelves of the neighborhood market.

1 stewing chicken (4 lbs.), cut into pieces
6 cups cold water
Salt
1 small onion
Flour
½ cup vegetable oil
1 tsp. curry paste
Juice of 1 lemon
Cooked rice

Simmer the chicken in the water with 1 teaspoon salt and the onion added for 4 to 5 hours, or till meat drops from the bones. Strain the liquid and boil it down to measure 2 cups; set aside. Discard the bones and dredge the chicken meat lightly with flour. Brown chicken quickly in the heated oil in a heavy skillet. Add the curry paste and simmer for 1 minute. Add the reserved broth and salt to taste. Simmer for 20 minutes. Add lemon juice at the last minute. Sauce should be rich and thick. Spoon the sauce on top of hot cooked rice. Serve with Major Grey's mango chutney.

HAWAIIAN CURRIED CHICKEN   ❉   ❉   *6 servings*

3 frying chickens (2½ lbs. each), halved
Flour
½ cup vegetable oil
4 onions, chopped fine
2 tsps. curry powder
3 garlic cloves, mashed
1 cup water
1 tsp. salt
6 cups canned tomatoes with juice

½ tsp. freshly ground black pepper
½ tsp. ground sage or 1 tsp. chopped fresh sage leaves
3 green peppers, minced
1 cup chicken broth
1 cup seeded raisins
½ cup browned slivered almonds

Flatten the chicken halves with a mallet or the flat side of a cleaver. Dredge the pieces with flour and set aside. Heat 6 tablespoons of the oil and brown the onions lightly in it; remove onions. Brown the chickens lightly on both sides. Remove the chickens and arrange the pieces in a baking pan. In oil remaining in the pan fry the curry powder to a dark brown. Add garlic and simmer for 3 minutes. Add the water, salt, browned onions, tomatoes, black pepper, sage, and green peppers. Mix well and simmer for a few moments. Pour the mixture over the chicken halves. Bake in a moderate oven (350°F.) for 2 hours or longer, basting often with the curry sauce and chicken broth. The liquid should be almost absorbed when chicken is done, with only enough left to make a thick rich gravy. Place chickens on a large platter and mound hot boiled rice high over them. Heat remaining 2 tablespoons of oil to boiling and drop the raisins into it for just a few moments to puff them. Lift them out of the oil and scatter the raisins and almonds over the rice. Mayor Grey's chutney and pickles are served with this.

HAWAIIAN CURRIED
CHICKEN IN PINEAPPLES   ❋   *4 servings*

1 roasting chicken (4 lbs.) cut into pieces	2 Tbs. curry powder
	5 Tbs. flour
6 cups lightly salted water	5 Tbs. vegetable oil or butter
4 medium-sized onions	½ cup seeded raisins
2 celery stalks, diced	Salt
2 fresh pineapples with leaves	Juice of 1 lemon

Simmer the chicken gently in the salted water with the onions
and celery. Remove the meat when tender and cut it into small
pieces; discard bones. Boil the broth down till it measures 4
cups; set aside. While the chicken is cooking, split the pineapples
lengthwise and scoop out the centers; be careful not to break
the shells. Cut the pulp into small chunks; there should be about
3 cups. Wrap the pineapple leaves in aluminum foil to keep
them from scorching and heat the fruit in a slow oven while
making the curry.

Fry the curry powder and flour in the heated vegetable oil
till curry is dark brown. Strain the chicken broth into the top
part of a double boiler. Add the fried curry mixture, the pineapple chunks, raisins, and the chicken pieces. Add salt to taste.
Simmer over boiling water for 15 minutes. Add lemon juice
just before taking from the heat. Sauce should be thick and
rich. Spoon the mixture into the prepared pineapple shells.
Unwrap the leaves to serve. Serve hot boiled rice with these
stuffed pineapples, along with a variety of pickled fruits and
chutneys.

HULA-HULA HAWAIIAN
CHICKEN CURRY   ❋   *6 servings*

1 small onion, minced	1 cup coconut milk (see p. 16)
6 Tbs. butter or olive oil	1 cup clear chicken broth
2 Tbs. curry powder	3 cups small bits of cold cooked chicken
2 Tbs. flour	
2 Tbs. chopped green gingerroot or 1 tsp. ground ginger	1 tsp. salt, or more

Brown the onion lightly in the butter and remove onion from skillet. Fry the curry powder in remaining butter to a dark brown, then stir in flour and simmer for 1 minute, or till a smooth paste is formed. Return onion to the pan and add the gingerroot, coconut milk, broth, and chicken. Simmer for 15 minutes, or till only a little thick rich liquid is left. Add salt to taste at the last. Serve with hot boiled rice and pickles. This makes a fiery curry; if that is not relished cut down the amount of ginger used.

AMERICAN CURRIED CHICKEN I

❈ ❈ *6 servings*

1 stewing chicken (4 lbs.)
4 cups water
1 tsp. salt
½ cup butter or vegetable oil
3 large onions, chopped fine
1 tsp. curry powder
1-inch piece of green gingerroot, sliced fine, or ½ tsp. ground ginger
1 garlic clove, mashed (optional)
1 raw potato, grated
6 peppercorns
1 cup coconut milk (see p. 16)
1 cup canned tomatoes

Put the chicken in a large pot with the water and salt. Simmer the chicken for 2 to 4 hours, till tender. Discard bones and cut meat into pieces; set aside. Boil down the liquid till it measures 2 cups; reserve. Heat the butter and brown the onions in it; remove onions from skillet. Fry the curry powder and ground ginger in remaining fat till dark brown. (If gingerroot is used, add it later with the liquid.) Add the garlic to the curry mixture and simmer for a few minutes. Add browned onions, the potato, peppercorns, gingerroot if used, coconut milk, tomatoes, and chicken pieces. Simmer for 15 minutes, or till sauce is thick and rich. Add chicken broth as it is needed. Serve hot boiled rice separately with chutneys, roasted nuts, onion rings, etc.

AMERICAN CURRIED CHICKEN II   ❃ ❃ *6 servings*

1 stewing chicken (3 lbs.)	1 tsp. curry powder, or more
6 cups cold water	1 garlic clove, mashed
Salt	¼ tsp. brown sugar
1-inch piece of green gingerroot or ½ tsp. ground ginger	1 cup coconut milk (see p. 16)
1 Tb. butter or vegetable oil	4 cups milk
1 small onion, chopped fine	1 Tb. instant potato made into a thin paste with water

Put the chicken in a large pot with the water and 1 teaspoon salt; simmer till tender. When cool enough to handle, cut the meat into small pieces. Meanwhile, soak the gingerroot in hot water for 1 hour, then peel it and slice very thin. Heat the butter and brown the onion; remove onion from pan. Fry the curry powder dark brown, add the garlic, and simmer for 3 minutes. Stir in the sugar, coconut milk, and gingerroot. In the top part of a double boiler combine chicken pieces, browned onion, fried curry mixture, milk, potato, and ½ teaspoon salt or more as needed. Simmer for 30 minutes over boiling water, or till mixture is thick and rich. Serve rice separately, with Major Grey's mango chutney, slices of hard-cooked egg, fried onion rings, rings of green pepper, etc.

LOUISIANA CURRIED CHICKEN   ❃ ❃ *6 servings*

1 large frying chicken (3½ lbs.), cut into pieces	2 cups okra, frozen or fresh, chopped fine
8 cups cold water	3 large tomatoes, chopped
Salt	¼ tsp. freshly ground black pepper
4 celery stalks, diced	2½ cups uncooked rice
6 parsley sprigs	Green-pepper rings
2 onions, chopped	Slices of raw okra
6 slices of bacon	
1 tsp. curry powder	
1 large green pepper, chopped fine	

Cover the chicken with the water and add 1 teaspoon salt, the celery, parsley, and half of the onions. Simmer for 2 hours, or till meat drops from the bones. Discard bones and cut meat into pieces; set aside. Boil the broth down till it measures 2 cups, strain, and reserve. Fry the bacon crisp and set aside for garnishing. In bacon fat remaining in skillet fry the rest of the onions, then the curry powder. Add the reserved broth, green pepper, okra, tomatoes, black pepper, chicken meat, and salt to taste. Cover and let simmer for 15 minutes, then add the rice; cover, and simmer again for 15 to 20 minutes, till most of the liquid is absorbed. Turn curry out on a platter and garnish with the bacon crisps, green-pepper rings, and raw okra cut paper-thin.

CHICKEN KABAB ✷ ✷ ✷ *4 servings*

2 onions, chopped fine
2 garlic cloves, mashed
2 whole cloves
4 peppercorns
½ cup yogurt
½ tsp. ground ginger

½ tsp. chili powder
1 Tb. vinegar
1 tsp. salt
1 frying chicken (3 lbs.), whole
½ cup oil or melted butter

Grind the onions, garlic, cloves, and peppercorns together to a smooth paste. Add yogurt, ground spices, vinegar, and salt. Pour over the whole chicken in a large bowl. Prick the chicken well with a fork and turn often during the next two hours to allow yogurt mixture to soak in. Roast on a rotating grill, or bake in a moderate oven (350°F.) for 2 hours, or till meat is tender, basting often with the hot oil. Serve on *chapati* or biscuits, with raw-onion rings, green-pepper rings, and wedges of lemon.

CURRIED CHICKEN BALLS
(North India)   ✷   *4 servings*

1 stewing chicken (4 pounds)
6 cups cold water
Salt
½ cup vegetable oil
1 small onion, minced

1 Tb. curry powder
1½ tsps. mixed herbs
2 eggs, lightly beaten
½ cup bread crumbs
1 cup tomato juice

Simmer the chicken in 6 cups water with 2 teaspoons salt till the meat drops from the bones. Remove meat to a bowl and mash it till it forms a paste. Boil down the cooking liquid till it measures 2 cups; set aside. Heat 2 tablespoons of the oil and brown the onion in it; add onion to mashed chicken. Brown the curry powder in the oil and add the mixture to the chicken. Let the chicken cool.

When the chicken is cool, add the mixed herbs, the eggs, and bread crumbs. Mold the mixture into balls the size of walnuts. Heat remaining oil and in it fry the chicken balls to golden brown. Mix the reserved broth and the tomato juice and pour over the meatballs. Cover and simmer over low heat for 2 hours. Add more liquid if needed. Gravy should be rich but scant when served. Spoon out the chicken balls on top of hot boiled rice and dribble the curried gravy over them. Mango chutney and pickles go well with these.

CURRIED CHICKEN LIVERS   ✻   4 servings

Here is an excellent curry for the chafing dish, one which can be prepared ahead of time, refrigerated, and reheated with improved flavor a day or two later for a late Sunday-morning breakfast or patio supper.

4 Tbs. butter or vegetable oil
1 onion, minced
16 fresh chicken livers, washed and dried, or frozen chicken livers, defrosted

2 tsps. curry powder
2 Tbs. flour
2 cups milk or chicken broth
1 tsp. salt
½ cup sliced mushrooms

Heat the butter and brown the onion lightly in it; remove onion. In butter remaining brown the chicken livers, adding more butter if needed; remove livers from pan. Fry the mixed curry powder and flour till dark brown. Return the onion and livers to skillet, and add the milk and salt. Simmer for 20 minutes, or till livers are well done. Add the mushrooms for the last 5 minutes of cooking. Spoon the livers on top of hot boiled rice or serve on Indian bread (see Chap. 14) or on dry toast.

NOTE If extra butter or oil must be added during the browning of the livers, make sure it is already very hot before adding, as a cold fat added gives a greasy-tasting dish.

VARIATION Minced chicken livers may be browned in curried butter and added to soufflés, omelets, or scrambled eggs.

CURRIED CHICKEN-LIVER PATTIES   ❊   5 servings

Unsweetened tart pastry, unbaked
16 chicken livers
4 Tbs. butter or vegetable oil
1 small onion, minced

1 tsp. curry powder
1 Tb. flour
1 cup milk
1 tsp. salt

Make tart pastry, roll it out into a thin sheet, and use about two thirds to line 10 muffin rings. Cut out 10 circles of pastry to make covers to fit. Chill while making the filling.

Wash the chicken livers, dry them, and mince into small pieces. Heat the butter and brown the onion lightly in it; remove onion. Fry the mixed curry powder and flour till dark brown. Return onion to pan with curry mixture, and add the milk, minced livers, and salt. Put the mixture in the top part of a double boiler and let cook over boiling water for 5 minutes, or till the mixture is rich and thick. Fill the pastry-lined muffin rings. Moisten the edges of the pastry and put on the covers, pinching the edges to seal them. Make a small hole in each cover for steam to escape. Bake in a very hot oven (450°F.) for 20 minutes, or till pastry is golden brown. Serve hot or cold with Major Grey's chutney.

VARIATION Brown the chicken livers in butter, then add to bottled curry sauce (see Chap. 3). Spoon the mixture onto pastry circles and fold over to make turnovers, or use to fill small pies.

CURRIED PIGEON   ❊ ❊ ❊   *4 servings*

2 pigeons	1 cup coconut milk (see p. 16)
4 Tbs. ghee or vegetable oil	1 tsp. salt
4 onions, chopped fine	4 Tbs. minced watercress or
2 Tbs. curry powder	fresh coriander leaves
1 tsp. ground cinnamon	4 raw potatoes, grated
1 tsp. ground nutmeg	4 Tbs. grated coconut
1 garlic clove, mashed	Juice of 1 lemon

Pluck, draw, wash, and quarter the pigeons. Heat the *ghee* and brown the onions lightly in it; remove onions from pan. Fry the curry powder and spices to dark brown in remaining *ghee* and stir in the mashed garlic. Simmer for 3 minutes, adding a little water if needed. Return the onions to the mixture and add the coconut milk, salt, watercress, potatoes, and grated coconut. Add the pigeons, cover, and simmer for 30 minutes, or till flesh is quite tender, basting often. Add a little more water if needed. Add the lemon juice 5 minutes before serving. Sauce should be rich and scant. Arrange the pigeons on a mound of rice and spoon the sauce over them. Serve with chutneys and relishes.

CURRIED DUCK   ❊ ❊ ❊   *4 to 6 servings*

1 large duck (5 lbs.)	½ cup vinegar
4 Tbs. olive oil	2 tsps. salt
1 Tb. curry powder	¼ green pepper, minced
6 garlic cloves, mashed	½ tsp. sugar
½ tsp. freshly ground black pepper	

Cut the duck into pieces and wash and dry. Heat the oil in a heavy kettle. Fry the curry powder to dark brown. Mix with the garlic, black pepper, vinegar, and salt. Add duck pieces and let marinate in a cold place for 3 hours, turning meat often to allow it to soak up flavor. Remove meat from kettle. Heat the oil marinade to very hot. Brown the duck, adding more oil if needed. Add the green pepper and a little water. Let the mixture barely simmer, covered, over very low heat for 3 to 4 hours, till meat is cooked and curry is ready. Add a little water

if duck sticks. Add the sugar just before curry is taken from
the heat. Serve with hot boiled rice and chutney.

Vindaloos

Vindaloos are dishes which use only vinegar and no water in the
preparation of meat. Pork and fish-tasting fowl such as duck, etc.,
are usually prepared *vindaloo* style. Also mustard oil is usually
used in the cooking.

PORTUGUESE DUCK
VINDALOO (Goa)   ✳   ✳   *4 servings*

1 large duck (5 lbs.)
1 Tb. curry powder
4 Tbs. mustard oil
2 garlic cloves, mashed
6 small paper-thin slices of green

gingerroot or ¼ tsp. ground
ginger
1 tsp. salt
1 cup vinegar

Cut the duck into pieces ready for cooking. Fry the curry powder in heated mustard oil to a dark brown shade. Stir in the
garlic and simmer for 3 minutes. Add the gingerroot, salt, and
vinegar. Add duck pieces. Cover and simmer over very low
heat for 1 hour or more, till meat is tender. Add only vinegar
and no water to keep from sticking. Meat should be quite dry
when served on top of hot boiled rice. Mango chutneys and relishes are served with *vindaloos*.

PORTUGUESE CHICKEN
VINDALOO (Goa)   ✳   ✳   *4 servings*

1 lb. chicken meat without bones
1 large onion, chopped fine
4 Tbs. mustard oil
½ tsp. ground cuminseed
½ tsp. ground ginger or 1-inch
piece of green gingerroot
8 garlic cloves

4 red chilies, ground
4 green chilies, ground
1 cinnamon stick, 2 inches
6 whole cloves
1 raw potato, grated
1 cup vinegar
1 tsp. salt

Cut chicken into very small bits. Brown the onion in the heated mustard oil and remove onion from skillet. Fry cuminseed, ginger, garlic, and all the chilies in remaining oil, then return the onion to the pan. Add the cinnamon and cloves, the potato, vinegar, and salt; mix well. Add the chicken and simmer for 1 hour, or till meat is well done. Add more vinegar if needed to keep from sticking, but no water. *Vindaloo* is very dry when spooned out on hot boiled rice or Indian breads. Serve with Major Grey's mango chutney.

Chapter 9

FISH AND SHELLFISH
CURRIES

FISH forms the main part of the diet of most people living in the coastal regions of the Far East. The first odors to greet a person on an incoming steamer are those of spices and fish. That strange dark fretwork, swaying for endless miles along the sands, which so mystifies the newcomer consists only of small fish strung out in the sun to dry, before going into the millions of black curry pots of India, or into the double-sealed zinc-lined tin boxes that will carry them to the tables of gourmets across the seas—at exorbitant prices.

The fish in these tropical waters are as strange and exotic in shape, flavor, and coloring as are the fruits on the land. There are some 1,800 known varieties, ranging from the giant deep-sea sharks to the tiny shrimps that teem in the muddy waters of the paddy fields. These shrimps are gathered eagerly for the curry pots, or dried, they are used as fertilizer for the impoverished land.

The Indian cook manages to concoct a tasty curry out of whatever fish is at hand. Shrimps or prawns, or shellfish of any kind is most favored. On Friday, however, the famous *kedgeree* appears on the *sahib's* table. Properly speaking, a kedgeree (also spelled kichri or kichree) is merely a mixture of rice, cold cooked fish, and numerous other ingredients such as *dal*, other vegetables, hard-cooked eggs, etc., cooked with curry spices to a dry *pulao* form. The Indians' kedgeree (Hindi *khicari*), however, has no fish in it.

Since only the big cities in India have refrigeration as yet, the majority of people living in villages still have to depend for their curries on dried fish or fish preserved by means of lime juice, salt, or spices.

There is an endless list of fish recipes, but all include curry powder.

Dried fish are soaked in water spiced with turmeric, chili powder, and lime juice for several hours, then dried, coated with ground turmeric and chili powder, and fried in mustard oil.

Large fresh fish are usually boiled or baked but are prepared first by drying well, rubbing inside and out with curry powder, and sprinkling with lime or lemon juice. They are allowed to stand for an hour or more before being put into boiling salted water, or into the oven.

Often, too, these large fish are stuffed with *pulao* (see p. 26) before cooking. Villagers make a mixture of ground turmeric, chili powder, and lime juice, enclose it in a banana skin, and place the packet inside a fish before baking.

Fish of the larger, coarser kind are often cut into chunks and pickled in a paste made of turmeric, chili powder, and lime juice. These, placed in clay jars, covered with vinegar and tamarind pulp, are stored in the little dark storehouse at the end of the compound and will last for many months.

Saffron can be used instead of turmeric for flavor and preserving, but is too expensive for the poorer people.

Here are a few basic methods of preparing fish in the Indian manner.

BOILED Such fish as haddock, sablefish, salmon, mullet, sole, mangofish, etc., are used. For 2 pounds of fish, cover with boiling water and add ½ red chili, juice of 1 lime, 1-inch piece of green gingerroot, 1 teaspoon salt. Simmer the fish gently for 20 minutes, or till fish is tender but still firm; drain. Serve with slices of lemon and fresh onion cut into rings, either raw or fried in hot oil.

BAKED Cut a 2-pound fish into fairly large pieces. Chop 1 large onion and fry it in 2 tablespoons mustard oil or butter. Add 1 teaspoon curry powder and when it is browned, add 1 cup water. Pour over the fish in a baking dish. Cover fish with slices of fresh tomatoes and season with salt to taste. Cover the pan and bake in a hot oven (400°F.) for 30 minutes, or till fish is tender but still firm. Serve with lemon and pickles.

Fish kababs (see below) may also be baked; they need to be basted during the process just as when being broiled. Also whole fish, stuffed or unstuffed, may be baked.

BROILED   Rub any small fish with a mixture of equal quantities of ground turmeric, ground red chilies, and freshly ground black pepper. Broil over an open fire or under a broiler, basting often with hot mustard oil or butter, till fish is cooked as desired. If using dried fish, soak them first in water to cover for 2 hours before seasoning.

Broiled fish kababs are also very popular. To make these, cut larger fish into 2-inch chunks and marinate the chunks in a mixture of lime juice, ground turmeric, and chili powder for 2 hours. Thread on skewers with slices of fresh onion, green gingerroot, tomato wedges, or other suitable vegetables. Broil the kababs over an open fire or under a broiler, basting often with very hot mustard oil or *ghee*. Be sure the basting oil is hot, for cold oil gives a greasy taste to the finished kabab.

FRIED   Rub fish inside and outside with curry powder, sprinkle with lime juice, and let stand for 1 hour; drain. Dip into lightly beaten egg and then into bread crumbs or flour. Fry in hot olive or mustard oil. If using dried fish, soak them first, as above, before seasoning.

BIRIANAS and PULAOS   For recipes for this method of preparing fish with rice, see Chapter 11.

CEYLON CURRIED DRIED FISH   ❊   *6 servings*

2 lbs. dried fish of any kind
1 large onion, chopped fine
¼ cup mustard oil or butter
4 coriander seeds, ground
1 dried red chili, ground
3 tsps. mustard seeds, ground
1 cup coconut milk (see p. 16)
1 cup sliced raw potato

2 small eggplants, peeled and diced fine
1 fresh green chili, chopped fine
4 bananas, cut fine
1 Tb. dal (see p. 26)
1 tsp. salt, or more
Juice of 1 lime

Soak the dried fish in cold water for 2 hours. Drain and dry. Brown the onion lightly in the heated mustard oil; remove onion. Crush the spices together in a mortar and fry in the fat remaining in the skillet till dark brown. Add the coconut milk, potato, eggplants, green chili, bananas, *dal*, and salt. Add fish and cover. Let simmer for 1 hour, or till the fish and vegetables are soft. Add lime juice just before serving. Serve hot boiled rice and mango chutneys or tart pickles.

PHILIPPINE CURRIED FISH   ❋   *4 servings*

1 cup coconut milk (see p. 16)
¼ cup buttermilk
1 lb. fish, any kind
2 onions, chopped fine
3 Tbs. mustard oil or butter

¼ tsp. curry powder
1-inch piece of gingerroot or ¼ tsp. ground ginger
½ tsp. salt, or more

Mix the coconut milk and buttermilk and pour the mixture over the fish. Simmer over low heat till the fish is almost done, about 15 minutes if fresh fish is used, but longer if dried, even though it has been soaked beforehand. Fry the onions in the heated mustard oil and remove onions. In remaining oil fry the curry powder till dark brown. Return onions to the skillet and add the liquid from the fish, the gingerroot, and salt. Simmer for 5 minutes, then add the fish and simmer again till fish is well done but still firm, about 10 minutes. The sauce should be thick. Spoon it out on top of hot boiled rice.

HAWAIIAN CASSEROLE OF CURRIED FISH   ❋   *8 servings*

3 lbs. any flaky white fish (halibut, swordfish, etc.)
½ cup butter
1 large onion, chopped fine
½ tsp. curry powder
2 Tbs. flour

4 cups milk
1 tsp. salt, or more
4 eggs, beaten
4 Tbs. chopped parsley
1 drop of Tabasco, or less
¼ cup grated cheese

Steam the fish till well cooked. Flake and arrange in a greased casserole dish. In a heavy pan heat the butter and brown the onion lightly. Remove and in remaining butter fry the curry powder till dark brown. Stir in the flour and simmer till the mixture bubbles up, about 3 minutes. Add the milk and salt and cook over low heat, or in a double boiler over boiling water, till a smooth sauce is formed. Remove a small portion of this sauce and mix it with the beaten eggs. Stir eggs into the pan and simmer all for a few minutes longer. Add the chopped parsley and the Tabasco if desired. Pour over the fish in the casserole dish and sprinkle top with the grated cheese. Bake in a very hot oven (450°F.) for 10 minutes, or till nicely browned.

NOTE   The curries used in the Pacific Islands and West Indies are much milder than those used in the Far East. Often potatoes, yams, or pumpkin are used with them instead of rice.

ENGLISH KEDGEREE   ❋ ❋   *4 servings*

6 Tbs. mustard oil or butter
3 onions, chopped fine
⅛ tsp. ground cayenne pepper
⅛ tsp. ground saffron or turmeric
⅛ tsp. ground allspice
4 peppercorns

2 cups water
1 Tb. lime juice
1 bay leaf
1 tsp. salt, or more
2 cups uncooked rice
2 cups flaked cooked fish

Heat the oil in a large heavy pot and brown the onions in it lightly; remove onions. Mix the spices well and fry to dark brown in remaining oil. Return onions to the curry mixture and add the water, lime juice, bay leaf, salt, and rice. Simmer for 20 minutes, till rice is beginning to get soft and half of the liquid is absorbed. Stir in the fish and simmer again till kedgeree is quite dry. Serve chutney and wedges of hard-cooked eggs with this.

VARIATION   This dish may be prepared with raw fish. In that case cut the fish into chunks and simmer in lightly salted water till just tender. Reserve the cooking liquid to use in place of the water in the recipe.

CURRIED FILLETS OF SOLE   �֍   *10 servings*

½ cup mustard oil or butter
1 small onion, chopped fine
1 Tb. curry powder
2 cups clear broth

1 tsp. salt
10 fillets of sole or similar fish
Juice of 1 lemon

Heat the oil in a heavy skillet. Brown the onion lightly and remove it. In remaining oil fry the curry powder to a dark brown.
Add the broth, browned onion, and salt and simmer for 5 minutes. Place the fillets in the skillet so they are covered with the
liquid. Simmer for 20 minutes, or till fish is white and cooked
firm but not mushy, and only a dribble of the liquid is left. Mix
this dribble with the lemon juice at the last minute and pour
over the fillets before serving.

Lobsters

Lobsters are bought live. The motion of the tail indicates their
freshness. If the shell is dirty and crusted, it is a sign of age and the
meat of that crustacean will be tough. Medium-sized lobsters are
the choicest. Tie the claws fast before attempting to cook and
wash in cold water.

Use enough water to cover the lobsters. Bring the water to a
boil in a large deep kettle and add 1 tablespoon salt for each
quart of water. If the lobster meat is to be used later in a highly
salted or seasoned dish, reduce the amount of salt accordingly.
Toss lobsters head first into the boiling salted water. This method
destroys life instantly. Bring water again to a boil and simmer for
10 minutes or longer, according to size and age of lobster, and
according to your personal taste. Lobster meat becomes tough and
stringy if cooked too long; if uncooked, the spawn will not be red.
Remove the scum which forms on top of the water during the
simmering.

If lobsters are to be eaten plain from the shell, rub the shell with
a little olive oil to give it a perfect appearance. Break off the claws,
then split the carcass lengthwise. Crack the claws with a hammer

to make it easier to get at the meat. If the lobster meat is to be used in other preparations, care must be taken to keep it in as large pieces as possible while removing it from the shell. Parsley and lemon are the standard accompaniments to lobster.

SINGAPORE CURRIED LOBSTER ✳ ✳ *6 servings*

3 lobsters (1½ lbs. each)
8 cups boiling water
Salt
¾ tsp. whole cloves
⅛ tsp. ground cayenne pepper
1-inch piece of green gingerroot or ½ tsp. ground ginger
1½ tsps. ground cinnamon

½ cup butter or vegetable oil
4 onions, chopped coarsely
2 tsps. curry powder
2 garlic cloves, mashed
2 tsps. sugar
3 cups coconut milk (see p. 16)
2 cucumbers, diced
2 Tbs. tamarind or lemon juice

Drop the lobsters into the boiling water to which has been added 1 tablespoon salt, the cloves, cayenne, gingerroot, and cinnamon. Simmer for 10 minutes; lift out lobsters and drain. Boil the cooking liquid till it measures 4 cups; strain and reserve 1 cup for the sauce. Split the lobsters lengthwise; throw away the dark vein and the small sac behind the head. Crack shells and claws and take out the flesh, keeping it in as big chunks as possible.

Heat the butter in a heavy skillet and brown the onions lightly; remove onions. In remaining butter fry the curry powder to dark brown; stir in the mashed garlic and simmer for 3 minutes, till a smooth paste is formed. Add the sugar and stir for another moment. Return the onions. Add the coconut milk, 1 cup of the reserved lobster liquid, and the cucumbers; mix well. Simmer for 20 minutes, or till cucumbers are tender. Add the lobster meat and salt to taste and simmer for 10 minutes longer. Add tamarind juice just before serving. The sauce should be thick. Serve on a bed of hot boiled rice garnished with lemon slices, tomato wedges, etc.

HAWAIIAN CURRIED
LOBSTER   ❋   ❋   *2 servings*

1 cup grated fresh coconut or ⅓ cup dried coconut

1 cup milk or ½ cup chicken broth

2 Tbs. butter or vegetable oil

2 tsps. curry powder

1 Tbs. flour

½ tsp. salt, or more

1 lobster (1½ lbs.), cooked, or 1 cup canned lobster

Rice ring (see p. 61)

If using dried coconut, soak it in the milk for about 30 minutes. Heat the butter and stir in the mixed curry powder and flour. Simmer for 3 minutes, or till a smooth paste has formed. Add the fresh coconut and chicken broth or the dried coconut and all the milk. Season with salt to taste. Simmer for about 10 minutes, till a smooth sauce is formed. Add the lobster meat. (If canned lobster is used, wash it well in cold water and drain before adding.) Simmer for 10 more minutes, or till mixture is rich and creamy; add very little more milk or broth if needed. Spoon this sauce into the center of a ring mold of hot boiled rice. Serve with chutney and lemon slices.

BENGAL CURRIED LOBSTER
BALLS   ❋   *4 servings*

1 large lobster (2 lbs.), boiled

2 tsps. coriander seeds

1 egg, beaten

1 cup bread crumbs

1 onion, chopped fine

2 Tbs. mustard oil or butter

½ tsp. freshly ground pepper

½ tsp. ground ginger

1 bay leaf

1 garlic clove, mashed

1 tsp. salt

2 cups hot water

Juice of 1 lime

Remove the meat from the cooked lobster; there should be about 1½ cups. Mash the meat well with the coriander seeds and form into small balls. Dip lobster balls into the beaten egg, then roll in the bread crumbs and set aside. Brown the onion in the heated oil and remove onion. Fry the spices till dark brown, adding a little liquid if needed. Simmer for 3 minutes.

Add the browned onion, bay leaf, garlic, and salt. Brown the lobster balls, then add the hot water and lime juice. Cover and let simmer for 10 minutes, or till most of the liquid is absorbed.

NORTH INDIAN SHELLFISH KOFTAS
4 to 6 servings

2 lbs. shellfish
6 cups water
3 tsps. salt
½ cup mustard oil or butter
1 onion, chopped fine
1 tsp. curry powder

1 garlic clove, mashed
2 eggs, well beaten
½ cup bread crumbs
1 cup boiling water
Juice of 1 lemon

Simmer the shellfish in the 6 cups water with 1 teaspoon salt till tender, about 5 minutes for shrimps, about 8 minutes for crabs, and 10 to 12 minutes for lobster, depending on the weight. Shell the crustaceans and mash the meat in a bowl; let it cool. Heat 3 tablespoons of the oil and brown the onion lightly in it; remove onion. Fry the curry powder to dark brown in the saucepan. Add the garlic and simmer for 3 minutes till a smooth paste is formed. Mix browned onion and curry mixture with the mashed fish. Add remaining salt. Form the mixture into balls the size of walnuts. Dip into the eggs and roll in the bread crumbs. Heat remaining oil in the skillet and fry the balls lightly. When all are browned, add the boiling water and the lemon juice, cover, and simmer gently for 15 to 20 minutes.

HAWAIIAN CURRIED SHELLFISH TIMBALES ❊ ❊ *10 servings*

1 tsp. curry powder
1 Tb. flour
2 Tbs. vegetable oil or butter
½ cup milk
1 tsp. salt
2 eggs, beaten well

8 cups cooked lobster or crab-meat pieces, or shrimps
1 Tb. chopped parsley
½ tsp. freshly ground black pepper
Juice of 1 lemon

Butter 10 small molds, ½-cup size or slightly larger. Mix the curry powder and flour and brown well in the heated oil. Add the milk and salt. Let simmer for 3 minutes, or till sauce is thick and smooth. Spoon out a small portion of the hot sauce into the beaten eggs and mix well; add egg mixture to the sauce and simmer again till sauce is thick. Mash the lobster or whatever shellfish you are using and add it to the sauce with the parsley, black pepper, and lemon juice. Add extra salt to taste if needed. Fill the buttered molds with this mixture. Set them in pan of hot water and bake in a moderate oven (350°F.) for 20 minutes, or till timbales are cooked.

CURRIED OYSTERS ❊ ❊ ❊ *6 servings*

6 dozen fresh oysters, shucked
1 Tb. butter or vegetable oil
1 onion, minced

1 tsp. curry powder
½ tsp. curry paste
Lemon slices

Drain the oysters over a bowl. Measure the liquid; if there is less than 2 cups, add enough water to make 2 cups. Heat the butter and brown the onion lightly in it; remove onion from the pan. In remaining butter fry the curry powder to dark brown. Add the browned onion, curry paste, and 2 cups liquid. Simmer for 10 minutes, till a smooth sauce is formed. Add the oysters and simmer for 3 minutes. Serve oysters carefully, taking care that each has its coating of the sauce. Serve with Indian breads and slices of lemon.

CURRIED SCALLOPS ❊ ❊ ❊ *6 servings*

1 Tb. curry powder
1 Tb. cornstarch
6 Tbs. vegetable oil or butter
2 cups milk

⅛ tsp. freshly grated nutmeg
1 tsp. salt, or more
2 dozen scallops, fresh or frozen

Cornstarch or corn flour is a flour made from the heart of the corn kernel. It is used in the East much more than ordinary wheat flour for curries, puddings, etc., for Indians claim it gives a more delicate flavor and texture.

Mix the curry powder and cornstarch together and stir into the heated oil. Simmer for 3 minutes, or till a smooth paste is formed. Add the milk and nutmeg. Add salt to taste and simmer for 20 minutes, or till a rich thick sauce is formed. Add the scallops for the last 15 minutes and simmer till they are cooked soft but not mushy. Serve at once. If scallops are left standing, they tend to toughen. Spoon out the sauce on top of hot boiled rice.

CURRIED SHRIMPS OR PRAWNS I ❀ ❀ *6 servings*

2 lbs. fresh shrimps or prawns
6 cups water
2 tsps. salt
½ cup mustard oil or butter
1 onion, chopped fine
2 Tbs. curry powder
3 Tbs. cornstarch

1-inch piece of green gingerroot or ¼ tsp. ground ginger
1 garlic clove, mashed
2 carrots, minced
1 celery stalk, diced
1 cup pineapple juice

Simmer the shrimps in the water with 1 teaspoon salt for 5 minutes, or till cooked soft but not mushy. Shell and devein them and set aside. Boil the cooking water till it measures 3 cups; strain and reserve. Heat the oil in a heavy iron skillet. Brown the onion lightly and remove it. Mix the curry powder and cornstarch and fry till dark brown. Let it simmer for 3 minutes, or till a smooth paste is formed. Return the onion and add reserved shrimp liquid, the gingerroot, garlic, carrots, and celery. Add remaining salt and simmer over low heat for 30 minutes, or till a smooth rich sauce is formed and the vegetables are cooked. Add the shrimps for the last 10 minutes, with more salt if needed. Add the pineapple juice just before serving and remove the gingerroot. Spoon out on top of hot boiled rice and serve Major Grey's chutney with it.

CURRIED SHRIMPS OR PRAWNS II ❊ ❊ *4 servings*

1½ lbs. fresh shrimps or prawns
6 cups water
1 tsp. salt
1 garlic clove
1 bay leaf
⅛ tsp. ground cayenne pepper
½ cup mustard oil or butter

2 onions, chopped fine
1½ Tbs. curry powder
1 Tb. flour
1 unpeeled large tart apple, finely diced
6 peppercorns
Lemon wedges

Simmer the shrimps in the water with the salt, garlic, bay leaf, and cayenne pepper for 5 minutes, or till just tender. Shell and devein the shrimps and set aside. Boil the cooking liquid till it measures 3 cups; strain and reserve. Heat the oil in a heavy kettle and brown the onions; remove onions. In remaining oil fry mixed curry powder and flour till dark brown. Simmer for 3 minutes, till the mixture becomes a smooth paste. Return the onions and add the apple, peppercorns, and reserved shrimp liquid. Simmer for 20 minutes, or till apples are tender and sauce is reduced by half. Add the shrimps and heat for 5 minutes, till they are heated through. Add seasoning if needed. Serve with hot boiled rice in a separate dish and garnish with wedges of lemon.

NOTE If preferred, 3 cups chicken broth may be used in place of the shrimp cooking liquid.

CURRIED SHRIMPS OR PRAWNS III ❊ ❊ *4 servings*

3 Tbs. butter or vegetable oil
1 small onion, minced
1 Tb. curry powder
2 Tbs. flour or instant potato
1 celery stalk, minced
½ unpeeled tart apple, diced

1 cup milk
½ tsp. salt, or more
1½ cups cooked or canned shrimps
Lemon slices

Heat the butter and brown the onion lightly in it; remove onion from skillet. Mix the curry powder and flour and fry to a dark brown in the butter. Let simmer for 3 minutes, or till a smooth paste is formed. Return the onion and add the celery, apple, milk, and salt. Turn the mixture into the top part of a double boiler and simmer over boiling water for 30 minutes, or till the sauce is rich and smooth. Add the shrimps for last 10 minutes. (If using canned shrimps, rinse well in cold water and dry before adding to the sauce.) Serve rice separately, and pass lemon slices.

NOTE If instant potato is used for thickening instead of the flour, mix it into a smooth paste with a little water and add it with the shrimps for the last 5 minutes.

GOA SHRIMP CURRY   ❋   ❋   *6 servings*

2 lbs. shrimps
¼ cup mustard oil or butter
1 onion, chopped fine
1 Tb. coriander seeds, ground
6 garlic cloves, mashed
6 green peppers, sliced thin

½ cup coconut milk (see p. 16)
3 cups shredded fresh coconut
   (about 1 coconut), or 1 cup
   dried coconut
1 tsp. salt, or more
1 Tb. tamarind or lemon juice

Simmer the shrimps in lightly salted water for about 5 minutes; cool. Shell and devein them and mash them in a large bowl. Heat the oil and brown the onion lightly in it; remove onion. Fry coriander in the oil remaining and add the mashed garlic. Simmer for 3 minutes, or till a smooth paste is formed. Return the onion to the skillet with the curry mixture and add the green peppers, coconut milk, and coconut. Add salt to taste and the mashed shrimps. Cover and let simmer for 20 minutes, or till a thick rich sauce is formed. Add the tamarind juice just before serving. Spoon out on top of hot boiled rice or serve with Indian breads.

THAILAND BAMBOO PRAWN CURRY
❀   *4 servings*

1 lb. fresh prawns
½ cup mustard oil or butter
1 small onion, chopped fine
1 tsp. curry powder
⅛ tsp. ground cayenne pepper
½ lb. bamboo shoots, fresh or canned, minced

1 cup coconut milk (see p. 16)
1 Tb. shredded coconut
1 tsp. salt, or more
Juice of 1 lime

Simmer the prawns in lightly salted water for 5 minutes, or till soft. Shell and devein them and mash them in a bowl. Heat half of the oil in a heavy skillet. Brown the onion lightly and remove it. In the same pan fry the curry powder and cayenne to a dark brown. Return the onion and add the bamboo shoots, coconut milk, and shredded coconut. Add the mashed prawns, the salt, and the lime juice. Simmer till all liquid is absorbed.

Let the mixture cool, then form it into small balls. Heat the remaining oil and fry the prawn balls in it till golden brown. Serve on top of hot boiled rice; or use as appetizers for the cocktail hour.

MALAY CURRIED SHRIMPS
❀   *4 servings*

1 lb. fresh shrimps
4 cups boiling water
Salt
1 onion, minced
2 Tbs. vegetable oil
1 tsp. curry powder

1 garlic clove, mashed
1 cup coconut milk (see p. 16)
1 cucumber, diced
1 cup small chunks of fresh coconut
Lemon slices

Simmer the shrimps in the water with 1 teaspoon salt for about 5 minutes, or till cooked. Remove the shrimps, shell and devein them, and cut into halves. Boil down the liquid till it measures 1 cup. Brown the onion lightly in the heated oil and remove onion from pan. Fry the curry powder in the same pan till dark brown. Add the garlic and simmer for 3 minutes, or till a thin paste has formed. Return the onion to the pan and add the coconut milk and shrimp liquid, cucumber and coconut chunks. Salt to taste. Simmer for 30 minutes, or till cucumber is tender and the sauce reduced to about half. Add the shrimps and heat. Serve hot rice separately with garnishes of lemon slices.

CALCUTTA CURRIED GRAY
SHRIMPS   ❋   *4 servings*

1½ lbs. gray shrimps
2 Tbs. vegetable oil or butter
1 Tb. curry powder
3 slices of lentil or whole-wheat bread (see Chap. 14)

½ cup sour cream
1 cup yogurt or buttermilk
1 tsp. salt, or more
Garnishes

The gray shrimp is a species found only in the sea waters around Calcutta. It is delicate in taste. Simmer the shrimps in lightly salted water for about 5 minutes, or till tender. Shell and devein them and dry thoroughly.

Heat the oil and fry the curry powder in it till dark brown. Add the dried shrimps and brown lightly; remove shrimps. Soak the bread slices in the sour cream and yogurt. In the top part of a double boiler put the sour-cream, yogurt, and bread mixture, the fried curry, and salt. Simmer for 10 minutes, stirring often. Add the shrimps and simmer for 10 more minutes. The sauce should be very thick and rich when done. Spoon on top of hot boiled rice. Garnish with wedges of lemon, tomato, etc.

HAWAIIAN CURRIED
SHRIMPS   ❋   ❋   *6 servings*

3 whole pineapples with leaves
3 cups chopped cooked shrimps
6 Tbs. butter
1 Tb. curry powder
3 cups thick white sauce (see p. 17)

1 lb. mushrooms, chopped fine
½-inch piece of green gingerroot or ¼ tsp. ground ginger
½ tsp. salt, or more
½ cup bread crumbs
½ cup grated cheese

Split the pineapples lengthwise, including the leaves. Scoop out the pulp, leaving ½-inch-thick shells. Heat the shells in a slightly warm oven (not over 200°F.). Protect the leaves from scorching by wrapping in aluminum foil. Chop the pineapple pulp fine and mix with the shrimps. Set aside.

Heat the butter in a heavy skillet and fry the curry powder to dark brown. Add the white sauce and simmer for 1 minute. Put the sauce in the top part of a double boiler and add the mushrooms, gingerroot, and salt. Simmer for 15 minutes, till sauce is very thick. Remove the gingerroot. Add the pineapple and shrimp mixture; stir well. Spoon out into the warmed pineapple shells. Sprinkle the tops with the bread crumbs and cheese mixed. Arrange under the broiler and toast till the cheese mixture is nicely browned. Arrange the pineapples on a big platter and bank dry hot boiled rice around them. Serve with hot mango pickles and lemon wedges.

NOTE Lobster or crabmeat may be used instead of shrimps.

SINGAPORE CURRIED SHRIMPS ❋ ❋ *6 servings*

2 lbs. fresh shrimps in shells
8 cups water
Salt
1 tomato, quartered
3 parsley sprigs, minced
2 whole cloves
½ tsp. minced fresh basil
1 garlic clove, mashed
Grated rind of 1 lime
2 shallots, minced
1 celery stalk, chopped fine

1 carrot, chopped fine
1 unpeeled tart apple, chopped fine
½ tsp. freshly ground black pepper
½ tsp. ground marjoram or 1 tsp. minced fresh marjoram
¼ tsp. grated nutmeg
½ tsp. ground cayenne pepper
2 Tbs. butter or vegetable oil
1 Tb. curry powder

Cover the shrimps with the water and add 1 teaspoon salt. Simmer for 5 minutes. Strain the liquid and boil down till it measures 4 cups; set aside. Shell and devein the shrimps. In a heavy kettle simmer the tomato, parsley, cloves, basil, garlic, lime rind, shallots, celery, carrot, apple, black pepper, marjoram, nutmeg, cayenne, and reserved cooking liquid. Heat the butter and fry the curry powder in it till dark brown. Add to the ingredients in the kettle. Simmer for 30 minutes, or till vegetables and apple are soft and the liquid is reduced by half. Strain through a sieve. Put the shrimps into the strained sauce and simmer for 10 minutes. The curry should have just a very little liquid when served. Serve hot boiled rice separately as well as a variety of chutneys and pickles.

NILGIRI CURRIED SHRIMPS   ❈   *8 servings*

2 lbs. fresh shrimps or 1 lb. canned shrimps
½ cup plus 2 Tbs. butter
1 onion, minced
1 garlic clove, mashed
½ tsp. ground thyme
½ tsp. ground mace
½ tsp. grated nutmeg
½ tsp. minced fresh parsley
½ tsp. minced fresh chervil
½ tsp. minced shallots
½ tsp. minced fresh tarragon
½ tsp. salt, or more
1 cup dry sherry, or more
1 cup bread crumbs

Prepare shrimps first. If canned, wash well in cold water and drain. If fresh, simmer in lightly salted water for 5 minutes, then shell and devein. Heat the ½ cup butter and fry the onion in it. Mix in the garlic and remove both from the pan. Mix the thyme, mace, and nutmeg and fry in the same skillet. Simmer for 3 minutes, or till a smooth paste is formed. Return the onion and garlic and add the fresh herbs, salt, and sherry (or water if preferred). Mix remaining butter with the bread crumbs. In a greased casserole alternate layers of shrimps and buttered bread crumbs, sprinkling each shrimp layer with some of the curry mixture. End with a layer of bread crumbs. Bake in a hot oven (400°F.) for 20 minutes, or till nicely browned on top. This is a popular dish in the Nilgiri Hills of South India where the *memsahibs* tend their own herb gardens. Serve with hot boiled rice or Indian breads, and chutneys.

CURRIED MADRAS PRAWNS   ❈   *4 servings*

1 Tb. butter or vegetable oil
2 Tbs. minced onion
1 tsp. curry powder
2 large fresh tomatoes, chopped coarsely
½ tsp. salt, or more
1 lb. Madras prawns, cooked, shelled, and deveined
Juice of 1 lemon

Heat the butter and brown the onion lightly in it; remove onion from skillet. In the same pan fry the curry powder till dark brown. Simmer for 3 minutes, till a smooth paste has formed. Add a drop of water if needed to keep from burning. Return the onion and add the tomatoes and salt. Simmer for 10 minutes, then add the prawns. Add more water if needed to make a very thick sauce. Add lemon juice at the last minute. Serve with hot boiled rice in a separate dish and various relishes.

Chapter 10

CURRIED EGGS

SINCE EGGS contain the germ of life they are forbidden to many orthodox Hindus. However, as in the case of meat eating, allowance is made for certain castes, such as the fighting men, hunters, etc., whose need for stronger foods is known to the gods. Today, since chickens are no longer just scavengers, but many are being raised in a sanitary way, many of these old taboos are breaking down. And there are always those vast millions of other Indians, the noncastes and non-Hindus, who depend much for their daily fare on eggs curried in one form or other. Since eggs in India are only half the size of American eggs, care must be taken when using Indian recipes. The recipes in this chapter call for American eggs. Also, perhaps as a double precaution because of germ-laden soil, in India eggs are usually cooked separately before they are used, even in cooked curry dishes.

Eggs are liked all over the world, but an egg can be spoiled by the wrong method of cooking. Eggs should always be at room temperature before being lowered into cool water. Bring the water slowly to a boil and then just simmer for 20 minutes. Put the cooked eggs under cold running water as soon as they are taken from the heat and they will be easy to shell.

To stuff hard-cooked eggs, halve them and remove and mash the yolks well. Mix the yolks with an appropriate seasoning and pile the mixture very lightly into the hollows of the egg whites. These can be eaten cold or can be heated in a hot oven for 10 minutes and served in a sauce. Curry-stuffed eggs make delicious appetizers as well as excellent luncheon and supper dishes.

EGG DAL CURRY   ❄ ❄   *6 or 12 servings*

2 cups dal (see p. 26)
12 hard-cooked eggs
2 Tbs. butter or vegetable oil
1 tsp. curry powder

½ cup coconut milk (see p. 16)
1 Tb. vinegar or lemon juice
1 tsp. salt, or less

Soak the *dal* in water to cover for 1 hour, or till it softens into a paste. Shell the eggs but leave them whole. Heat the butter and fry the curry powder to dark brown in it. Add the coconut milk, *dal*, vinegar, and salt. Simmer this mixture for 15 minutes, or till a thick sauce is formed. Drop in the peeled eggs and heat for 5 more minutes. Serve with hot boiled rice. The eggs are served whole.

EGG-BALL CURRY (Koftas)   ❄   *6 or 12 servings*

12 hard-cooked eggs
8 Tbs. butter
4 onions, chopped fine
2 tsps. curry powder
4 tsps. ground turmeric
½ tsp. ground ginger
8 garlic cloves, mashed
4 cups minced cooked lamb

2 Tbs. dal (see p. 26)
2 cups water
1 tsp. salt
1 parsley sprig, minced
12 green chilies, minced
2 tsps. poppy seeds
2 raw eggs, lightly beaten
Vegetable oil for frying

Shell the eggs but leave them whole. Heat the butter and brown the onions lightly in it; remove onions from pan. Mix curry powder and ground turmeric and ginger and fry in remaining butter till dark brown. Stir in the mashed garlic and simmer for 1 minute longer. Add the browned onion, cooked lamb, *dal*, water and salt. Cover and let simmer for 30 minutes, or till all liquid is absorbed. Put the parsley, chilies, and poppy seeds in a mortar and grind into a paste. Add half of the beaten egg to the spices and stir into the lamb mixture, blending thoroughly. Form in 12 soft balls with one of the hard-cooked eggs in the center of each. Dip the balls into the remaining beaten egg and fry in the oil until golden brown. Handle carefully to prevent eggs losing their coats. These may also be baked in a hot oven for 10 minutes. Serve with curried tomato sauce (see below).

CURRIED TOMATO SAUCE   ❀   *about 2½ cups*

4 Tbs. butter
2 onions, minced
2 tsps. curry powder
6 Tbs. ground turmeric
4 large ripe tomatoes, chopped

¼ tsp. ground cayenne pepper
1 tsp. salt
3 cups boiling water
Fresh mint or coriander leaves, minced

Heat the butter and brown the onions in it; remove onions. In remaining butter fry the curry powder and turmeric to dark brown. Return the onions and add the chopped tomatoes. Stir well, then add cayenne, salt, and boiling water. Simmer for about 15 minutes, or till a smooth sauce is formed. Serve with egg-ball curry (above) or with whole hard-cooked eggs heated in it. Sprinkle minced leaves over the completed dish.

CURRIED STUFFED EGGS   ❀   *6 servings*

2 Tbs. butter
1 tsp. curry powder or paste
2 Tbs. flour
1 cup milk
1 tsp. salt

6 hard-cooked eggs
2 Tbs. malt vinegar
½ tsp. dry mustard
2 Tbs. mayonnaise

Heat the butter and in it fry the mixed curry powder and flour till well browned. Add milk and salt. Stir and simmer till the mixture becomes a smooth sauce. Shell and halve the eggs. Remove the yolks and mash them in a bowl with the vinegar, mustard, and mayonnaise. The mixture should be light but firm enough to make a filling for the egg whites. Stuff the egg whites and arrange them in a serving dish. Spoon the curry sauce over them; there should be just enough to mask each egg.

P & O CURRIED EGGS   ❀   ❀   *8 servings*

12 hard-cooked eggs
4 Tbs. butter
1 Tb. minced onion
1 Tb. curry powder
1 Tb. soy sauce
½ cup mayonnaise

1 Tb. minced parsley
⅛ tsp. ground cayenne pepper
⅛ tsp. freshly ground black pepper
Salt
Parsley sprigs for garnish

Shell the eggs, halve them, and remove the yolks. Mash yolks well. Heat the butter in a skillet and brown the onion; remove onion. In remaining butter fry the curry powder to dark brown. Add browned onion, fried curry, soy sauce, mayonnaise, minced parsley, and red and black peppers to the yolk mash. Add salt to taste. Beat till light and spoon lightly into the egg-white hollows. Arrange egg halves in a greased baking dish and cover with a good curry sauce (see Chap. 3). Bake in a moderate oven (350°F.) for 20 minutes. Garnish with parsley sprigs and serve with hot boiled rice.

COCONUT CURRIED EGGS ❈ *5 servings*

2 Tbs. minced onion
2 Tbs. ghee
½ tsp. ground turmeric or saffron
1 cup shredded fresh coconut

1 Tb. lemon juice
1 cup coconut milk (see p. 16)
½ tsp. salt, or more
5 hard-cooked eggs, sliced

Brown the onions lightly in the heated *ghee*. Stir in the turmeric and fry for a minute longer. Add the coconut, lemon juice, coconut milk, and salt. Simmer for 5 minutes, or till a smooth paste is formed. Arrange the egg slices in a baking dish. Spoon the coconut mixture on top of them and place in the oven for 10 minutes, or till most of liquid is absorbed, but do not allow the mixture to dry out. Serve with plain boiled rice or *dal* (see p. 26).

CURRIED POACHED EGGS

Add 1 teaspoon of a good curry paste and a pinch of salt to 2 cups water. Bring to a boil. Slip raw eggs from a saucer into the boiling liquid. Stir the water as the eggs cook to help keep a rounded shape. Poach to your taste. Lift out with a skimmer and drain briefly on absorbent paper before serving. Serve on *popadams* or other Indian bread.

CURRIED SCRAMBLED EGGS ❋ *2 servings*

4 eggs
2 small onions, minced
4 Tbs. butter

½ tsp. curry powder
1 large tart apple, sliced
1 cup tomato sauce or chili sauce

Beat the eggs only lightly and put aside. Fry the onions lightly in the heated butter; remove onions from the pan. In butter remaining fry the curry powder to dark brown. Let simmer for 3 minutes, till a smooth paste is formed. Return the onions to the pan and add the apple and the tomato sauce. Cover and let simmer for 15 minutes, or till the mixture is a smooth sauce. Stir in the beaten eggs and cook till set. Serve this piled on rice or noodles.

CURRIED VEGETABLE OMELET ❋ ❋ *4 servings*

½ cup dal (see p. 26)
6 eggs
1 onion, minced
¼ tsp. freshly ground black pepper

⅛ tsp. coriander seeds
5 cardamom pods
½ cup yogurt
½ tsp. salt
½ cup butter or vegetable oil

Soak the *dal* in water to cover until it softens to the consistency of paste. Beat the eggs lightly and add the softened *dal*. Add the onion and pepper. Grind the coriander seeds and cardamom pods in a mortar till well crushed; then add them to the egg mixture. Mix well and add yogurt and salt. Heat the butter in a heavy skillet and pour in the egg mixture. Cook gently till the omelet has set, then fold over just once. Serve with tamarind jam or sweet chutney.

Chapter 11

DRY CURRIES

D RY CURRIES are known by various names, according to the country where they are made and the preparation used. In America, Greece, Turkey, and other Near Eastern countries, they are labeled as *pilafs* or *pilaffs*. In India, Malay, further East, and elsewhere they are listed as *pellows, pillaws, pooloos, pulaos,* or *pullaos,* but all pronounced by the foreigner as "plows," sounded with an explosive *p*-low.

Pulao, as it is called in South India, is simply raw rice cooked along with meat and other ingredients till soft and fluffy. Each community or country has its own blend of curry spices for its own distinctive dish.

Pulaos lend themselves to many variations. Much of their popularity, however, is due to the garnishments which go with them, especially for festive occasions. A *pulao* is garnished in much the same way as a *biriana* (see p. 132). The American housewife is experimenting with these dishes more and more for Sunday suppers, patio parties, etc., and originating her own varieties of garnishes which can be equally tempting even if less ornate.

STANDARD TURKISH PILAF   ❋   *4 servings*

Turkish dishes are much milder than those of India and farther East, for Turks prefer more delicate seasoning.

1 cup uncooked rice	1 tsp. salt
½ cup olive oil or butter	¼ tsp. ground cinnamon or
2 cups water	other spice
Pulp of 1 tomato	⅛ tsp. saffron

(*120*)

Wash the rice, then dry it and fry till brown in the heated oil. Place it in a heavy kettle with the water, tomato (optional), salt, and cinnamon. Simmer till all liquid is absorbed and the rice is dry and fluffy. Mound the rice on a platter and sprinkle the saffron over it. Add meat or vegetables on top.

FESTIVE TURKISH PILAF   �֎   *8 servings*

1 lb. uncooked rice
¾ cup olive oil or butter
1 cup water
½ tsp. salt
1 onion, minced
1 cup slivered almonds

1 cup seeded raisins
1 hard-cooked egg, sliced
1 onion, cut into rings
1 fresh green pepper, cut into thin rings

Wash and dry the rice. Heat ¼ cup of the oil and brown the rice in it; then add the water, salt, and minced onion. Simmer for 20 minutes, or till rice is dry and all liquid is absorbed. (Here various spices may be added if desired.) Heat remaining oil and brown the almonds very lightly in it; watch carefully, as the nuts scorch in an instant. Remove almonds and puff the raisins. Remove, and use along with almonds, egg slices, and onion and pepper rings to garnish the platter of rice. Any meat or vegetable is placed on top of the rice. Serve with chutney and mango pickle.

HINDU NONMEAT PULAO   ✳   *4 servings*

1 cup olive oil or butter
1 large onion, minced
2 cups uncooked rice
1 garlic clove, mashed
¼ tsp. ground saffron
1½ cups water
1 tsp. salt
12 whole cloves
12 cardamom pods

1 cinnamon stick, 2 inches
6 whole allspice berries
1 Tb. extra butter
¼ cup seeded raisins
2 Tbs. almonds
1 onion, cut into rings
1 green pepper, cut into thin rings

Heat the oil in a heavy kettle and fry the onion. Add the rice which has been washed and dried. Add mashed garlic, the saffron mixed with the water, and the salt. Mix well and add the whole spices. Simmer, covered, for 20 minutes, or till rice is dry and fluffy and all liquid is absorbed. Do not remove the spices. Turn out on a platter. Heat the tablespoon of butter and puff the raisins, then brown the almonds slightly. Garnish the rice with raisins, almonds, and onion and green-pepper rings. Curried meat sauces may be served with this, or plain fried meats, but the vegetarian Hindu regards this as a complete meal. He livens it by serving with it many intriguing chutneys, jams, and sweets as well as fresh fruits, but not salads as served in the West.

AMERICAN PULAO　　❊　❊　❊　　*4 servings*

1 cup plus 2 Tbs. vegetable oil or butter
2 onions, chopped fine
1 cup uncooked rice
1 cup boiling water or clear broth
½ tsp. salt
1 tsp. peppercorns
1 cinnamon stick, 2 inches, cracked
4 cardamom pods
4 whole cloves
2 bay leaves
2 Tbs. raisins
1 Tb. slivered almonds
⅛ tsp. ground saffron

Heat the cup of oil in a heavy kettle and brown the onions. Remove onions and fry the uncooked rice which has been washed and dried. Fry for a few moments, then return onions to the pan and add water, salt, peppercorns, cinnamon stick, cardamoms, cloves, and bay leaves. Cover and let simmer till all liquid is absorbed and the rice is dry and fluffy. (If this method of cooking is followed, there will be no need to boil the rice first and then dry it out in a colander.) Heat remaining oil and in it puff the raisins, then drain on absorbent paper. In the same pan brown the almonds very lightly, then drain on paper. Pile the rice on a platter and sprinkle the raisins and almonds on top, then dust with the ground saffron.

NOTE　Whole spices are left in the rice, to be removed by the diner from his individual portion.

MISSION HOUSE PULAO   ❋   *6 servings*

1 frying chicken (3 lbs.)
1 lb. stewing beef
6 cups water
1 tsp. salt
1-inch piece of green gingerroot
   or ½ tsp. ground ginger
3 large onions, chopped fine
1 garlic clove, mashed (optional)
2 cardamom pods

4 whole cloves
4 black peppercorns
1 cinnamon stick, 4 inches
1½ cups uncooked rice
4 Tbs. raisins
4 Tbs. almonds
4 Tbs. butter or oil
Few onion rings
Few green-pepper rings

In a heavy kettle put the chicken, beef, water, salt, gingerroot, onions, and garlic. Simmer, covered, for 2 to 4 hours, or till meats are tender. Remove the meats from the liquid and take the flesh from the bones. Discard bones and set meat in oven to keep warm. Strain the broth and boil down till it measures a little over 2 cups. Combine the broth, meat, whole spices, and uncooked rice which has been washed and dried. Cover closely and simmer (or bake in oven) till all liquid is absorbed and the rice is dry and fluffy. Raisins may be added to the rice and cooked for the last few minutes. Or they may be used as garnish on top of the rice after it is turned out on platter. If used as a garnish, heat the raisins as well as the almonds in the butter before sprinkling over the rice. Arrange onion and pepper rings around the edge. Serve chutney with this.

NOTE Whole spices are left in the rice for serving.

ARMENIAN PILAF   ❋   ❋   ❋   *2 servings*

1 Tb. butter or lamb drippings
1 Tb. curry powder
1 cup uncooked rice
1 cup tomato juice or chopped
   pulp

1 cup diced cooked lamb
1 cup broth
½ tsp. freshly ground black pepper
½ tsp. salt, or more

Use a heavy iron kettle. Heat the drippings and brown the curry powder. Add the uncooked rice and fry it for 5 minutes, stirring constantly with a wooden spoon. Add the tomato juice, lamb, broth, and seasonings. Cover and simmer for 30 minutes, or till liquid is all absorbed and the rice is dry and fluffy. Serve chutneys and relishes with this.

NOTE Mutton or goat meat are the meats most commonly used in the Near East and North India, hence mutton drippings are used largely in cooking. Chutneys and spices are most necessary to liven up these meats and, often, to hide the strong odor.

MUTTON OR GOAT-MEAT PULAO   ✵   *4 servings*

6 dried chilies
½ tsp. cuminseeds
6 whole cloves
1-inch piece of green gingerroot or ½ tsp. ground ginger
1 Tb. vinegar
5 garlic cloves, mashed
1 Tb. sugar

3 cups lamb broth or water
1 neck of mutton or goat, chopped
1½ cups uncooked rice
1 tsp. salt
Tomato wedges
Green peppers, cut into narrow strips

Grind the chilies, cuminseeds, cloves, and gingerroot in a mortar, sprinkling with vinegar during the process. Tie the spices in a muslin bag and drop into a heavy kettle with the garlic, sugar, broth, and meat. Cover and simmer for 2 hours, or till meat is almost tender, adding more broth if liquid begins to get too low before meat is cooked. Add the uncooked rice and the salt 30 minutes before dish is to be served. Cover the kettle and simmer again till all liquid is absorbed and the rice is dry and fluffy. Remove the spice bag and turn out rice on a platter. Garnish with tomato wedges and green-pepper strips, etc. Chutneys and sweet pickles are served with this.

NOTE If a richer *pulao* is desired, the rice can be fried in ½ cup oil or butter before adding it to the kettle. Instead of mutton or goat, this dish may be made with breast of lamb or riblets, about 2 pounds, or about 1 pound of shoulder chops.

MOGHLI PULAO (Moslem)   ❊   *6 servings or more*

1½ cups mutton drippings or butter

2 onions, chopped fine

1 lb. mutton, chopped fine

1 broiling chicken (2 lbs.), cut into large pieces

1 cup water

1 cup yogurt or curd (see p. 30)

1½ lbs. uncooked rice, washed and dried well

1 tsp. salt

1 garlic clove, mashed (optional)

1 tsp. ground ginger

1 tsp. extra butter

1 cinnamon stick, 4 inches

1½ tsps. cardamom pods

1½ tsps. whole cloves

1½ tsps. black peppercorns

Almonds, raisins, pepper rings, fried onion rings, etc., for garnish

½ tsp. ground saffron

Heat the fat in a heavy kettle and first fry the onions lightly, then the mutton; remove onions and mutton. Fry the chicken pieces till well browned. Return onions and mutton to kettle with the chicken. Add water, yogurt, uncooked rice, salt, and garlic. Fry the ginger for 1 minute in the hot butter and add to the meats. Add the cinnamon, cardamoms, cloves, and peppercorns whole. Cover the kettle and let simmer for 1 hour, or till chicken is tender. Remove the pieces of chicken, but let the other ingredients simmer till all liquid is absorbed and the rice is dry and fluffy. Place the pieces of chicken on a platter and mound the rice over them. Garnish with the almonds and raisins puffed (see p. 87) and pepper and onion rings. Sprinkle ground saffron lightly over all. A variety of chutneys and sweet and sour relishes are usually grouped around this imposing-looking *pulao*.

CASSEROLE OF CHICKEN PULAO   ✳   *12 servings*

4 large stewing chickens, (4 lbs. each), cut into pieces
4 tsps. salt
2 Tbs. peanut oil
4 onions, chopped fine
4 whole cloves
1 cinnamon stick, 4 inches

4 peppercorns
1 garlic clove, mashed
2 cups uncooked rice
½ tsp. ground saffron
Raisins puffed in hot oil
Onion rings
Green-pepper strips

Put the chickens in a large kettle, cover with water, and add 3 teaspoons of the salt. Simmer for 2 to 4 hours, or till tender. Remove the meat and discard bones. Boil down remaining liquid till 4 cups remain; strain and reserve. Brown the meat in the peanut oil, then remove meat. Fry the onions in the same skillet and add the meat, reserved broth, whole spices, garlic, and uncooked rice. Stir in remaining salt, adding extra salt as needed. Bake in a covered casserole in a hot oven (400°F.) for 1 hour, or till all liquid is absorbed and the rice is dry and fluffy. Sprinkle lightly with saffron before taking to the table, and arrange the raisins, onion rings, and pepper strips around. Serve chutneys and relishes.

PULAO FOR STUFFING CHICKEN   ✳   *about 5 cups*

4 Tbs. butter or vegetable oil
1 onion, minced
1 tsp. curry powder
1 small garlic clove, mashed
2 cups chicken broth

1 cup pineapple juice
4 Tbs. seeded raisins
4 Tbs. pistachios, chopped
1½ cups uncooked rice
1 tsp. salt, or more

Heat the butter in a heavy skillet and brown the onion in it; remove onion. Fry the curry powder till dark brown. Add garlic and simmer for 3 minutes, till a smooth paste is formed. Return onion to the pan and add broth, pineapple juice, raisins, pistachios, and rice. Season with salt. Cover tightly and simmer over low heat for 15 minutes, till rice is half done. Strain off the liquid; reserve it for other uses if you wish. Use the *pulao* to stuff chickens or other poultry. This is enough for 1 large chicken or 2 smaller birds.

PINEAPPLE-BAKED FRYING CHICKENS ❋ *6 servings*

2 frying chickens (3 lbs. each), whole
Salt
2½ cups pulao for stuffing chicken (see p. 126)
1 cup diced pineapple, fresh or canned
2 cups pineapple juice
Slices of orange, lime, and mango for garnish

Wash and dry the chickens and prepare them for roasting whole. Sprinkle with salt inside and outside. Stuff with *pulao* and sew the openings or skewer shut. Put the birds in a large casserole and add the diced pineapple and pineapple juice. Cover the casserole tightly. Bake in a hot oven (400°F.) for 1 hour, or till chicken is tender. Remove the birds to a platter. Thicken the pan juices with a little flour mixed with water, if you like gravy. Garnish the platter with slices of orange, lime, and mango, and with pineapple chunks from the casserole.

KORMA-STUFFED CHICKEN ❋ *6 servings*

1 plump roasting chicken (about 4½ lbs.)
1 Tb. butter or vegetable oil
1 onion, minced
2 Tbs. korma (see p. 20)
2 cups pulao for stuffing chicken (see p. 126)
Juice of 2 limes
Salt
½ cup melted butter
1 cup water

Prepare the chicken for stuffing and set aside. Heat the butter in a heavy skillet and brown the onion. Remove skillet from heat and add the *korma* and *pulao* and half of the lime juice. Season with salt to taste. Stuff the chicken loosely with this mixture and fasten the openings. Bake in a moderate oven (350°F.) for 2 to 4 hours, or till meat is tender. Baste often with a mixture of remaining lime juice, melted butter, and water. When the bird is ready, place it on a platter and pour the thick rich liquid and any escaped stuffing around it. Serve with chutneys and relishes.

NOTE   Pigeons, duck, quail, pheasant, and birds of all kinds can be cooked this way.

PULAO-STUFFED CHICKEN   ❊   *6 servings*

2 large onions, chopped fine
4 Tbs. butter or vegetable oil
1 large roasting chicken (4 lbs.)
2 tsps. salt
2 cups chicken broth
1 cup uncooked rice

1 cinnamon stick, 4 inches
6 whole cloves
½ cup seeded raisins
1 cup flour
1 cup water

Brown the onions lightly in the heated butter; remove onions. Prepare the chicken by washing well; dry the bird and sprinkle inside and out with 1 teaspoon salt. In a separate bowl mix the browned onions, remaining salt, the broth, rice, and whole spices. Cover tightly and simmer for 30 minutes, or till all liquid is absorbed and the rice is dry and fluffy. Add the raisins to this mixture and more salt if needed. Stuff the chicken, fastening the openings well.

Make a thick paste of the flour and water and coat the whole chicken with it. Tie the bird in a muslin bag and put into a large kettle of boiling water. Let the bird simmer for 3 to 4 hours, or till meat is tender. Remove from muslin cover and put on a platter. Garnish with nuts, puffed raisins, green-pepper strips, onion rings, etc. Serve with mango chutney and pickles.

PULAO WITH KABABS   ❊   ❊   *6 servings*

2 lbs. lamb or beef
4 Tbs. olive or peanut oil
2 Tbs. minced onion
1 tsp. curry powder
1 garlic clove, mashed

6 peppercorns, cracked
3 bay leaves
1 cup lemon juice
1 cup bourbon or water
1 tsp. salt, or more

Cut the meat into 1-inch cubes. Heat the oil and fry the onion in it, then remove onion. Fry the curry powder in the same pan. Combine onion and curry mixture in a deep bowl. Add the garlic, peppercorns, bay leaves, lemon juice, bourbon, and salt to taste. Add meat cubes and let them marinate for 1 hour, turning often. Meanwhile prepare the *pulao*.

4 Tbs. butter or vegetable oil
1½ cups uncooked rice
½ cup blanched almonds
½ cup seeded raisins
1 cup broth
⅛ tsp. ground saffron

Heat the butter and brown the mixed rice and nuts. Add the raisins and broth. Do not add salt. Cover and simmer over low heat for 30 minutes, or till rice is soft and all liquid is absorbed. Sprinkle with saffron and keep warm in oven till kababs are ready.

Drain the meat cubes and thread them on skewers with chunks of vegetables such as onions, fresh tomatoes, fresh mushrooms. Broil over an open fire or in a broiler, turning to brown on all sides. Place a skewer on top of a mound of *pulao* to serve. Pass bowls of chutney and mango pickles.

AMERICAN CHICKEN PULAO ❄ *6 servings*

1¼ cups vegetable oil or butter
5 large onions, chopped fine
2 cups uncooked rice
4 cups chicken broth
10 coriander seeds
⅛ tsp. cuminseeds
2 cardamom pods, crushed
1 cinnamon stick, 4 inches
4 cups diced cold cooked chicken
1 tsp. salt, or more
1 cup seeded raisins
1 cup unsalted cashews, peanuts, or almonds

Heat 1 cup of the oil and fry the onions in it till they are a clear pale brown; remove onions. Brown the uncooked rice for 5 minutes, adding more hot oil if needed to keep it from sticking. (Do not add cold oil or it will leave a greasy taste.) Return onions to rice and add the broth. Tie the coriander seeds, cuminseeds, and cardamon pods in a small muslin bag and add the spice bag and the cinnamon stick to the rice. Add chicken and salt to taste. Simmer for 30 minutes, or till liquid is absorbed and the rice is dry and fluffy. Remove the spice bag but leave the cinnamon stick in the rice.

Heat remaining oil and in it puff the raisins and brown the

unsalted nuts. Pile the *pulao* on a large platter and garnish with the raisins and nuts.

AMERICAN BEEF OR LAMB PULAO ❋ *4 servings*

¼ cup vegetable oil
1 onion, chopped fine
2 tsps. curry powder
¼ tsp. ground ginger (optional)
2 cups beef broth

2 cups cubed cold cooked lamb
  or beef
½ unpeeled cooking apple, diced
1 tsp. salt, or more
1 cup uncooked instant rice

Heat the oil and brown the onion in it; remove onion from skillet. Fry the curry powder and ginger till dark brown. Return onion to skillet and add the broth, cold meat, apple, and salt. Cover and let simmer for 15 minutes, or till only half of the liquid remains. Add the instant rice and simmer till it is dry and fluffy and all liquid is absorbed. Toss lightly on a platter and serve with hot mango chutney and relishes.

NOTE This is a hot curry and the ginger may be omitted if a milder one is desired.

PULAO OF SHRIMPS OR PRAWNS ❋ ❋ *6 servings*

1 cup mustard oil or butter
3 large onions, chopped fine
3 garlic cloves, mashed
4 cups uncooked rice
1 cup coconut milk (see p. 16)
4 whole cloves
4 cardamom pods

1 blade of mace
1 cinnamon stick, 4 inches
1 tsp. salt, or more
2 cups cooked shrimps or
  prawns
Garnishes

Heat the oil and brown the onions lightly in it. (Mustard oil gives a finer flavor to fish foods than any other fat.) Add the garlic, uncooked rice, coconut milk, whole spices, and salt to taste. Cover and let simmer for 30 minutes, or till liquid is absorbed and rice almost dry. Add the cooked shrimps or prawns for the last 10 minutes. Turn out *pulao* on a platter and garnish with wedges of lemon and tomato, hard-cooked eggs, etc. Serve with a bowl of Major Grey's chutney.

BENGAL SHRIMP PULAO   ✳   ✳   *6 servings*

2 lbs. fresh shrimps **or** 1 lb.
   canned shrimps
8 Tbs. butter
2 Tbs. minced onion

2 Tbs. korma (see p. 20)
1½ cups yogurt or curd (see p. 30)
½ tsp. salt

Prepare shrimps first. If canned wash well in cold water and drain. If fresh simmer in lightly salted water for 5 minutes, then shell and devein. Heat the butter in a heavy skillet and brown the onion lightly. Add the *korma* and simmer for 3 minutes. Add the yogurt or curd and salt and turn the sauce mixture into the top part of a double boiler. Simmer over boiling water for 10 minutes, stirring constantly. Add the shrimps and cook for another 15 minutes, or till mixture is quite dry. Serve hot boiled rice in a separate dish along with chutneys.

Marinated Meats for Pulaos

Strong-flavored meats such as pork, duck, goose, etc., are used largely for *pulaos* in the East, but they are first marinated for some hours in a mixture which will tenderize them and camouflage the taste. When fowl is used whole, several large gashes are made in the sides and a marinade mixture is rubbed in well. Haunches and other large cuts of pork or game are pricked all over with a fork or skewer and a marinade is rubbed in before the meat is put on the spit. Smaller portions of meat are steeped well in a marinade, and turned often during the process.

YOGURT MARINADE

¾ cup yogurt or curd (see p. 30)
2 Tbs. korma (see p. 20)

1 Tb. sliced green gingerroot
1 Tb. lime juice
½ tsp. salt

Mix all ingredients and pour over the meat. Steep for 4 hours or more. If a larger cut is used, double or triple the recipe.

DUCK PULAO   ❊   ❊   ❊   ❊   *4 servings*

1 duck (4 lbs.), cut into pieces
1½ cups yogurt marinade (see p. 131)
¼ cup vegetable oil
1 onion, chopped fine
1 garlic clove, mashed
2 cups broth or water
1½ cups uncooked rice

1-inch piece of green gingerroot, sliced fine
4 cardamom pods
1 cinnamon stick, 4 inches
4 peppercorns
4 whole cloves
1 tsp. salt

Put the duck pieces in a deep bowl and pour the marinade over them. Let them steep for 4 hours. Drain the duck pieces and broil them until golden brown and tender.

Heat the oil and brown the onion in it. Add the garlic, broth, rice, spices, and salt. Cover and simmer for 30 minutes, or till liquid is absorbed and the rice is dry and fluffy. Serve the broiled duck on top of the *pulao*.

VARIATION When duck is ready to broil, cut the meat into inch pieces. Brown them in the oil after the onion is cooked and let the duck finish cooking with the rice.

Birianas

Birianas are Moslem dishes; they are all prepared in the same way but differ in their garnishings. *Birianas* may be made with pigeon, duck, chicken, lamb, or fish, but never from pork. Since they are used mostly for festive occasions such as weddings, durbars, etc., they often change their names in honor of respected or royal guests. They differ from the ordinary curry dish in several ways. Though butter or oil is used lavishly in the preparation, the dish ends up much drier. The rice is uncooked when added, and is put on top of the meat to cook with it; usually it is added during the last 15 minutes only, in order that it may not become too mushy. The spices are not ground, but added whole and not removed before serving. The diner calmly takes the large pieces of stick cinnamon and whole cloves from his mouth and without embarrassment drops them on the side of his plate.

Garnishes for these dishes are elaborate. They take the place of the Westerner's green salads which are taboo in a land where the soil is so germ laden. For some occasions there will be flower-petal designs, or ornate patterns traced in puffed raisins or toasted nuts, or slices of candied orange and pineapple. The decorations used for festal dishes are beautiful beyond description. It is not uncommon at a special banquet to see a whole lamb, the haunch of a wild boar, or whole fowls sheathed entirely in silver or gold tissue as thin as a cobweb. And these are smothered in great mounds of snowy rice, festooned with fresh petals of roses, jasmine, or frangipani. Clever scroll patterns are done in cashews, almonds, pistachios, balanced by the green of cucumbers and other vegetables and the leaves of mint and coriander. Just before serving, too, rosewater or jasmine perfume is sprayed over the dish and guests. To accompany the main dish, gleaming brass trays are piled high with fruits from secluded gardens—purple grapes, strange-colored melons, pink and gold mangoes, ruby red pomegranates, vivid green oranges, tangerines, limes, tamarinds, figs, mangosteens, custard apples, plantains—these and peaches and pears from the snow-capped mountains in the North.

Of course this display is typical of the wealthier Moslems, but down in the village, in the humble courtyard there behind the mud wall, the meal the housewife sets before her husband on a fresh plantain leaf—a small bowl of curried sauce and mound of rice—is equally a thing of beauty, ringed round with marigold, lemon, coriander, and mint leaves.

CHICKEN BIRIANA   ❋   ❋   ❋   *4 servings*

2 cups yogurt
1 tsp. salt
¼ tsp. freshly ground black pepper
1 frying chicken (3 lbs.), disjointed
6 Tbs. vegetable oil or butter
1 large onion, chopped fine
6 garlic cloves, mashed
3 cardamom pods, ground
½ tsp. ground cuminseed
2 green chilies, sliced fine
1-inch piece of green gingerroot, sliced paper-thin

10 mint leaves, shredded
1 cinnamon stick, 2 inches
6 whole cloves
2 cups water
2 cups uncooked rice
⅛ tsp. ground saffron or turmeric
¼ cup raisins, puffed (see p. 87)
Slices of hard-cooked eggs
¼ cup toasted nuts
Few sweet onion rings, raw or fried

Season the yogurt with ½ teaspoon salt and the pepper and spoon it over the chicken. Let chicken stand for 1 hour, turning pieces often. Heat the oil in a heavy skillet. Brown the onion lightly; remove onion from the pan and blend the garlic with it. In remaining oil in the skillet fry the cardamom and cuminseed. Drain and dry the chicken pieces and add them to the pan along with chilies, gingerroot, mint, cinnamon, and cloves. Return onion and garlic mixture and add the water. Cover pot tightly and let all simmer for 2 hours. Then add the rice, remaining salt, and the saffron, and simmer again till all liquid is absorbed and the rice is fluffy.

Pile on a large platter, leaving the whole spices in the mixture. Garnish with raisins, hard-cooked egg slices, nuts, and onion rings. Circle the platter with many small bowls of chutney, sweet pickles, preserves, shredded coconut, and sweets. A hot curry sauce may also be served, but remember a *biriana* is supposed to be mild.

LAMB BIRIANA   ❊   ❊   ❊   ❊   *4 servings*

1 lb. lamb stewing meat with bones
1 lamb shinbone with meat
6 cups cold water
Salt
3 onions, chopped fine
½ cup lamb drippings or butter
1 cup uncooked rice

3 garlic cloves, mashed
1 cinnamon stick, 4 inches
6 cardamom pods
4 whole cloves
6 white peppercorns
1 blade of mace
½ tsp. ground ginger
⅛ tsp. ground saffron

Put the lamb with all the bones in the cold water and add 2 teaspoons salt. Simmer for 2 to 4 hours, or till tender. Remove from the liquid and take the meat from the bones; discard bones. Boil liquid down till it measures 3 cups; set aside. Brown the onions lightly in the drippings. Add the reserved broth, uncooked rice, the meat, garlic, whole spices, and the ground ginger if you wish a fiery curry. Add salt if needed. Cover and simmer, or bake in a moderate oven (350°F.), for 30 minutes, or till all liquid is absorbed and the rice is dry and fluffy. Toss out lightly onto a platter and sprinkle very lightly with saffron.

MAHARAJAH'S PULAO FOR A FEAST

1 young lamb
Salt
Lamb biriana (see p. 134)
  enough to fill lamb

Boiling fat, a large quantity
Garnishes
Rosewater

Trim the lamb and split it lengthwise on the underside. Sprinkle it with salt inside and out, but sparingly. Then stuff with the *pulao*. Skewer the opening shut and arrange the lamb on a spit over a slow but steady fire. The spit must be turned constantly and the meat must be basted constantly with boiling fat. Broil the lamb for 6 to 8 hours according to its size and the texture of the flesh. When cooked, remove it from the spit and let it cool. Arrange garnishes (orange sections, grapes, pistachios and almonds, crystallized fruits, flowers) around it. Sprinkle rosewater freely over all.

Chapter 12

VEGETABLE CURRIES

IN EASTERN LANDS where there are so many persons who
do not eat meat, it is natural that a great variety of vegetable
dishes should have been evolved over the centuries. Also, the
colonial powers introduced many Western vegetables. However,
vegetables are seldom cooked or served as a separate dish. They
are usually cooked with curry spices and other ingredients, the
less tender vegetables, or those requiring longer cooking, being
either minced first or added at the outset, while the more tender
varieties are added later, some just before the dish is done.

Many vegetables are dried and stored for later use, to provide
for days of dreaded droughts and famines. The most used of
these are lentils, beans, and peas, legumes which are dried and
compressed into small hard cakes called *dal*. For ways to prepare
and use *dal*, or for substitutes for it, see Chapter 4.

White wheat flour is seldom used in a *pukka* Indian curry. For
thickening sauces, the most widely used substance is a flour made
of the dried legumes, which is also called *dal*, or a little of the
pressed cake made of mashed legumes. Often no thickening is
used, but only a little liquid is added in preparing the dishes, and
the vegetables are simmered down till they have the required
texture.

There are a few rules for the preparation of vegetables. All
vegetables grown in the Indian peninsula must be well washed in
a solution of permanganate of potash to make them safe before
going into the curry pot or, even more important, before being
used raw in a salad or garnish. Green gingerroot or coconut are
also used largely with vegetables. The gingerroot should be well
pounded; Indian cooks claim that the whole spice gives a better

flavor than ground ginger. The juice of lime, lemon, or tamarind is usually added to any vegetable curry just before it is taken from the heat. Whole seeds, such as aniseed, mustard, poppy, or sesame, are sprinkled on cooked bland vegetables to add flavor.

Vegetable curries, like meat curries, are known by various names according to the method of cooking:

BHAJI (*bhajhee, bajee, bhaja*), a vegetable curry which uses the leaves of vegetables such as beets, cauliflower, pumpkin, radishes, spinach, squash, etc.

BHURTHA, a mash of one or more vegetables, which is served cold. These often take the place of potato to serve with meat or fish, or sometimes they are served instead of bread.

CHAKEE, a curry which blends three or more vegetables, boiling or parboiling the hard ones first, adding the soft ones last, and simmering all with yogurt, spices, coconut milk, etc. These are eaten either hot or cold; when hot they are usually served with boiled rice.

FOOGATH, a tasty fried cake made from mixtures of cold cooked vegetables, spiced with green gingerroot and curry powder, then fried in hot fat or oil.

Vegetables are also used in cutlets and fritters, or they may be stuffed with curry mixtures. In fact, vegetables with spices are used as surprisingly tasty main dishes, instead of being just a mere accompaniment to meats. Some fruits are also treated as vegetables and are prepared and served in the same ways.

There are many vegetables available in the Far East. Some are familiar to us, others are strange. Here is a list of some of them.

Artichoke
Asparagus
Bamboo shoots
Beans, many varieties, as amaranth beans, field beans, long beans or drumsticks
Beets, white and red
Cabbage
Cauliflower
Corn (American or Indian corn)
Cucumber

Eggplant (aubergine or brinjal)
Gourds, many varieties, as ash gourd or bitter gourd
Jerusalem artichokes
Lettuce
Lotus roots
Mushrooms
Okra (lady's fingers)
Onion
Palm hearts (cabbage palm)
Peas

Potatoes (Irish or white potatoes)
Pumpkin, white and yellow
Radishes, white and red
Spinach
Sweet potatoes
Tomatoes
Turnips
Vegetable marrow (zucchini or green summer squash)
Water chestnuts
Watercress
Yams, several varieties

There are many other vegetables which have no English names. Barks of several trees are also used like vegetables, as are some tree blossoms, the neem flower, for instance. Many plants usually used as herbs or spices are prepared as vegetables. Some are familiar herbs like mint, mustard, parsley, and sage, but there are more unusual plants like fenugreek and the many varieties of chilies.

CURRIED APPLES AND CELERY   ❋ ❋   *4 servings*

½ cup butter or vegetable oil
6 cups chopped unpeeled apples
1 Tb. curry powder
⅛ tsp. ground cayenne pepper or dash of Tabasco

1 cup diced celery
1 cup tomato juice
1 tsp. salt

Heat the butter and brown the apples lightly in it; remove apples from pan. In the same pan fry the curry powder (and cayenne if used) to a dark brown, or till spices form a smooth paste, about 3 minutes. Return apples to the pan and add all other ingredients. Cover and simmer for 30 minutes, or till celery is tender. This mixture should be almost dry. Spoon on top of hot boiled rice.

FOOGATH OF BANANA   ❋ ❋   *4 servings*

12 quite green bananas
4 Tbs. butter or vegetable oil
1 tsp. curry powder

2 Tbs. shredded fresh coconut
1 cup coconut milk (see p. 16)

Skin and cut the bananas into ½-inch pieces; soak in water to cover for 1 hour. Heat the butter and fry the curry powder in it till it is dark brown. Simmer about 3 minutes, till a smooth paste is formed. Add drained bananas, coconut, and coconut milk. Cover and simmer for 30 minutes, or till bananas are soft. Spoon on top of curried dishes as a vegetable, or use as main dish.

Carrots

Carrots prepared in an Indian way make a new eating experience. Here are some of the ways to use the humble carrot by itself. However, it also plays an important part in the various curried vegetable dishes.

Boil carrots in gingered water till tender, then cut into strips and coat with honey, butter and minced candied gingerroot.

Boil carrots in salted water till soft, then mash and mix with ground almonds and chopped parsley.

Boil carrots in salted water till very soft. Drain and rice them and mix with mushrooms to add to cream soup.

Boil carrots in salted water till tender, then mash and mix with raisins; use as a stuffing for baked tomatoes.

Shred raw carrots and add to gelatin molds. Serve yogurt with them instead of mayonnaise.

Boil carrots and yellow turnips in salted water till tender. Mash and season with caraway seeds and butter.

Boil carrots in salted water till tender. Mash and mix with fresh chopped mint leaves and butter.

CURRIED CARROTS AND
PEAS ❊ ❊ *4 servings*

1 lb. carrots, washed	1 tsp. chili powder
Salt	2 Tbs. butter or vegetable oil
½ tsp. ground cuminseed	1 cup shelled fresh green peas

Scrape the carrots and cut them into thin rounds. Boil them in water to cover with 1 teaspoon salt till they are tender but still quite firm; drain. Mix the cuminseed and chili powder. Heat the butter and fry the spices to a dark brown in it. Simmer for 3 minutes, adding a little water to keep from scorching. Add the carrots, peas, and extra salt if needed. Cover tightly and simmer over low heat till the peas are tender, adding only a drop or two of water if needed to keep them from sticking. The mixture should be thick and quite dry when spooned out onto hot boiled rice.

CURRIED CAULIFLOWER   ❊   *4 servings*

1 large cauliflower
1 cup yogurt
1 onion, minced
2 garlic cloves, mashed
1 tsp. ground ginger
1 tsp. sugar
2 Tbs. butter or vegetable oil

2 onions, chopped coarsely
1 tsp. salt
2 cups hot water
½ tsp. ground cinnamon
¼ tsp. grated nutmeg
¼ tsp. ground coriander

Separate the cauliflower into flowerets and rinse. Put the yogurt in a large bowl and add the minced onion, garlic, ginger, and sugar. Add the cauliflowerets to this and let them stand for 2 hours, turning pieces several times. Heat the butter in a large saucepan and brown the chopped onions in it; add the cauliflower with its yogurt dressing. Add salt and water and simmer for about 30 minutes, till the vegetable is tender but not mushy. Most of the liquid should be absorbed and only a small amount of the thick sauce should remain. Remove from the heat and sprinkle with mixed cinnamon, nutmeg, and coriander.

Eggplant

This fine vegetable does not enjoy the popularity in North America it receives in other parts of the world. In Spain it is used as commonly as the potato in England, or bread in France. It is included in almost every dish in the Near East, especially in Turkey, along with garlic or sesame and caraway seeds. Lamb or, more often, the tough mutton, is stuffed with eggplant and saffron mixtures, or as often the other way round—eggplant is stuffed with spiced mutton.

Eggplant is known by many different names—*brinjals* in India, *aubergines* in France and Spain, the Chinese squash in South

America, the purple passion fruit in the Near East, and the mad, or raging, apple in mid-Europe where one monarch of ancient times is said to have died mad after living on it exclusively for many days.

Perhaps because of its exotic color, or because it belongs to the deadly nightshade family, or because of the bitter brown liquid which appears on the cut surfaces, many superstitions have sprung up about it over the ages. In the West many people regard the eggplant liquid as a poison which must be extracted by soaking the vegetable in brine before using it. In the far East, however, this extract is regarded as life-giving and the vegetable is never presoaked or parboiled. Apart from its food value, it is also one of the most beautiful of vegetables. There are three varieties, white, striped, and deep purple, all are used extensively and decoratively. Eggplant grows plentifully all over India and it is used there in many recipes.

EGGPLANT CURRY   ✿   ✿   *4 to 6 servings*

4 small eggplants	1 cup water
½ cup vegetable oil	2 Tbs. lemon juice
1 Tb. coriander seeds	1 tsp. ground saffron
4 dried red chilies	½ tsp. salt, or more
1 onion, chopped	1 Tb. brown sugar
2 Tbs. grated coconut	1 Tb. butter
1 garlic clove	2 green chilies
1 tsp. sesame seeds, roasted	½ tsp. mustard seeds

Wash the eggplants well. Cut lengthwise into quarters, retaining the skins. Steep in salted water for 1 hour, then drain and dry. Fry the sections in the heated oil till lightly browned, then remove eggplants. In the same skillet put the coriander, red chilies, and chopped onion. Brown lightly. Grind the coconut and garlic together and add to the onion mixture. Stir the roasted sesame seeds into the water and lemon juice. Stir in the saffron, and salt to taste. Put all in the skillet and simmer, covered, for 5 minutes. Add the sugar and eggplants, keeping the pieces whole. Simmer for 5 minutes, then remove from the heat. In another skillet heat the butter and fry the green chilies and the mustard seeds. When seeds begin to jump, pour the mixture into the curried eggplant. Serve with hot boiled rice in a separate dish.

FRIED EGGPLANT ❄ ❄ *4 servings*

1 large eggplant
1 tsp. ground saffron

½ tsp. salt
½ cup vegetable oil

Wash the eggplant and cut it into thick slices. Skin may be removed or left on. Mix the saffron and salt and rub it over the eggplant slices. Let them stand for 1 hour, then press out the moisture from the slices with the hands. Heat the oil and fry the slices till nicely browned.

CURRIED BRINJALS ❄ ❄ ❄ *4 servings*

4 small round brinjals (egg-plants)
Salt
1 lb. raw lamb or beef, ground
1 onion, minced
3 Tbs. uncooked rice

1 small tomato, chopped fine
1 sprig of fresh mint or 1 tsp. mint sauce
4 Tbs. butter or vegetable oil
1 tsp. curry powder
4 cups chicken broth

Wash the eggplants carefully and wipe dry. Cut off the tops, taking care not to tear the skin; reserve the tops. Scoop out the pulp carefully. Sprinkle the insides of the shells with salt and let stand for 1 hour or more. Sprinkle the pulp with salt and press down in a colander with a weight; let drain for 30 minutes. Rinse out the shells with cold water and drain.

Meanwhile mix the raw meat, onion, and uncooked rice with the tomato and mint. Heat the butter in a heavy skillet and fry the curry powder till it is dark brown; simmer for about 3 minutes. Add this curry mixture to the other ingredients and add ½ teaspoon salt, or more to taste. Add the chopped drained pulp. Mix all thoroughly and use to stuff the drained eggplant shells. Fasten on the tops with food picks. Stand the eggplants upright in a casserole or baking dish half-filled with the chicken broth. Bake in a moderate oven (350°F.) for 1 hour or more, or till the rice in the shells is soft and the liquid absorbed. Spoon some of the broth over the shells constantly while baking. Any liquid left in dish should be used as a gravy.

EGGPLANT MASH (Bhurtha)   ❋   *4 to 6 servings*

1 large eggplant
1 tsp. salt
1 tsp. mustard oil
1 onion, minced

Juice of 1 lemon
Pinch of ground cayenne pepper

In the village the eggplant is buried whole in hot ashes and left till soft. This would be a fine method for the camper.

In the kitchen, peel the eggplant and cook in lightly salted water till soft, then drain and mash. Add the other ingredients, mix well and chill. Serve with cold meats and curries.

EGGPLANT AND POTATO MOOLEES   ❋   *4 servings*

4 small eggplants or 1 large one
4 medium-sized potatoes
1 large coconut
2 cups hot water
4 Tbs. butter or vegetable oil
2 onions, chopped
1 garlic clove, mashed

4 green chilies, cut into thin strips
½ tsp. ground ginger
½ tsp. ground turmeric
1 tsp. salt, or more
2 Tbs. vinegar

Wash the eggplants and cook in boiling salted water till tender. Remove skins. Pare the potatoes and cook for about 15 minutes, till fairly tender. Crack open the coconut, scrape out the pulp, and grate it. Steep it in the hot water. Heat the butter and brown the onions lightly in it. Add the garlic, chilies, ginger, turmeric, and salt. Simmer for 5 minutes, or till a smooth paste is formed. Squeeze the coconut from the water and add only half of it to the curried mixture. (Use the remaining coconut pulp for other recipes.) Add the potatoes, eggplants, and the liquid the coconut steeped in. Simmer for 5 more minutes. Just before removing from heat add the vinegar. This curry should be almost dry. It may accompany meat or fish curries, but it is usually served as the main dish by the Hindu. Wrapped in a plantain leaf, it is eaten cold by the traveler.

CURRIED LEEKS   ❀   ❀   ❀   *4 servings*

1 cup butter
3 leeks with green tops, chopped fine
½ tsp. curry powder
1 cup fresh lima beans

1 cup fresh green snap beans
1 cup shelled fresh green peas
3 tomatoes, cut into wedges
1 cup boiling water
1 tsp. salt

Heat the butter and brown the leeks lightly in it; remove leeks from pan. In remaining butter brown the curry powder to dark brown. Return leeks to the pan and add all other ingredients. Simmer for about 30 minutes, till vegetables are tender but not mushy. This is a standard curry. Spoon on top of hot boiled rice.

LENTIL CURRY   ❀   ❀   ❀   ❀   *6 servings*

2 cups dried lentils
3 Tbs. butter or vegetable oil
2 onions, chopped fine
1 tsp. curry powder

1 cup water
1 tsp. salt
6 hard-cooked eggs, halved

Soak the lentils overnight in salted water; use 1 teaspoon salt to 2 cups water. In the morning drain them. Heat the butter and brown the onions lightly in it; remove onions. In remaining butter fry the curry powder to dark brown. Add 1 cup water with the browned onions, the drained lentils, and the salt. Cover and simmer for 1 hour, or till lentils are tender. Add more salt if necessary. Arrange the warm egg halves on a platter and pour the lentil curry over them. When served the mixture should be quite dry. Serve chutneys and relishes with this.

CURRIED MUSHROOMS   ❀   ❀   *4 servings*

¾ lb. mushrooms
4 Tbs. butter or vegetable oil
2 large onions, chopped fine
1 tsp. ground turmeric

1 tsp. chili powder
1 garlic clove, mashed
½ cup water
½ tsp. salt

Wash and dry the mushrooms, then peel and slice them. Heat

the butter and brown the onions lightly in it; remove onions from pan. Mix the turmeric and chili powder and fry in remaining butter till dark brown. Stir in the mashed garlic and simmer for 3 minutes, or till mixture becomes a smooth paste. Return the onions and add the mushrooms, water, and salt. Simmer for 10 minutes, till mushrooms are tender. Mixture should be very thick when done. Spoon on top of hot boiled rice.

CURRIED MUSHROOM
STEMS ❃ ❃ *4 servings*

This is a good way to prepare mushroom stems when you have used all the caps for stuffing or some other fancy dish.

1 lb. mushroom stems
2 medium-sized onions, chopped fine
4 Tbs. butter or vegetable oil
1 tsp. curry powder

½ cup tomato juice
1 tsp. salt
½ tsp. grated nutmeg
½ tsp. ground cinnamon

Wash the mushroom stems and slice them. Brown the onions lightly in the heated butter and remove onions. Fry the curry powder to a dark brown and simmer till a smooth paste is formed. Add the tomato juice, onions, mushroom stems, and salt. Cover and simmer for 20 minutes, or till stems are tender and all the liquid is absorbed. Sprinkle with nutmeg and cinnamon and spoon on hot boiled rice.

Okra or Lady's Fingers

This small green vegetable is used in the East for many vegetable dishes as well as in pickles and soups. Known as *bhindis* or *bhendies*, it is often boiled, then fried in *foogaths* (see p. 149), then used in curries and chutneys. It is used fresh also, by the *sahibs*, sliced very thin in green salads.

SIMPLE OKRA CURRY ❋ ❋ *4 servings*

2 cups whole okra
1 cup water
Salt
4 onions, chopped fine
4 Tbs. butter or vegetable oil
2 tsps. dry mustard
1 tsp. ground turmeric

1 tsp. ground coriander
1 tsp. ground chilies
1 tsp. ground ginger
1 bay leaf
1 garlic clove, mashed (optional)
2 Tbs. shredded fresh coconut
½ cup tamarind or lemon juice

Wash the okra well in permanganate of potash if in India; in the United States just wash in water. Boil in the 1 cup water with 1 teaspoon salt, covered, for about 20 minutes, till okra is slightly tender but not mushy. There should be very little liquid left and this should be added to the mixture later. Brown the onions lightly in the heated butter; remove onions. Mix the spices well together in a mortar and fry in the butter to dark brown. Return onions to the pan, add the bay leaf, garlic, coconut, and 1 teaspoon salt. Add the okra and any liquid left from the first boiling. Stir in the tamarind juice. Simmer for 10 minutes, or till curry is thick and rich. Spoon out on top of hot boiled rice.

NUT AND GREEN-PEA CURRY ❋ ❋ *4 servings*

8 small onions, minced
6 Tbs. butter or vegetable oil
2 tsps. curry powder
1 tsp. rice flour or cornstarch
1 tsp. ground ginger
2 garlic cloves, mashed

½ cup unsalted ground nuts (cashews, almonds, or peanuts)
½ cup coconut milk (see p. 16)
1 tsp. salt
2 cups shelled green peas
Crisp fried onions

Brown the onions lightly in the heated butter and remove from the pan. Mix the curry powder, flour, and ginger and fry in remaining butter till dark brown. Simmer for about 3 minutes, till a smooth paste is formed. Return the onions and add the garlic, ground nuts, and coconut milk. Add salt. Simmer this mixture for 15 minutes, then add the green peas. Simmer for 20 minutes longer, or till peas are tender but not mushy. Add more salt if necessary. Spoon out on top of hot boiled rice and garnish with the crisp fried onions.

NOTE Another substitute for the rice flour is 1 tablespoon undiluted condensed pea soup which serves well as a thickening.

PARSNIP CURRY ✳ ✳ ✳ *4 servings*

This rather bland vegetable is particularly suited to curries.

1 lb. parsnips	1 tsp. chili powder
2 Tbs. butter or vegetable oil	1 cup water, or more
1 onion, minced	1 tsp. salt
½ tsp. ground cuminseed	1 small green pepper, cut into
3½ tsps. ground turmeric	fine strips

Peel and dice the parsnips and set aside. Heat the butter and brown the onion lightly in it; remove onion. Blend the ground spices and fry in remaining fat. Simmer for 3 minutes, or till a smooth paste is formed. Stir in the onion again. Add the water, parsnips, and salt. Bring to a boil and simmer for 30 minutes, or till parsnips are tender but not mushy. Add more water if needed as the parsnips cook, but the sauce should be almost dry when served. Add more salt to taste if necessary. Garnish with the strips of green pepper.

CURRIED GREEN PEPPERS ✳ *4 servings*

2 onions, chopped separately	1 garlic clove, mashed
2 Tbs. butter or vegetable oil	8 green peppers, seeded and
½ tsp. mustard seeds	sliced fine
½ tsp. ground ginger	1 cup water
1 tsp. sugar	1 tsp. salt

Brown 1 chopped onion lightly in the heated butter and remove it from the pan. Mix the mustard seeds and ground ginger and fry in remaining butter till seeds pop. Add the sugar and garlic and simmer till a smooth paste is formed and the color is dark brown. Return the onion. Add the green peppers, water, and salt. Cover the pan and simmer for 20 minutes, till peppers are tender but still firm. Spoon out on top of hot boiled rice. While the peppers are cooking, fry the remaining onion to crisp brown and use as a garnish for the finished dish.

CURRIED STUFFED GREEN
PEPPERS   ❊   *8 servings*

8 fresh green peppers	¼ tsp. ground cinnamon
2 Tbs. butter or lamb drippings	¼ tsp. grated nutmeg
1 large onion, minced	¼ tsp. ground coriander
1 garlic clove, mashed	½ tsp. salt
3 cups ground lean lamb	Curry sauce for peppers (see below)
1 tsp. curry powder	low)
½ tsp. ground ginger	Yogurt

Wash the peppers and cut off the tops; reserve the tops. Scoop out and discard seeds and membranes. Heat the butter and brown the onion and garlic lightly in it. Add the lamb, curry powder, and all the spices mixed together. Simmer for 5 minutes, then add the salt. Fill the peppers with the mixture and fasten on the tops with food picks. Stand the peppers upright in a baking dish and surround with curry sauce (see below). Cover the baking dish and bake in a moderate oven (350°F.) for 1 hour, or till meat and vegetables are done. If stuffing appears to become too dry while cooking, add a little yogurt to the sauce in the bottom of the dish.

CURRY SAUCE FOR
PEPPERS   ❊   ❊   *about ½ cup*

2 Tbs. butter or vegetable oil	½ cup yogurt
1 onion, minced	½ tsp. salt
1 tsp. curry powder	

Heat the butter and fry the onion in it; remove onion. In the same pan fry the curry powder till dark brown. Return onion and add the yogurt and salt. Simmer for 3 minutes, or till a smooth sauce is formed.

CURRIED POTATOES   ❊   ❊   *4 servings*

2 large raw potatoes	2 Tbs. butter or vegetable oil
2 cups water	½ tsp. curry powder
Salt	1 large tomato, chopped

Peel the potatoes and cut into thick slices. Parboil in the water with ½ teaspoon salt for 10 minutes; then set potatoes aside and reserve about 1 cup of the cooking water. Heat the butter in a heavy skillet and fry the curry powder to a dark brown. Simmer for 3 minutes, or till a smooth paste is formed, adding some of the cooking water if needed to keep from sticking. Add the tomato, potatoes, and remaining cooking water. Add salt cautiously. Cover and simmer for 15 minutes, or till the potatoes are soft and the sauce thick. Spoon this on top of curried meats, or use as a main dish. These are usually garnished with chopped chives, fried onions, or shredded coconut.

SPICED MASHED POTATOES
(Foogath)   ❈   *2 servings*

1 tsp. dal (see p. 26)	1 Tb. water, or more
1 tsp. mustard seeds	½ cup mashed potato
2 Tbs. butter or vegetable oil	Salt
½ tsp. ground ginger	1 Tb. lemon or tamarind juice
½ tsp. ground turmeric	2 Tbs. shredded fresh coconut
1 green pepper, sliced fine	

Soak the *dal* in a little water till it becomes pasty. Mix it with the mustard seeds and fry in the heated butter till the seeds begin to pop. Stir in the ground ginger and turmeric; fry till dark brown. Add the green pepper and water and simmer for about 15 minutes, till the pepper strips are tender and almost transparent but still crisp. Add the mashed potato and salt to taste. Heat for 5 minutes longer. The mixture should be quite dry when done. Stir in the lemon juice after taking from the heat. Spoon mixture on top of meat curries or eat as a main dish. Sprinkle coconut on top when the dish is served.

CURRIED POTATO CAKES   ❈   *3 servings*

Mix 1 cup each of cold mashed potatoes and cooked green peas with 1 tablespoon of chopped green chilies and a good pinch of mixed ground ginger and coriander. Add salt to taste. Form into small flat cakes. Dip into beaten egg and fry in hot butter or vegetable oil till well browned.

POTATO BALLS   ❋   ❋   ❋   ❋   *4 servings*

¼ cup mustard oil
1 small onion, minced
½ tsp. ground turmeric
1 tsp. ground chilies
1 cup hot water

2 large raw potatoes, diced
1 garlic clove, mashed
1 tsp. salt
Juice of ½ lemon, or more

Heat the oil and brown the onion lightly; remove onion. In remaining oil fry the turmeric and chilies for 3 minutes. Put in a large saucepan and add the other ingredients. Cover and simmer till potatoes are soft enough to mash and all the liquid is absorbed. Mash and mix thoroughly. Roll the mixture into small balls and chill before serving. To serve hot, brown the balls in additional hot mustard oil.

POTATO MASH (Bhurtha)   ❋   ❋   *6 servings*

6 large potatoes
1 green chili, minced
1 large onion, minced

1 tsp. sesame oil
1 tsp. salt
Juice of 1 lemon

Boil the potatoes till very tender, drain well, and mash. Mix with the other ingredients and chill. Serve with cold meats or curry.

AMERICAN CURRIED
SPINACH   ❋   ❋   *4 servings*

¼ cup vegetable oil
1 tsp. curry powder
⅛ tsp. paprika
2 pkgs. (10 ozs. each) frozen
spinach

½ tsp. dry mustard
½ tsp. salt, or more

Heat the oil and fry the mixed curry powder and paprika in it to a dark brown, but take care not to scorch the mixture. Cook the spinach, covered, using only the liquid that thaws from it and enough more to keep it from burning. As soon as it is tender but not mushy, stir in the curry mixture and dry mustard and add salt to taste.

NOTE Frozen zucchini, squash, and pumpkin are tasty when curried this way.

BARBADOS TOMATO CURRY ❋ *4 servings*

2 Tbs. butter or olive oil
1 tsp. curry powder
1 cup uncooked rice
2½ cups stewed tomatoes
Juice of 1 lime

1 Tb. minced chives
1 tsp. Worcestershire sauce
Salt
2 cups grated sharp cheese

Heat the butter in a heavy skillet and fry the curry powder in it to a dark brown. Stir in the rice and cook till it bubbles up. Add the tomatoes, lime juice, chives, Worcestershire sauce, and salt to taste, about ½ teaspoon. Cover and simmer for 30 minutes, or till the rice is dry and fluffy. Arrange in a well-greased baking dish and sprinkle with the grated cheese. Place under a broiler till top browns nicely. This curry is especially good with fish dishes.

HAWAIIAN TOMATO CURRY ❋ *4 servings*

6 firm red tomatoes
2 Tbs. butter or vegetable oil
1 tsp. curry powder
2 Tbs. bread crumbs
½ cup grated cheese

1 tsp. guava jelly
½ cup tomato catsup
1 tsp. salt
Extra butter

Peel the tomatoes and scoop out the pulp carefully. Stand the tomato shells in a buttered baking dish in readiness for stuffing. Heat the butter and fry the curry powder in it till dark brown. Mix the bread crumbs and cheese with the curry powder and butter. Add the jelly, catsup, and salt and mix in the chopped tomato pulp. Fill the tomato shells with the mixture. Pour a little water (about ½ cup) around the bottom of the tomatoes. Dot the top of each shell with butter. Bake in a moderate oven (350°F.) for about 20 minutes, or till tomatoes are cooked but not mushy. Serve hot boiled rice in a separate dish.

SPICED ZUCCHINI   ❊   ❊   ❊   *4 servings*

1½ lbs. small zucchini
2 Tbs. butter or vegetable oil
1 small onion, minced
1 tsp. ground cuminseed
1 tsp. sugar

2 cups water
2 green chilies, sliced thin
1 tsp. salt
1 Tb. mashed potato or instant potato

Scrub and peel the zucchini and cut them into small pieces, slices, or dice. Heat the butter and brown the onion lightly in it; remove onion from pan. In the remaining butter fry the cuminseed for 3 minutes. Stir in the sugar and add the water. Return onion to the pan and add the green chilies, zucchini, and salt. Cover and simmer for 20 minutes, or till vegetables are soft. Add the potato for the last 5 minutes. Mixture should be quite dry. Spoon out on top of hot boiled rice or Indian breads.

NOTE   The green Italian squash called zucchini, which is known in England as vegetable marrow, is not the only vegetable that can be cooked this way. Pumpkin and other kinds of squash can be prepared in the same fashion.

VEGETABLE PULAO   ❊   ❊   ❊   *4 servings*

4 cups diced raw vegetables
4 cups boiling water
Salt

1 onion, chopped fine
2 Tbs. butter
2 Tbs. korma (see p. 20)

For vegetables use a mixture of several of these: carrots, green and yellow snap beans, green peas, turnips, pumpkin, squash. Parboil them in the water with 1 teaspoon salt added for 15 minutes; remove vegetables. Simmer the liquid till it measures 2 cups; reserve it. Brown the onion lightly in the heated butter. Stir in the *korma* and simmer till a dark brown smooth paste is formed. Add the vegetables, reserved liquid, and salt to taste. Simmer for about 30 minutes or longer, till the curry is quite dry. Serve with hot boiled rice.

CURRIED VEGETABLE
LOAF ❋ *6 to 8 servings*

4 cups diced mixed vegetables
4 cups boiling water
1½ tsps. salt
½ cup dal (see p. 26)

¼ cup vegetable oil
1 tsp. curry powder
Juice of 1 lime

Cook the vegetables in the boiling water with 1 teaspoon salt for 15 minutes. Set aside the vegetables and boil down the liquid till it measures 1 cup. Soak the *dal* in the vegetable liquid till it has become a paste. Heat the oil and fry the curry powder in it to a dark brown. Stir fried curry into the mixture of vegetables. Add the softened *dal*, remaining salt, and the lime juice last; mix well. Press into a greased baking dish or a bread pan (9 by 5 by 3 inches). Bake in a moderate oven (350°F.) for 20 minutes, or till vegetables are cooked into a firm loaf. This loaf is used cold as well as hot.

CURRIED COCONUT
VEGETABLE ❋ ❋ *4 servings*

1 cup grated fresh coconut or ½ cup shredded dried coconut
1 cup cider vinegar
¼ cup vegetable oil or ghee
4 onions, chopped fine

1½ tsps. curry powder
1 cup each of diced squash, pumpkin, tomato, cauliflower
1 tsp. salt, or more
Juice of 1 lime

Steep the coconut in the vinegar for 1 hour, then press through a sieve and set both pulp and liquid aside. Heat the oil and brown the onions lightly in it; remove onions. Fry the curry powder to dark brown in the oil left in the pan. Put the diced vegetables in a kettle and cover with boiling salted water. Boil for about 20 minutes, till just tender but not too soft. Drain the vegetables and mix with the browned onions, curry mixture, the coconut pulp and liquid. Let simmer till all liquid is absorbed. Add the lime juice just before serving. Spoon out on top of hot boiled rice. Sweet-sour tamarind pickles or jam, or sweet mango chutneys are served with this.

Gandhi's Ashram Vegetables

Vegetarian dishes were the only ones ever served in Gandhi's ashrams, the religious communities or retreats where his disciples met and lived. People who visited him, however, tell how appetizing these simple meals were. Vegetables were shredded or minced to allow for quick cooking and they were cooked with as little liquid as possible, thus retaining the health-giving minerals and vitamins and the natural flavors. Vegetables were never mushy, merely tender.

ASHRAM VEGETABLE
CURRY ❋ ❋ *3 servings*

1 cup chopped carrot
1 cup chopped pumpkin
1 cup chopped turnip

1 cup chopped fresh tomatoes
1 cup fresh green peas
½ tsp. salt, or more

Cook the vegetables together in boiling salted water to cover for about 20 minutes, till they are tender. Force the vegetables through a sieve and spoon on top of hot boiled rice; or serve with simple curried eggs (see p. 117). A sweet chutney or relish is served with this.

Chapter 13

YOGA DISHES

YOGA is a way of life. A disciple or follower of that way of life is known as a yogi. Yogis claim that by practicing their regimen they gain increased powers in the mental, spiritual, physical, and psychical world. Their claims seem to be supported by the reports of many observers.

Yogis adhere strictly to a prescribed diet. They eat no meats, but live on whole grains, nuts, fruits, and vegetables which are cooked slowly and in the smallest amount of liquid possible. Thus they conserve richness of flavor and the precious mineral content. Honey is used for sweetening instead of refined white sugar. They drink only milk, rich goat's milk preferred. Basically all these foods are very simple, and in addition only small portions are served.

Yogis believe in a controlled diet rather than fasting; only the ascetics undertake those amazing long fasts. Yogis stress the conditions under which the one meal a day should be eaten—with thankfulness, time for relaxation, a peaceful mind, and a straight spine—all aids to the perfect digestion which the Creator ordained for man.

Many Indians become yogis, but not all yogis are Indians. According to recent statistics this is one of the fastest-growing cults in the world today. The most famous disciple was Mahatma Gandhi.

Gandhi believed in the doctrine of the Jains, one of the most ascetic and intellectual groups of nonconformists to Brahmanical Hinduism. Therefore he ate no meats of any kind, nor any eggs, not just from the habits of a lifetime, but from a spiritual convic-

tion which he was able to sustain even when living in England
while studying law. Few people know that in those student days
he ran a small vegetarian club in London for the benefit of his
own countrymen there. He himself lived all his days on such a
diet as this sample of his menus:

Mushroom nut roast with some whole grains added
Juices of carrot, celery, and lime
Prunes stuffed with cottage cheese
Yogurt ice cream

Instead of using refined white flour in preparing foods, yogis
use ground whole grains. Substitute for 1 cup of white flour any
of these:

½ cup barley flour
1½ cups rolled oats
½ cup potato flour

1 scant cup rice flour
1½ cups rye flour
1 cup corn flour (cornstarch)

YOGA NUT ROAST   ❀   ❀   ❀   *6 servings*

2 cups nuts, any kind
2 cups whole-wheat bread
crumbs
1 cup tomato pulp, fresh or
canned
1 onion, minced
2 Tbs. peanut oil

2 eggs, well beaten
2 cups minced celery
1 tsp. grated lemon rind
1 cup sliced mushrooms
½ cup water
Salt

Chop or grind the nuts and mix in a bowl with the bread
crumbs and tomato pulp. Fry the onion in the heated oil and
add it along with the eggs, celery, and lemon rind. Simmer the
mushrooms for 5 minutes in the water and add both mushrooms
and liquid to the mixture in the bowl. Add salt to taste. Put in a
greased baking dish and bake in a moderate oven (350°F.) for
30 minutes, or till celery is cooked. Baste with a small amount of
mixed hot peanut oil and water if the roast appears to become
too dry while cooking.

NOTE Curry spices fried, or fresh herbs, may be added to
this roast if a spicier dish is desired. This is eaten hot or cold.

YOGA CURRIED CASHEWS ❋ *4 servings*

½ cup cashews
1 cup coconut milk (see p. 16)
1 tsp. curry powder
1½ tsps. mustard seeds
3 Tbs. butter

2 lbs. fresh snap beans, sliced fine
½ cup cider vinegar
1 tsp. salt

Soak the cashews in cold water for 1 hour, then drain. Simmer them in the coconut milk for about 30 minutes, till tender. Fry the curry powder and mustard seeds till dark brown in the butter, then add the cashews and the milk they were simmered in, the beans, vinegar, and salt. Cover and simmer for about 20 minutes, till mixture is thick and the beans are soft. Serve with hot boiled rice.

YOGA COCONUT CURRY ❋ *2 servings*

1 coconut
1 tsp. lemon juice
3 Tbs. sesame oil
2 Tbs. minced onion
⅛ tsp. ground turmeric or saffron

⅛ tsp. ground coriander
⅛ tsp. chili powder
1 cup coconut milk (see p. 16)
3 hard-cooked eggs, sliced

Crack open the coconut and extract the pulp. Grate the pulp; there should be about 3 cups. Mix it with the lemon juice and let stand for 1 hour. Heat the oil and fry the onion lightly in it; remove onion from pan. In oil remaining fry the spices which have been well mixed together. Add the coconut and lemon juice and coconut milk and simmer over very low heat for 10 minutes. Pour this mixture over slices of hard cooked eggs. Serve with hot boiled rice or Indian bread.

PEANUT CAKES ❋ ❋ ❋ *4 servings*

1 cup whole cornmeal
1½ cups boiling water
Salt
1 cup ground peanuts or ¼ cup peanut butter

1 tsp. minced parsley
1 Tb. chopped watercress
½ cup peanut oil or butter

Cook the cornmeal in the boiling water with ½ teaspoon salt in the top part of a double boiler over boiling water. Remove from the heat and add the peanuts, parsley, and watercress. Add salt to taste. Replace pot over boiling water and steam for another 2 hours, or till mush is very thick. Cool. Cut into ½-inch slices. Fry in hot peanut oil till nicely browned.

NOTE Peanuts are known as monkey nuts in most English-speaking countries in the Far East. In Africa they are called ground nuts.

YOGURT PANCAKES ❋ *2 servings, or more*

1 cup yogurt
1 cup dry cottage cheese or curd (see p. 30)
1 tsp. honey
½ cup ground nuts, any kind
½ tsp. salt
¼ cup vegetable oil, for frying

Mix the yogurt, cottage cheese, and honey in a bowl. Stir well till honey is dissolved. Add the nuts and salt and beat all to a thin batter. Add more nuts if the mixture is too thin. Cook on a hot oiled griddle as you would cook pancakes. Serve honey, butter, maple syrup, or jaggery, the heavy dark Indian molasses, with these pancakes.

YOGA PARSNIP PANCAKES ❋ ❋ *2 servings, or more*

2 cups cold mashed cooked parsnips
1 Tb. honey
2 Tbs. whole-wheat flour
2 eggs, well beaten
¼ tsp. ground ginger
¼ tsp. salt
1 cup vegetable oil

Put the parsnips in a bowl and add the honey, whole-wheat flour, beaten eggs, ginger, and salt. Heat a griddle and pour on just enough oil to keep pancakes from sticking. Cook the parsnip mixture like pancakes, adding a little oil for each one.

YOGA BEAN-SPROUT CURRY   ❋ ❋   *2 servings*

4 Tbs. butter or nut oil
1 tsp. curry powder
2 onions, chopped fine
1 green pepper, minced

1 cup water
½ tsp. salt
1 cup drained bean sprouts

Heat the butter and fry the curry powder to dark brown. Add the onions, green pepper, water, and salt. Simmer for 3 minutes, till a smooth sauce is formed. Add the bean sprouts. Cover and simmer for 20 minutes, or till sprouts are tender but not mushy. Serve hot boiled brown rice with this curry.

YOGA BEAN CURRY (Foogath)   ❋   *4 servings*

½ cup dried kidney beans
1 parsley sprig
1 lb. unpeeled radishes, grated
1½ tsps. mustard seeds
3 Tbs. butter or vegetable oil

5 Tbs. shredded fresh coconut
1 small green chili, chopped
1 tsp. salt
Juice of 1 lime

Soak the beans in water to cover overnight; drain. Grind the parsley and radishes together in a blender or mash in a large mortar. Add whole mustard seeds. Heat the butter and simmer this mixture for 4 minutes. Add the coconut, chili, drained kidney beans, and salt. Bring to a boil, then turn heat low. Cover and simmer for 15 minutes, or till mixture is thick. Add a little water if needed to keep from scorching. Add lime juice just before taking from the heat and more salt if necessary.

YOGA CABBAGE   ❋ ❋ ❋   *4 servings*

1 medium-sized cabbage, shredded
½ cup butter or vegetable oil
2 Tbs. honey

1 egg, beaten well
1 cup yogurt
2 Tbs. lemon juice
1 tsp. salt

Heat the butter and wilt the cabbage in it without browning for 5 minutes. Add the honey, cover, and simmer for 15 minutes. Mix the beaten egg, yogurt, and lemon juice in a bowl. Add salt and pour over the cabbage. Heat, but do not allow to boil. Serve hot with boiled brown rice.

YOGA RED CABBAGE   ❋   ❋   *3 servings*

½ cup shredded red cabbage   ½ cup yogurt
1 cup shredded pineapple, fresh   ½ tsp. salt
    or canned

Toss all ingredients together and serve on a green lettuce leaf.

YOGA GINGERED
CUCUMBERS   ❋   ❋   *6 to 8 servings*

¼ cup peanut oil or butter   ½ tsp. grated lemon rind
6 cucumbers, sliced thin   ¼ cup lemon juice
1 tsp. ground ginger   ¼ tsp. salt

Heat the oil and fry the cucumbers gently in it till soft. Remove from the pan and let them drain on paper. Fry the ginger to dark brown in the oil in the pan. Add the lemon rind and juice and simmer for 3 minutes. Add salt to taste. Put cucumbers in a shallow serving dish and dribble the sauce over them. Sprinkle a pinch of ginger on top. These are used as pickles or relishes with the very bland yoga rice dishes.

YOGA EGGPLANT   ❋   ❋   ❋   *4 servings*

1 large eggplant, peeled   1 garlic clove, mashed
3 tomatoes, sliced   1 cup olive or peanut oil
1 cup whole-wheat bread crumbs   ½ tsp. salt

Slice the eggplant and arrange on the bottom of a greased baking dish. Put tomato slices on top. Mix the bread crumbs with the mashed garlic and the oil and sprinkle the mixture all over the vegetables. Sprinkle salt on last. Bake in a moderate oven (350°F.) for 1 hour, or till eggplant is soft.

YOGA PARSLEY CURRY   ❋   ❋   *4 servings*

¼ cup peanut or olive oil
1 tsp. curry powder
4 cups cold cooked rice, not too
　soft

1 cup minced fresh parsley
1 Tb. ground almonds
½ tsp. salt
1 Tb. lemon juice

Heat the oil and fry the curry powder to dark brown. Remove
the pan from the heat and add the mixture to the cold rice along
with the parsley, almonds, salt, and lemon juice. Toss very
lightly, taking care not to jam down the grains of rice. Put in
a greased pan and bake in a moderate oven (350°F.) for 20
minutes, or till the curry browns lightly on top.

YOGA GREEN PEPPERS   ❋   ❋   *4 servings*

4 large green peppers
1 small onion, minced
¼ cup peanut or sesame oil
¼ tsp. ground ginger
¼ tsp. ground turmeric
1 Tb. minced fresh parsley

1 Tb. chopped watercress
¼ cup seeded raisins
¼ cup chopped nuts
¾ cup uncooked brown rice
2 cups water
½ tsp. salt

Prepare the green peppers for stuffing first. Cut off the tops and
remove seeds and membranes. Wash and drain the peppers.
Brown the onion lightly in the heated oil. Add ginger and turmeric. Simmer for about 3 minutes, till a smooth paste is formed.
Remove from the heat and add parsley, watercress, raisins, and
nuts. Cook the brown rice in the water with the salt added for
10 minutes only. Drain; there should be about 2 cups of partly
cooked rice. Add the curried mixture to it. Fill the green pepper
shells lightly. Stack peppers upright in a baking dish and add a
little water to cover the bottom of the dish. Cover and bake in a
moderate oven (350°F.) for 30 minutes or less, till rice is soft
but not mushy.

YOGA SWEET POTATOES   ❄   *6 servings*

6 sweet potatoes
½ cup butter
1 cup grated fresh coconut
1 cup sweet cider

½ tsp. ground cinnamon
½ tsp. grated nutmeg
1 tsp. salt

Bake the potatoes in their skins till soft. Split lengthwise and scoop out the soft pulp; keep the skins intact and reserve for baking later. Mix the pulp with the butter, coconut, cider, and spices; add the salt or more to taste. Pile the mixture lightly into the potato skins. Bake in a hot oven (400°F.) for 10 minutes, or till potatoes are slightly browned on top.

YOGA TOMATO CURRY   ❄   *4 to 6 servings*

½ cup sesame oil
2 onions, chopped fine
½ tsp. ground chilies
½ tsp. ground ginger
1 garlic clove, mashed

10 tomatoes, peeled and chopped
1 cup coconut milk (see p. 16)
1 cup grated fresh coconut
½ tsp. salt

Heat the oil and brown the onions lightly in it; remove onions. In oil remaining in the pan fry the mixed ground chilies and ginger. Stir in the garlic and simmer for 3 minutes, or till a smooth paste is formed. Add the tomatoes and coconut milk. Cover and simmer for about 15 minutes, till the sauce is smooth and thick. Stir in the grated coconut and the salt and simmer for 5 minutes longer. Serve with hot boiled rice or Indian breads.

YOGA RICE AND CABBAGE   ❄   *4 servings*

½ cup mustard or sesame oil
1 tsp. curry powder
1 cup uncooked rice
½ cup grated coconut
1 Tb. dal (see p. 26)

1 cup coconut milk (see p. 16)
1 small cabbage, shredded
1 tsp. salt
Juice of 1 lemon

Heat the oil and fry the curry powder to dark brown. Stir in the rice which has been well washed and dried. Simmer till it bubbles up. Add all other ingredients. Cover and let simmer for 30 minutes, or till rice is dry and all liquid is absorbed. Add a spoonful more of coconut milk if curry becomes too dry while cooking.

YOGA RICE AND LENTILS   ✻   *8 servings*

2 cups dried lentils	4 peppercorns
6 cups cold water	1 bay leaf
2 cups uncooked brown rice	1 cinnamon stick, 4 inches
1 tsp. shaved gingerroot or ¼ tsp. ground ginger	1 tsp. salt
	Melted butter
6 whole cloves	

Soak the lentils in the cold water for 1 hour. Wash the rice thoroughly and drain it. Drain lentils and put them in a large heavy kettle. Add the rice, gingerroot, cloves, peppercorns, bay leaf, and cinnamon stick. Add enough boiling water just to cover, and the salt. Cover and simmer for 30 minutes, or till all moisture is absorbed and the rice is dry and fluffy. Leave whole spices in when serving. Serve melted butter with this plain but wholesome dish, to be dribbled over the top.

VARIATION   Instead of lentils, dried yellow split peas may be used. The proportions of rice and legume may be varied and the spices may be changed; it is delicious in all versions.

YOGA PEA PULAO   ✻   ✻   ✻   *4 servings*

4 Tbs. butter	1 cup boiling water
1 large onion, chopped fine	1 tsp. salt
⅓ cup seeded raisins	¾ cup shelled green peas, fresh or frozen
1 cup uncooked brown rice	
1 Tb. honey	⅛ tsp. ground turmeric

Heat the butter in a heavy skillet and brown the onion lightly in it; romove onion. In remaining butter fry the raisins till they puff up. Remove raisins and drop them on absorbent paper to drain. In butter remaining in the pan brown the rice and add the honey, browned onion, boiling water, and salt. Cover and simmer for 20 minutes. Stir in the fresh peas and continue to cook for about 10 minutes longer, or till rice is dry and fluffy and all liquid is absorbed. If using frozen peas, add them for the last 5 minutes only. Turn out on a serving platter and sprinkle with the turmeric and puffed raisins.

Yoga Dressings and Sauces

Since most yoga dishes are saltless and lightly spiced, dressings are often served along with them. Here are a few of these unusual recipes.

AVOCADO DRESSING   ❄   ❄   *about 1 cup*

Mash well the pulp of 1 ripe avocado. Add 1 teaspoon honey, 1 teaspoon lemon juice, and a sprinkle of salt. As a variation, use ground ginger in place of the salt.

BANANA COCONUT
DRESSING   ❄   ❄   *about 1½ cups*

Mash the pulp of 1 ripe banana. Add 1 cup coconut milk (see p. 16), 1 tablespoon honey, and a pinch of salt and mix well.

YOGA CARROT SAUCE   ❄   *about 3½ cups*

1 lb. carrots, grated   ½ medium-sized onion, minced
1 tsp. salt   1 Tb. lemon juice

Mix all ingredients well together. Chill before serving and serve while fresh.

PEANUT-BUTTER DRESSING   ❄   *¼ cup*

2 Tbs. peanut butter   1 Tb. lemon juice
¼ tsp. grated fresh horseradish   1 Tb. sour cream
¼ tsp. salt   Paprika

Mix together all ingredients, using just enough paprika to color the mixture. Chill and serve with radishes, cucumbers, or other cold vegetable salads.

Chapter *14*

INDIAN BREADS

BREAD AND RICE are seldom served together at ordinary Indian meals, but with many curries a great variety of breads is eaten instead of rice, especially in certain parts of the country.

CHAPATI is unleavened bread made of whole-wheat or other flours. The flour is mixed with milk, water, or other liquids. The dough is cut into rounds and fried on a griddle. There are many variations of this. These are served hot as soon as they are cooked.

PARATHO is a bread which is made in much the same way as a *chapati*. After the dough is rolled out and ready for the griddle, the individual rounds are brushed with melted butter, and then fried.

POPADAM is a paper-thin biscuit or wafer made from potato or lentil flour. Some are plain, others are flavored for spicy appetizers. There is a trick to cooking these *popadams;* they curl up and double in size while cooking, and they must be kept flat by pressing lightly with a towel when they are in the pan and just beginning to curl.

PAPPAR starts as a small spiced ball made from *dal* and white flour with butter, ground cuminseed and aniseed, black pepper, and salt added. The balls are dropped into boiling sesame oil, to emerge as tiny paper-thin biscuits.

BAISANI ROTI is a bread made from a mixture of white flour and other cereal grains, spiced with onion and chili peppers. It is deep-fried in oil.

FANCY ROTI is made from white flour spiced with ground cuminseed, aniseed, and turmeric, with minced pistachios and almonds added. These are fried in saffron oil.

Most of these are now imported in cans, ready for curry lovers in America. They can be bought at import shops and food specialty stores.

CHAPATI I

2 cups whole-wheat flour   Water
1 tsp. salt

Mix the flour and salt with enough water to make a stiff dough. Let it stand, covered with a cloth, for 30 minutes. Roll out into a sheet about ½ inch thick and cut into rounds the size of pancake. *Do not use any fat for cooking.* Heat a heavy iron griddle over high heat and fry the rounds till brown. They should look like unbaked crumpets. When ready to serve them, broil under moderate heat and they will puff up light.

CHAPATI II

2 cups whole-wheat flour   Melted butter for frying (about
1 cup water, or more   1 cup)

Add enough water to the whole-wheat flour to make a stiff dough. *Add no salt.* Knead well, then cover with a damp cloth and let stand at room temperature for 3 hours. Knead again and shape into egg-sized balls. Roll these out into thin round cakes. Heat a well-buttered iron skillet and fry the *chapati*, one at a time, till brown spots appear on them. Turn and fry on the other sides till the cakes puff up. While they are still in the pan, press gently around the edge of the cake to make it puff up in the middle. Take finished bread from the skillet and butter one side only. To keep hot and soft till serving time, wrap in a cloth. A good cook is judged by the size and lightness of her *chapati*.

CHAPATI III

¾ cup white flour   ¼ cup cold water, or more
3 tsps. salt   Melted butter
3½ Tbs. butter

Sift the flour and salt together and cut in the 3 tablespoons of butter. Add enough water to make a dough like a piecrust. Work the dough till it is crumbly, then add a little more water to make a soft dough. Divide into small round balls. Work with one portion at a time. Flatten out a ball of dough on a floured board, brush it with melted butter (½ tablespoon), and dust lightly with flour. Roll into a ball again. Repeat the process in 5 minutes. Then roll the ball into a flat cake. Heat a heavy skillet to white heat. Bake the cake for 1 minute on each side. Brush well around the whole edge with melted butter and fry again till the cake puffs up. Cook only one at a time, as they demand care.

FANCY CHAPATI

4 Tbs. lentil or pea flour
6 Tbs. whole-wheat flour
1 Tb. minced fresh coriander or watercress leaves

1 tsp. grated onion
1 green pepper, minced
1 tsp. salt

Mix both flours and add the other ingredients. Roll out the dough, cut it into rounds, and bake on a greased griddle in the same fashion as Chapati II (p. 166).

N O T E   Lentil or pea flour is also called *dal*. The dried legumes are ground like grains. As a substitute use soybean flour, potato flour, or cornstarch.

LENTIL CHAPATI

1 cup dal (see p. 26)
3 Tbs. undiluted evaporated milk
5 Tbs. brown sugar

1 cup whole-wheat flour
½ tsp. salt
1 cup water, or less

Soak the *dal* in cold water overnight, then drain. Simmer in salted water for 30 minutes, or till soft. Mash well and set aside. Mix the other ingredients to form a soft dough. Knead well and divide into small balls. Let stand for 1 hour. Flatten out each ball into a flat cake. Make a dent in the middle and fill with some of the mashed *dal*. Form each again into a ball.

Let stand in a cool place for 1 hour. Roll out flat again and fry the flattened cakes on a hot greased skillet.

NOTE Instead of mashed soaked *dal*, undiluted canned pea soup may be used; or 1 cup dried lentils may be cooked until very dry and mashed.

YOGA BREAD

1 cup sesame, peanut, or soy oil   7 cups whole-wheat flour
1½ cups water   1 tsp. salt

Beat the oil and continue to beat while adding the water, drop by drop, till oil is frothy. Sprinkle in the flour quickly and lightly to hold the bubbles of air in the liquid. Add enough flour to make a stiff dough. Knead till the dough is rubbery. Cover with a damp cloth and let stand at room temperature overnight. In the morning knead again and add enough flour to shape into small loaves. Put in greased small bread pans and bake in a moderate oven (350°F.) for 1½ hours, or till nicely browned. This makes 2 loaves.

YOGA LENTIL BREAD

1 cup dried lentils or peas   2 hard-cooked egg yolks
⅛ tsp. grated nutmeg   1 cup vegetable soup or meat
⅛ tsp. celery salt   broth
2 eggs, slighlty beaten

Soak the lentils in cold water for 2 hours. Drain and barely cover with fresh cold water. Simmer for 30 to 45 minutes, till lentils are soft or all liquid is absorbed. Mash well. Add to the mash the nutmeg, celery salt, and beaten eggs. Mash the cooked egg yolks and add with the soup to the lentil mixture. Press this mixture into a well-greased pie plate. Set in a shallow pan of water to keep bottom from burning. Bake in a preheated moderate oven (350°F.) for 20 minutes, or till the bread is dry and suitable for cutting. Cut into small squares and serve with soup as you would serve croutons.

YOGA UNLEAVENED BREAD

3 cups whole-wheat flour
1 cup ice-cold water, or less
3 Tbs. peanut oil or butter

1 tsp. salt
3 egg whites, beaten stiff

Work the flour and ice water into a stiff dough. Knead well, then work in the oil and salt. Add the beaten egg whites, folding carefully. Spoon into greased muffin tins. Bake in a very hot oven (450°F.) for 20 minutes, or till muffins are slightly brown on top.

YOGA PUMPKIN BREAD

1 cake compressed yeast
1½ Tbs. warm water (85°F.)
3 Tbs. peanut oil or butter

2 cups mashed cooked pumpkin
3 cups whole-wheat flour
1 tsp. salt

Dissolve the yeast in the warm water. Add the oil and pumpkin and mix well. Add the flour and salt and knead till the mixture is a smooth firm paste. Cover with a damp cloth and let stand in a warm room for about 2 hours, or till the dough has doubled in bulk. Punch down, add a little more flour, and knead well again till a soft dough is formed. Shape into loaves and bake in a moderate oven (350°F.) for 40 minutes, or till the loaves are nicely browned. This makes 2 small loaves.

PURI

2 cups whole-wheat flour
½ cup water, or less

Vegetable oil

Work the flour and water together till a soft dough forms. Cover with a damp cloth for 1 hour, then knead well again till the dough is smooth and does not stick to the hands. Mold into small balls. Roll out the balls on a floured board to rounds the size of a large pancake. Put oil in a heavy frying pan to a depth of ½ inch and heat smoking hot. Put in 1 *puri* at a time. Press the biscuit gently with the back of a spoon till it puffs up. Cook to a light brown shade. Drain on paper. Continue until all the rounds are fried. Serve either hot or cold.

POTATO PURI

This Indian bread made from potatoes is a favorite in the North. They are as simple to make as plain *puri*. Mix equal quantities of whole-wheat flour and potato flour with enough milk to make a stiff paste. Roll out the paste as thin as possible on a floured board and cut into saucer-sized cakes. Fry the cakes quickly on a very hot well-greased griddle, adding more hot fat as needed. These plain unsalted cakes are served dry without butter. Curry is piled on top of them.

PURI FOR A PARTY   *100 puri*

½ cup vegetable oil
4 cups whole-wheat flour
1¼ cups cold water, or less
1 cup shredded coconut

½ tsp. ground cardamom
2 Tbs. seeded raisins, chopped
½ cup sugar
¼ cup coconut milk (see p. 16)

Mix the oil and flour with enough water to make a stiff dough. Knead well, then cover with a cloth and let stand in a cool place for 1 hour. Knead again and roll into small balls. Let stand for 1 hour longer. Roll out the balls into rounds the size of tiny pancakes.

Make the filling. Mix coconut, ground cardamom, raisins, and sugar. Add enough coconut milk to blend, but the mixture should be quite dry. Spoon out some of the filling on half of the little cakes and cover with the remaining rounds. Moisten the edges just enough to seal and flute them. Fry in hot vegetable oil until lightly browned and drain on absorbent paper.

CURRIED PASTRY

Fry 1 teaspoon curry powder in 2 tablespoons heated oil until well browned. Add to flaky piecrust and mix well. This crust can be rolled into large pieces and filled with curried meats or vegetables. Or shape it into smaller pasties and fill with curried meat mixtures for picnics. Or cut still smaller, to miniature size, and fill with highly spiced curry filling for delightful canapés for a party.

WHEAT-FREE ORANGE BREAD

2 cups barley flour
3 tsps. baking powder
½ tsp. salt
½ cup brown sugar
3 Tbs. peanut oil

2 eggs, well beaten
½ cup honey
½ cup water
Grated rind of 2 oranges

Sift together the barley flour, baking powder, and salt. Cream the sugar and oil together, then add the beaten eggs. Beat in the honey, water, and grated rind. Sift in the flour mixture bit by bit. When well mixed, pour into a well-greased bread pan (9 by 5 by 3 inches). Bake in a moderate oven (350°F.) for 1½ hours. This makes 1 loaf.

MOLASSES BREAD

¼ cup honey
¼ cup molasses
2½ cups whole-wheat flour
1 tsp. baking soda

1 tsp. salt
1 egg, well beaten
⅔ cup yogurt
½ cup sesame or peanut oil

Mix the honey and molasses. Sift the whole-wheat flour, soda, and salt together. Beat the egg and stir in the yogurt and oil. Mix honey mixture with yogurt mixture. Add the wheat flour, a little at a time, till a thick batter is formed. Beat well. Pour into a greased bread pan (9 by 5 by 3 inches) and bake in a moderate oven (350°F.) for 1 hour. This makes 1 loaf.

Chapter 15

SALADS, FRUITS, AND SALAD DRESSINGS

T HE NATIVES of India eat few green salads. Because of danger from cholera-infected soil they prefer cooked vegetables and the safer tree-fruits and nuts with which India is so well endowed. Nature, as though atoning for its extra-fiery spices, has given a great abundance of luscious fruits, some of them oversweet to Westerners. There are the papaya, many kinds of melon, custard apple, mangosteen, fig, date, pomegranate, breadfruit, pomelo, orange, lemon, lime, tamarind, banana, plantain, plum, guava—the list is very long and includes many fruits as yet unknown even to long-time residents of the country.

In India uncooked fruits are seldom cut up for use in salads as in the West. Rather, they are served whole as a dessert. Since these sweet fruits are a necessary adjunct to a hot curry meal, the *mem-sahib* evolved over the years a few fine combinations of greens and fruits, salads which are now found extensively on the tables of the Indians themselves. Thus fruits have come to be used as the chief salad ingredient when preparing a curry meal. Some of these fruits now in everyday use in India are actually native to the Western hemisphere which have been adopted and made at home in the same fashion as chili pepper.

Apples which come down from the cool hills are considered a great delicacy. They are cut into segments but left attached at the base so that the fruit appears like a lotus. Its center is heaped with a mixture of chopped figs and raisins and sour cream, all sprinkled with ground cinnamon or nutmeg and topped with almond slivers.

The avocado, a native of Central America, is now grown all over the subtropics. This fruit forms the early dawn breakfast (*chota hazri*) of many Europeans in both India and Africa. It is used extensively in hospitals for ulcer diets and for invalid and baby foods. Avocados are commonly served halved, in the skin but with the pit removed, with a dash of lemon or lime juice and salt and black pepper added. When sliced the avocado blends well with pomelo, grapefruit, banana, and other fruits. Never use mayonnaise or cream cheese with it because of its high fat content. Serve only tart juices with this buttery fruit.

Papaya is a melonlike fruit growing on a small tree. In the East the fruit is always seasoned with lime or lemon juice. The fruit is halved, the peel left intact, but the peppery seeds removed. Lime juice is sprinkled over the cut surface and the pulp is spooned out by the diner. This is a usual early-morning breakfast fruit and it is claimed by the old-timer to be a great pick-me-up after a late night. Sometimes the fruit is peeled, cut into cubes, and sprinkled with lime juice, then served as a dessert after curry. The papaya halves may be stuffed with lime-flavored yogurt or cream cheese. Papaya slices make a welcome addition to a fruit salad; and sometimes slices of the ripe fruit are added to curry dishes while they are being cooked. The leaves and juice of the papaya are used by the Indian cook to tenderize tough meat. Today extracts of this same fruit are used for commercial meat tenderizers.

The pomelo is a favorite fruit with both Indians and Europeans. It is similar to the grapefruit in size and appearance, but its segments are more distinct and the luscious pulp comes in several colors—green, pale yellow, pink, ruby red.

A pomegranate is also known as Eve's Apple, since many believe it was the original fruit which caused such havoc in the Garden of Eden. It is this apple with its jaunty little crown symbolic of royalty that was the most-used motif in the walls of the great temple at Jerusalem. Today this design is still included in ornate decorations for banquet tables. The ruby-red seeds, that Persephone ate while in Pluto's dark kingdom, add to the appeal of any salad. The juice from those seeds tints and flavors many of our fancy drinks. In fact, when distilled, this juice makes the popular syrup known as grenadine. In Eastern lands the seeds with their rich juice are added to many stuffings for festive spiced or curried dishes.

One of the vegetables used in Western salads which is also used in India is the cucumber, which is employed in various ways. Halved lengthwise, they are scooped out and stuffed with unsalted butter seasoned with sesame seeds. Or sliced into rounds, they are first salted to stand for an hour, then drained and sprinkled with grated lemon rind and lemon juice and minced preserved gingerroot.

The tender young sprouts of several vegetables are also used, not only in cooked dishes, but in fresh salads. Bean sprouts, which are those of the mung bean, are probably familiar, but also used in the East are bamboo shoots which are now available to the American cook in cans, and the sprouts of potatoes and other vegetables. The leaves of fresh mint, coriander, nasturtium, watercress, and other flavorful herbs are used widely for fresh salads to serve with curries, as well as for garnishes to decorate them.

TURKISH APPLE SALAD

Pare eating apples and hollow out the centers to form cups. To keep apples from discoloring while making the stuffing, dip the apples into a bowl of water to which the juice of a lemon has been added. Mix chopped figs and raisins with enough yogurt to bind the mixture. Season with ground cinnamon. Stuff the apples and serve on individual plates garnished with lemon leaves.

BANANA COCONUT
SALAD   ❊   ❊   *4 to 6 servings*

1 Tb. shredded dried coconut   3 ripe firm bananas, sliced fine
2 Tbs. warm milk   ½ tsp. salt

Simmer the coconut in the milk for 3 minutes, then add it to the bananas and salt. Serve as a bland salad with hot curried sauces.

SPICED BANANA SALAD ❋ ❋ *4 servings*

2 Tbs. butter
1 tsp. ground cuminseed
½ tsp. chili powder
½ cup yogurt

2 large ripe firm bananas,
  mashed
½ tsp. salt

Heat the butter and fry the mixed spices in it till dark brown. Stir in the yogurt and mashed bananas. Simmer for a few moments, then add salt and cool. Use this as a side dish or salad, or as a salad dressing.

STUFFED FIG SALAD ❋ ❋ *4 to 6 servings*

Stew 12 dried figs till they are plumped up and soft but not mushy. Cut a slit in each fig. Make a filling with ½ cup cream cheese, 1 teaspoon grated orange rind, 1 tablespoon yogurt, and 1 teaspoon honey. Stuff the filling into the slits and serve 2 or 3 figs to each person.

AMERICAN PAPAYA SALAD

Choose small papayas. Do not peel them, but halve them. Scoop out the black seeds. Make a filling of crushed pineapple, cottage cheese, and yogurt. Add just a few drops of lemon juice and salt to taste. Fill the papaya halves. Use a few of the black seeds as a decoration.

PERSIMMON SALAD BALLS

Choose persimmons that are quite ripe but not too soft. Separate the pulp from skin and pit. Add enough cream cheese to make a firm mixture. Shape into small balls. Dip them into lemon juice, then roll in shredded lettuce to form little mystery salad balls, which always delight guests.

NUT SALAD ❆ ❆ ❆ ❆ *6 servings*

1 cup roasted nuts, peanuts or cashews
3 sweet red peppers
1 Tb. white sugar
1 Tb. brown sugar
½ tsp. salt

1 cup sliced bamboo shoots
1 tsp. anchovy paste
1 cup shredded raw cabbage
1 cup shredded raw chicory
1 cucumber, sliced into rounds
1 Tb. minced celery leaves

Grind the nuts and sweet peppers together. Mix with the sugars, salt, bamboo shoots, and anchovy paste. Toss lightly to mix with the cabbage and chicory. Spoon this mixture out on the cucumber rings or on top of Indian breads. Sprinkle minced celery leaves on top.

ROSE SALAD FOR FEAST DAYS ❆ *4 servings*

1 large avocado
1 large red-pulped pomelo
Lettuce leaves
1 green pepper, minced
1 Tb. cream cheese
½ cup cooked lima beans
1 Tb. honey
1 Tb. lime juice

Juice of 1 lemon
3 large radishes, sliced thin
½ tsp. salt
½ cup slivered almonds, browned
1 Tb. pistachios
2 Tbs. pomegranate seeds
½ cup pink grapes

Peel the avocado and slice lengthwise. Peel the pomelo and divide it into segments; skin the segments carefully. Arrange the lettuce leaves on plates, and make a flower design on top with pomelo segments as petals and avocado slices as leaves. Make a center for the flower by mixing the green pepper, cream cheese, lima beans, honey, lime juice, lemon juice, and radishes. Add salt to taste. Garnish with the nuts, pomegranate seeds, and grapes.

MOROCCAN CARROT SALAD ❆ ❆ *4 servings*

1 cup chopped ripe olives
4 carrots, grated

1 small fresh red chili
½ onion, minced

Mix all ingredients and serve on overlapping thin slices of tomato.

ONION SALAD ❋ ❋ ❋ ❋ *6 servings*

4 large Spanish onions, chopped fine
½ cup coconut milk (see p. 16)
¼ green pepper, shredded
1-inch piece of green gingerroot, shaved thin

1 Tb. minced fresh coriander leaves
1 Tb. minced fresh mint leaves
1 Tb. chopped watercress
1 tsp. salt

Mix all ingredients together and serve on lettuce leaves or Indian bread as a salad with curry dishes.

RAINBOW ONION SALAD

Slice large sweet onions into rings. Prepare 3 or 4 bowls of diluted food coloring. Dip some of the rings into each bowl of coloring. Let stand for a few moments, then drain. Toss in a bowl of shredded lettuce. Dress the salad with honey and lemon juice and add salt to taste.

PUMPKIN SALAD

1 small red pumpkin
½ green pepper, sliced fine
½ tsp. dry mustard
½ tsp. ground cuminseed

½ tsp. ground ginger
½ tsp. salt
1 cup yogurt

Slice, peel, and seed the pumpkin. Cut into dice and boil them for 30 minutes, or till they are soft. Add the green pepper, mustard, cuminseed, ginger, and salt. Simmer for 10 minutes longer. The mixture should be quite dry when done. Let cool and stir in the yogurt. Serve hot or cold with curried dishes.

NOTE Yellow summer squash, zucchini, cauliflower, banana, cucumber, or cabbage may be spiced in this way and served as a cold salad with curry dishes.

Salad Dressings

CURRIED SALAD DRESSING   ❋   *about ⅓ cup*

½ tsp. curry powder   5 Tbs. malt vinegar
½ tsp. paprika   2 tsps. sugar
1 tsp. butter or vegetable oil ½ tsp. salt
½ Tb. minced onion   ½ cup cold vegetable oil

Fry the mixed curry powder and paprika in the butter till dark
brown. Add the minced onion and cook for 2 minutes longer.
Add the vinegar, sugar, and salt, and simmer till sugar is well
dissolved. Let cool, then add the cold oil. Put in a bottle and
shake well.

SINGAPORE DRESSING   ❋   *about ⅓ cup*

1 tsp. curry powder   5 Tbs. olive oil
1 tsp. dry mustard   1 Tb. lemon juice
1 tsp. brown sugar   1 Tb. vinegar
½ tsp. garlic salt   2 tsps. soy sauce
¼ tsp. salt

Put all ingredients in a jar and shake well before using. Or mix
in an electric blender. Use with fresh vegetable salads, not with
fruits.

YOGURT FRUIT-JUICE
DRESSING   ❋   *about 1¼ cups*

Add 1 raw egg yolk to ½ cup orange juice, ½ cup pineapple
juice, and 1 tablespoon lemon juice. Beat to a cream, then add
enough yogurt (about ½ cup) to give the consistency of a
dressing.

ORANGE YOGURT
DRESSING ❁ ❁ *about 1½ cups*

Mix 1 cup yogurt with ½ cup frozen concentrated unsweetened orange juice. Add a pinch of salt. Use for fruit salads.

EGG YOGURT DRESSING ❁ *about ½ cup*

Hard-cook 1 egg yolk. Mash the yolk with 1 raw egg yolk. Add just a pinch of cayenne pepper, ¼ teaspoon salt, and ¼ cup yogurt. Serve very cold.

COTTAGE-CHEESE
DRESSING ❁ ❁ *about ⅔ cup*

Mix ½ cup fairly dry cottage cheese with 1 mashed hard-cooked egg yolk, ¼ teaspoon garlic salt, ½ green chili minced, 3 radishes minced, and enough lemon juice to make a dressing with the consistency of rich cream. Use for vegetables or greens.

LOW-CALORIE COTTAGE-
CHEESE DRESSING ❁ *about 2 cups*

Mix 1 cup dry cottage cheese with 1 cup yogurt, 1 tablespoon minced onion, and the juice of ½ lemon.

LEMON HONEY DRESSING ❁ *about 1½ cups*

Juice of 1 lemon   ½ cup honey
1 egg, well beaten   1 cup cottage cheese
3 Tbs. yogurt, or curd (see p.   ½ tsp. ground mace
  30), or sour cream   ½ tsp. salt

Mix all ingredients together and beat well. Chill before use.

JERUSALEM ARTICHOKE
DRESSING   ❊   *about 1½ cups*

Boil 1 pound Jerusalem artichokes in the skins till soft. Cool
enough to handle, then slip off the skins and mash the pulp till
it is smooth. Add ¼ teaspoon onion juice, ¼ teaspoon honey,
¼ teaspoon curry paste, 1 teaspoon Worcestershire sauce and,
if desired, ¼ teaspoon garlic salt. Use to dress lettuce or to
stuff whole small tomatoes.

ALMOND SALAD DRESSING   ❊   *about ⅓ cup*

2 Tbs. ground almonds	2 tsps. honey
2 Tbs. yogurt	½ tsp. paprika
2 Tbs. lemon juice	1 tsp. grated horseradish
¼ tsp. salt	

Mix all ingredients together. Serve with radishes, cucumbers,
or tomato slices.

COCONUT DRESSING   ❊   ❊   *about ⅓ cup*

4 Tbs. grated fresh coconut	½ tsp. chili powder
1 onion, minced	¼ tsp. ground saffron
2 Tbs. grated lemon rind	

Blend these ingredients together and serve on slices of fresh
vegetables such as radishes, tomatoes, cucumbers.

CRANBERRY DRESSING   ❊   *about 2 cups*

Mix ½ cup water and ½ cup brown sugar. Bring to a boil and
boil for 5 minutes. Add ¼ pound washed cranberries (about 1
cup) and cook for about 5 minutes, until the berries have all
popped. Cool. Add ¼ cup chopped unsalted cashews, ½ cup
chopped ripe olives, ¼ teaspoon minced onion, and ¼ teaspoon
salt. Use for fruit salads.

Chapter 16

ACCOMPANIMENTS
TO CURRY

THERE IS no doubt that much of the popularity of curry, not only in the East but also in the West, derives from the interesting accompaniments or side dishes served with it. In some parts of India these side dishes are still called seven boys or eight boys, the term dating back to the time when seven or eight smartly turbaned houseboys used to file into the *sahib's* dining room, each bearing his own bowl of special savory to be added to the mound of rice already on the plate.

Some of the more popular side dishes are Bombay duck; raisins and currants puffed in hot oil, pickles and chutneys; candied gingerroot; onion rings, fresh, fried, and pickled; shredded or grated coconut; many other kinds of nuts, curried or seasoned in various ways; hard-cooked eggs, chopped; crisp curls of fried bacon; crisp fried fishes; cold shrimps; chopped fresh leaves of coriander, mint, parsley, and watercress; thin strips of fresh sweet green peppers; sliced radishes; curls of carrot or celery; fiery fried tiny potato balls; various breads; pickled fruits stuffed with relishes; spiced and candied fruits; jellies and jams.

Also toppings for small cocktail wafers are made of smoked salmon and minced onion; cream cheese and stuffed olives; black caviar with lemon; mashed walnuts and dates with cream cheese; tart jams such as guava and cranberry-pineapple mixed; chopped figs and anchovies with garlic salt; highly spiced tiny sausages; avocado slices with chopped chives and lime juice. For examples of other accompaniments, see the recipes for chutneys and pickles in Chapter 17.

In the old-fashioned English style of service, a sweet dessert was followed by a savory. Some of the dishes in this chapter would be served in that way, but any savory will make a good appetizer for the American style of service. Another term for these dishes is *sambal* which is a Malay word for a condiment, especially one made with pickles, coconut, and salted fish or roe, but it is used now for other kinds of savories as well. This term came into use in Indonesia and Malaysia where curry is a customary food and is often served.

Some accompaniments which are called chutneys and pickles are actually uncooked relishes or briefly cooked mixtures which are not preserved. These fresh chutneys must be eaten on the day they are made.

Bombay Duck

Bombay duck is not a duck but a dried fish. In the West today Bombay duck is perhaps the best known of all curry accompaniments, though strangely enough it is not so considered in India where it is used in an entirely different way. The fish is a small gelatinous phosphorous creature (*Harpodon nehereus*), known as the bummalo or bombil. It is found in the salt waters around India. It is dried in long lines stretched along the beaches in the sun, and the drying fish fill the air with an objectionable odor for miles around. When dried it goes into the native bazaar or is boxed to be sent abroad as one of the most expensive delicacies known. The dull, flat, rubbery-looking fish is most unappetizing as it comes from the box. Since the disagreeable odor of crisped Bombay duck lingers for many hours, it should be prepared several hours in advance and kept in a dry place till the curry is served. Allow one piece of the savory for each diner. Take the fish whole from the package and brown them quickly in a hot oven till each fish begins to curl at the edge and turn golden brown. Take from the oven and let cool; as it cools it will curl and crisp, within a minute or two. It is now an intriguing morsel waiting to be crumbled on top of a curry. Pile the fish on a serving platter; do this carefully to keep them whole. After the diner has added all the tidbits he desires to his curry, the fish is picked up in the fingers from the platter and crumbled with the fingers over the top of his curried dish. This is one of the reasons for the inevitable finger bowl presented when serving curry. The crisped fish may be served hot or cold. Even after the can or box has been opened, remaining fish may be kept for many months if wrapped in aluminum foil. For the American housewife, any dried fish such as codfish will serve equally well and at much less cost.

SPICED NUTS   ✳   ✳   ✳   ✳   *4 servings*

1 cup sugar
¼ cup hot water
⅛ tsp. cream of tartar
1 tsp. ground cinnamon

½ tsp. rosewater, or vanilla or orange extract
1½ cups nuts—cashews, almonds, or pistachios

Mix the sugar with the water, cream of tartar, cinnamon, and flavoring. Simmer till a soft ball forms when a little is dropped into cold water. Add the nuts and stir till the mixture crumbles into a sugary mass. Turn out on a lightly greased cookie sheet. Separate the mass into small clusters while still warm. Pile in a bowl and serve with curry as an accompaniment or sweet. Or, if desired, form the mixture into even smaller bits and add as a garnish to dry curries or *pulaos*.

CURRIED NUTS

Many curried nuts are now on the shelves of American markets. These are easy to prepare at home and any kind of nut may be curried—cashews, peanuts, walnuts, almonds, etc. Fry 1 teaspoon curry powder in ¼ cup vegetable oil until brown, then drop 1 cup nuts into the hot oil and brown lightly. Nuts have a tendency to scorch quickly, so stir all the while. Another way is to coat the nuts with the fried curry mixture and put them into a hot oven for 5 minutes, or till browned. Watch closely this way too and take from the oven as soon as they are done.

GARLIC NUTS

Add a pinch of garlic salt to olive oil or preferably nut oil. Heat and dribble over a pan of Brazil nuts. Bake slowly for 10 minutes. Drain on absorbent paper before serving.

SALTED PUMPKIN SEEDS

These long-time favorites in the East are rapidly gaining favor in America. Remove the seeds from a pumpkin and spread them out on a baking sheet. Bake in a slow oven (250°F.) for 15 minutes or longer, till the fibrous net around the seeds dries. Rub through the hands to remove the fibers and return the cleaned seeds to the baking sheet. Add ½ teaspoon salt to 1 cup butter or nut oil and dribble this over the seeds. Bake them slowly for another 15 minutes, or till quite dry. Use as garnishes for curries or as tidbits with cocktails.

CHEDDAR CHUTNEY SPREAD

1 lb. aged Cheddar, shredded   ½ cup mango chutney
1 tsp. ground ginger   3 Tbs. curry paste

Blend the ingredients in a bowl until well mixed. Store in refrigerator. Use as a spread for canapés or as a filling; or roll into small balls and chill to serve as a relish.

VARIATION   Add ½ cup finely chopped nuts to the mixture.

CURRIED CEREAL SNACKS

1 cup butter or vegetable oil   ⅛ tsp. ground ginger
½ tsp. curry powder   3 cups bite-sized cereal snacks

Heat the butter and fry the curry powder and ground ginger till dark brown. While butter is still bubbling, drop in the cereal snacks and brown for a moment only, stirring all the while. Toss out quickly on absorbent paper and let drain. Salt may be needed but taste first. Different kinds of oil give distinctive flavors, so if using oil instead of butter, experiment first to please your own taste.

GARLIC POPCORN SNACKS

Add garlic cloves to olive oil or butter and heat. Discard garlic and dribble the flavored oil over freshly puffed popcorn.

FISH SAMBALS OR SAVORIES I

2 cups mashed cold cooked fish
1 cup mustard or vegetable oil
1 small onion, minced
2 tsps. curry powder
1 tsp. ground turmeric or saffron
½-inch piece of green gingerroot, minced

1 Tb. vinegar or lemon juice, if needed
Salt
1 egg yolk, lightly beaten

Use any kind of fish, or a mixture of several varieties. Heat 3 tablespoons of the oil and brown the onion lightly in it; remove onion from skillet. In oil remaining fry the curry powder, turmeric, and ginger till all is dark brown. Simmer for 3 minutes, till a smooth paste has formed; add drops of vinegar or lemon juice if needed to keep it from sticking. Remove from the skillet and mix with the fish; mix in browned onion and add salt to taste. Shape the mixture into small balls the size of marbles. Dip into the egg yolk. Heat more of the oil in the skillet and fry the fish balls till nicely browned. If more oil is needed, be sure it is very hot when it is added as cold oil will give a greasy taste. Serve as an accompaniment to curries. The cook with originality can concoct a large variety of these *sambals*, using different seasonings or fresh herbs.

FISH SAMBALS OR SAVORIES II

2 cups mashed cold cooked fish
1 cup vegetable oil or butter
10 green chilies, minced
2 small onions, minced
1 garlic clove, mashed

1 tsp. curry powder
1 Tb. water or vinegar
½ tsp. salt
2 cups finely grated coconut

Prepare the fish. Heat 2 tablespoons of the oil and brown the green chilies and onions lightly in it; remove vegetables from the pan and mix with the mashed garlic. In oil remaining in the skillet fry the curry powder. Stir in the vegetable mixture and simmer for 3 minutes, or till a smooth paste is formed; add the water if needed to keep the paste from sticking. Add salt, mashed fish, and grated coconut; let the mixture cool. Roll into small balls. Heat enough of the remaining oil to cover the bottom of the skillet, and fry the fish balls in it till nicely browned. Add more oil as needed.

SHARK SAMBALS

Simmer shark meat with a few cloves and a few cardamom pods till it is soft enough to mash. Mash and shape into small cakes or balls. Fry in hot curried butter.

SMOKED-FISH SAMBALS

1 lb. smoked salmon
½ tsp. curry powder
1 Tb. butter or vegetable oil
1 Tb. mayonnaise
1 small onion, minced
Grated rind of 1 orange
1 cup sour cream

Mince or grind the salmon. Fry the curry powder in the heated butter till dark brown. Cool and mix with the mayonnaise, onion, orange rind, and sour cream. Fold in the minced salmon and mix well. Very little, if any, salt is needed in this mixture because the fish is salty. Form into small balls and chill before serving; or use as a spread on toast triangles.

NOTE Any variety of smoked fish can be used in the same way.

CURRIED SHRIMP SAMBALS

1 cup cold cooked shrimps
3 Tbs. preserved gingerroot, minced
3 Tbs. cream cheese
2 tsps. curry powder
1 Tb. vegetable oil or butter
¼ cup sour cream

Mash the shrimps well and mix in the gingerroot and cream cheese. Fry the curry powder in the heated oil. Cool and add to the shrimps. Mix in the sour cream last. Mixture should be firm enough to form into small balls.

MINIATURE-SHRIMP SAMBALS

1 cup mustard oil
¼ tsp. curry powder

1 cup cooked miniature shrimps

Heat the oil and brown the curry powder well. Drop the cooked shrimps into the hot oil. Let them cook for just 1 minute, till crisp. Drain on absorbent paper. Serve as sambals, to be picked up from the bowl in the fingers, or use as cocktail tidbits with food picks.

AMERICAN SHRIMP SAMBALS

1 lb. fresh shrimps
4 cups water
Salt
Juice of 1 lemon
2 garlic cloves, mashed
1 Tb. curry powder

1 Tb. butter or vegetable oil
¼ cup mango chutney
1 Tb. minced parsley
1 tsp. caviar
¼ cup mayonnaise, or less
Green and red chilies, shredded

Put the shrimps in the water with 1 teaspoon salt, the lemon juice, and garlic. Simmer for about 5 minutes, till shells are pink and flesh is firm. Drain, shell, and devein. Mash or grind the shrimps and put in a bowl. Fry the curry powder till dark brown in the heated butter and add to shrimps. Add the chutney, parsley, and caviar. Fold in just enough mayonnaise to make a smooth mixture, but do this cautiously since mixture must be thick. Add salt only if needed. Shape into balls and chill. Garnish with the shredded chilies. Or spread on crisp small crackers or toast, and broil to serve hot.

CHUTNEY HAM SAMBALS

⅛ tsp. curry powder
1 Tb. butter
¾ cup minced boiled ham

¾ cup mango chutney
¼ cup mayonnaise

Fry the curry powder in the butter till dark brown. Cool and stir into the minced ham and chutney. Add only enough may-

onnaise to make mixture thick. Form into small balls and chill
before using.

EGG SAMBALS

Hard-cook eggs. Cool and quarter lengthwise. Remove the
yolks and mash well. To the yolks add minced onion, minced
sweet green pepper, a sprinkle of freshly ground black pepper,
a little lemon juice, and salt to taste. Use the mixture to fill the
whites of the eggs. Chill well before serving with curry as a side
dish.

MANGO SAMBAL

Pare a ripe but firm mango and cut into slices. Sprinkle slices
lightly with ground ginger. Dribble over them a syrup made
from sugar and water, flavored with lime juice. Let stand for
some hours, then chill and serve as a sambal.

CHILI COCONUT SAUCE

Use equal amounts of ground ginger, minced onion, and minced
green chilies. Fry to dark brown in mustard oil or butter. Add
1 tablespoon of this mixture to 1 cup coconut milk (see p. 16).
Thicken with 1 teaspoon rice flour. Simmer for 10 minutes, till
a thick sauce is formed. Serve as a sauce or dip for fish.

HOT COCONUT SAMBAL
SAUCE

Soak 1 cup grated fresh coconut in 1 cup water for 1 hour.
Drain off the liquid and reserve it for use in curries. Mix the
pressed-out pulp with minced onion, a little ground ginger and
saffron, and lime or lemon juice. This makes a hot sauce or dip
for sambals.

SPICY DIP FOR SAMBALS

1 cup butter or vegetable oil
½ tsp. ground ginger
1 tsp. ground cuminseed
1 tsp. ground turmeric
⅛ tsp. ground cayenne pepper
1 garlic clove, mashed
1 large onion, minced

Heat the butter. Mix the ginger, cuminseed, turmeric, and cayenne and fry till dark brown. Add the mashed garlic and simmer the mixture till it is a smooth paste. Add the onion and simmer till it is clear and soft. Save this fiery sauce in a separate bowl and use as a dip for sambals or other appetizers. Caution your guests as to its strength.

FRESH COCONUT SIDE DISH

Add enough cream cheese to grated fresh coconut to make a smooth thick mixture. If thinning is needed, add a little coconut milk (see p. 16). Fry a very small amount of curry powder in butter and add to the mixture. Or add anchovy paste, or just a pinch of ground ginger. Season very lightly with salt to taste. Roll into small balls and chill well before serving.

YOGA COCONUT CHUTNEY

4 Tbs. grated coconut
½ tsp. chili powder
1 small onion, minced
2 Tbs. grated lemon rind
⅛ tsp. ground saffron
¼ tsp. salt

Mix all ingredients well. Chill. Serve this fresh chutney on the day it is made.

FRESH VEGETABLE SIDE DISH

2 cups fresh cottage cheese
1 cup grated fresh coconut
½ tsp. onion, minced
1 cucumber, diced fine
1 fresh tomato, diced fine
1 small green pepper, minced
1 tsp. salt
¼ tsp. ground black pepper

Toss all ingredients together lightly. Chill and serve in a small bowl as a side dish.

VEGETABLE SHREDS OR STRIPS

Carrots and celery in shreds or strips are often served. Heat carrot strips in a mixture of condensed frozen orange juice, honey, and salt. When tender and glazed, cool and serve cold. Sprinkle celery strips with carrot juice, salt, and lemon juice. Shred carrots and steep the shreds in lemon juice with salt to taste.

FRESH MINT PICKLE

Pound ½ cup fresh mint leaves in a mortar with 1 small onion. Season with salt and freshly ground black pepper. Add just enough lemon juice to make a thick paste. Serve with cold lamb.

FRESH MINT CHUTNEY

½ cup fresh mint leaves
1 onion
1 fresh green chili

1 tsp. white sugar
¼ tsp. salt
Juice of ¼ lemon

Grind mint leaves, onion, and chili together. Add the sugar, salt, and lemon juice. Mix well and let stand for a few hours before using. Serve this fresh chutney as a sauce or relish on the day it is made.

ONION CHATNI

Cut large sweet onions into rings and sprinkle them with minced chili peppers of varied colors. Sprinkle vinegar lightly on top. Serve the *chatni* as a fresh salad.

VEGETABLE RELISH

4 Tbs. butter
2 onions, chopped fine
2 garlic cloves, mashed
¼ tsp. chili powder
½ tsp. ground cuminseed

½ tsp. ground ginger
1 cup cider vinegar
1 tsp. salt
2 cucumbers, sliced thin
2 tomatoes, sliced thin

Heat the butter and brown the onions lightly in it; remove onions. Mix the garlic with the onions and stir well. Fry the spices in remaining butter and add them to the onion paste. Stir in the vinegar and salt and mix again to a smooth paste. Put cucumbers and tomatoes in separate bowls. Cover the slices with the onion and spice paste and let them marinate at room temperature for 1 hour. Arrange the slices of both vegetables in an attractive pattern in a shallow serving dish, and serve as a relish with curries.

WATERCRESS CHUTNEY

2 Tbs. minced watercress
2 Tbs. minced green pepper
1 garlic clove, peeled
1 tsp. ground cuminseed
2 tsps. dried coconut

2 tsps. warm milk
4 tsps. malt vinegar
1 tsp. sugar
½ tsp. salt

Chop the watercress, green pepper, and garlic together. Stir in the cuminseed. Soak the coconut in the warm milk for 20 minutes, then add to the watercress mixture. Mix the vinegar, sugar, and salt and stir till well dissolved. Add to the mixture and toss. This chutney should be quite dry. Serve this fresh chutney with curry dishes on the day it is made.

DARJEELING RELISH

2 Tbs. mustard oil or butter
1 small onion, minced
⅛ tsp. ground cayenne pepper
¼ tsp. ground ginger

1 Tb. rice flour
1½ cups coconut milk (see p. 16)

Heat the oil in a heavy skillet and brown the onion; remove onion. Mix the spices and rice flour and fry in remaining oil till dark brown. Stir in the coconut milk and add the browned onion. Simmer till a very thick sauce is formed. This relish is used with fish curries.

FRESH APPLE CHUTNEY

2 Tbs. shredded coconut
½ cup warm milk
2 large tart apples
1 Tb. salt
2 cups cold water

2 Tbs. minced onion
⅛ tsp. ground cayenne pepper or Tabasco
Juice of 1 lemon

Soak the coconut in the milk for 20 minutes, then drain. Peel and chop the apples. Add the salt to the cold water and soak the apples and minced onion in it for 10 minutes. Drain and mix with the cayenne and coconut. Add the lemon juice last. Mix gently. Serve this fresh chutney on the day it is made.

QUICK TOMATO-BANANA CHUTNEY

Mix equal amounts of chopped tomato and banana. Add 1 green chili minced finely. Add salt to taste and a little Worcestershire sauce to taste. Use this fresh chutney on the same day it is made. This is one of many quick relishes concocted by the old-timers in India.

DATE CHUTNEY

4 plump dates, pitted and chopped
½ small onion, chopped fine
2 garlic cloves, mashed

1 tsp. ground cuminseed
¼ tsp. ground cayenne pepper
½ tsp. salt
2 tsps. malt vinegar

Mix the dates, onion, garlic, cuminseed, and cayenne well together. Add the salt and vinegar last and mix into a smooth paste. This very peppery chutney is used sparingly with vegetable fritters or very bland curries only.

FRESH MANGO CHUTNEY

1 ripe firm mango
1 small onion, minced

1 tsp. minced green gingerroot
1 cup coconut milk (see p. 16)

Peel the mango and cut the pulp into small pieces. Mix the onion and gingerroot and add them to the coconut milk. Stir into the mango pulp and mix well. Serve this fresh chutney on the day it is made.

HAWAIIAN PAPAYA RELISH

1 ripe firm papaya
¾ cup cider vinegar
1½ cups sugar

1 large piece of preserved ginger-root

Peel the papaya, remove the seeds, and cut the pulp into small pieces. Mix the vinegar and sugar and add it to the papaya. Chop the gingerroot and add it. Simmer gently for about 30 minutes, till the fruit is clear and soft. Serve cold with curries.

TAMARIND CHUTNEY

1 lump of tamarind pulp the size of an egg
2 cups water
1 cup ripe firm gooseberries
1 Tb. butter

1 tsp. mustard seeds
½ tsp. chili powder
2 tsps. sugar
1 Tb. seeded raisins
½ tsp. salt

Soak the tamarind in the water for 20 minutes, then squeeze out the juice and strain. Fry the gooseberries just lightly in the heated butter and remove berries from the pan. Fry the mustard seeds in remaining butter till the seeds pop, then return the gooseberries and all other ingredients. Add the strained tamarind water last and simmer for about 30 minutes, till the mixture is like jam.

NOTE   Tamarind is a flavoring used largely in India instead of lemon or lime juice. Known also as the Indian date, the edible part of this fruit or pod comes from the pulp which is used fresh or dried. The dried pulp is like our dried citron and similar fruits. It must be soaked in water before using.

Chapter 17

CHUTNEYS, PICKLES, AND OTHER PRESERVES

D OWN IN that little clay-walled storeroom at the end of every Indian courtyard there are numerous large jars, many of them big enough to hide one of Ali Baba's thieves. They are usually filled with a most amazing assortment of relishes which are employed to pep up pallid vegetable dishes and stimulate jaded appetites. Indian pickles, if taken too greedily, will leave one gasping at the first mouthful, but if used in the Indian manner they will add just the touch needed to make the curry perfect. These delicacies have intriguing names—stuffed mangoes, pickled limes, kumquat chutney, pickled tamarind.

Chutney comes from the Hindi word *catni* which means to lick or taste. Most Europeans became acquainted with this tasty relish through Major Grey's recipe. The Major was an English army officer who evolved his famous recipe about 1860, using what Nature had provided at hand—green mangoes, hot peppers, and spices. His purpose was to hide the indifferent taste and texture of the meat then being served to his troops who were under siege. The relish was prepared in great quantities, barrels of it, and it became famous all over the world. But the poor Major did not copyright the name and it has now become the common one for almost any fiery sauce made to be served with curry. This means that the name is no guarantee of any particular recipe or ingredient.

It is wise for the hostess who is just becoming acquainted with curries to sample a few of the commercial brands of chutneys now on the market before serving them to her guests. Some are simply cheap jams made of carrots, sugar, currants, and gingerroot. Others are merely highly gingered applesauce. A proper chutney should have large segments of green mango and gingerroot visible through the glass container. There are many brands to choose from. Some are excellent and these are always expensive; but they make a good accompaniment for cold meats as well as for hot curries.

Most Indian pickles can now be bought at a good import house or any shop dealing in oriental foods. Pickled Indian limes, a great favorite in the Far East, are now obtainable and are rapidly growing in favor in Western lands.

If you make your own preserves, use a heavy kettle to cook in, and use only wooden spoons for mixing and stirring. The Indian cook claims that a metal spoon will spoil the flavor of the jam. Cook very slowly over low even heat to allow the full flavors to develop. Store in sterilized bottles, jars, or crocks.

For recipes for uncooked chutneys or relishes, see Chapter 16, Accompaniments to Curry.

SIMPLE PRESERVED MANGOES

Choose firm green mangoes just beginning to ripen. Peel and cut into large sections. For each pound of fruit, mix 4 cups water with 2 cups white sugar and boil for 5 minutes to make a syrup. Add the fruit and simmer over low heat to 220° F. on a candy thermometer, or till the mixture thickens and becomes jamlike. Seal in hot sterilized jars. Simmer the sealed jars in boiling water for 15 minutes. Crystallized gingerroot, chili peppers, and lemon slices may be added if desired, in quantities to the taste of the cook.

MANGO JAM

Cut up enough soft ripe mangoes to make about 2 quarts of pieces. Force the pieces through a sieve and remove all fibers. There should be about 5 cups of very smooth pulp. Add 4 cups sugar, 2 cups water, and ¼ teaspoon salt. Simmer for 45 minutes, or till the jam is very thick. Seal in hot sterilized jars.

MANGO CHUTNEY I

2 lbs. half-ripe mangoes
4 cups good cider vinegar
5 lbs. white sugar
½ lb. seeded sultana raisins

2 Tbs. whole cloves
4 small dried red chilies
½ lb. preserved gingerroot
1 Tb. salt

Pare the mangoes and cut into pieces about ½ inch thick and 1 inch long. Use a heavy iron kettle for the cooking. Bring the vinegar to a boil. Add the sugar and stir well. Bring to a boil again, then simmer for 5 minutes. Add the other ingredients and simmer till the fruit is transparent. Arrange the fruit, spices, and peppers in an attractive manner in a hot sterilized jar. Pour the hot syrup over them and seal. Let stand for several days or even weeks before using, as this chutney improves with age.

MANGO CHUTNEY II

1 lb. green gingerroot
30 full-grown but still green
  mangoes
2½ cups seeded raisins, ground
2 garlic cloves, mashed

1 lb. dried chilies, ground
1 cup almonds, slivered
4 cups white sugar
6 cups white-wine vinegar
1 cup salt

Steep the gingerroot in hot water for 1 hour, then peel and chop. Peel the mangoes and cut them into thick slices. Mix mangoes, raisins, garlic, and chilies in a bowl. Add chopped gingerroot and almonds. In another saucepan mix the sugar, vinegar, and salt. Bring to a boil and simmer till sugar is well dissolved. Set aside to cool. Pour the cooled syrup over the fruits and simmer till fruits are clear. Arrange fruits nicely in sterilized jars. Pour the syrup over them and seal while hot. Let stand for a least 1 month before using.

MANGO CHUTNEY III
(Army Recipe)

25 firm green mangoes just turning yellow
5 Tbs. coarse salt
¼ cup small chunks of fresh
green gingerroot
½ tsp. grated nutmeg
1 tsp. whole cloves
1½ tsps. allspice berries
4½ cups wine vinegar, or more

3 lbs. brown sugar
2 small hot onions, chopped fine
1 small garlic clove, mashed
1½ cups seeded raisins
½ cup dried currants
1 Tb. dried small red chilies
½ cup almonds, slivered
2 Tbs. preserved gingerroot

Peel the mangoes and cut them into ½-inch segments. Sprinkle
well with the coarse salt and let stand overnight. Wash off the
salt in the morning. Boil the green gingerroot in water for 30
minutes, then drain. Tie the spices in a muslin bag large enough
to allow swelling. Put the vinegar in a heavy kettle and add the
spice bag, sugar, and drained gingerroot. Simmer gently for
30 minutes, stirring often. Add the onions, garlic, raisins, currants, and chilies. Add half of the mangoes and simmer for 2
hours, stirring and watching carefully. Add the almonds and
preserved gingerroot and the rest of the mangoes. Simmer for
another 2 hours, or till the mixture is as thick as jam. Remove
the spice bag. Arrange the fruit and other ingredients in a
tasteful manner in hot sterilized jars, with almonds and raisins
showing through the glass. Seal. Stand in a cool place for several
weeks before using. This chutney can be kept for years.

NOTE This recipe makes about one fourth of the original
army recipe. The original recipe made enough chutney to fill
one clay jar for the storeroom in the compound.

MANGO CHUTNEY IV
(Bombay)

1 lb. green gingerroot
10 lbs. full-grown but still green
mangoes
2 cups white-wine vinegar
2 cups white sugar
2 garlic cloves, mashed

4 lbs. seeded raisins
1 lb. dried currants
2 Tbs. mustard seeds
4 Tbs. salt
4 dried chilies, chopped

Steep the gingerroot in hot water for 1 hour. Then peel and chop. Peel the mangoes and cut them into pieces, removing pits. The pulp should weigh about 6 pounds. Simmer in 1 cup of the vinegar. In another pot put remaining vinegar and the sugar and simmer till a syrup is formed. Add the gingerroot, mashed garlic, raisins, currants, mustard seeds, and salt. Let simmer for 10 minutes, then add the mangoes and vinegar in which they simmered. Use a stone jar for steeping. Arrange the chilies around the walls of the jar and the fruits about them. Pour the syrup over all. Stand the jar out in the hot sun for 4 days before finally bottling the chutney. This is a sweet chutney. The Indian housewife prepares it in this way during the hot season when there is no danger of rains.

APPLE CHUTNEY

4 lbs. firm tart apples	2 lbs. seeded raisins
2 tsps. ground cinnamon	2 garlic cloves, mashed
14 whole cloves	2 lbs. brown sugar
1 tsp. allspice berries	1 tsp. salt
4 cups spiced or herb vinegar	

Pare and slice the apples. Tie the spices in a muslin bag and drop the bag into the vinegar in a heavy kettle. Add all other ingredients and simmer for 1 hour, or till mixture is of jam thickness. The time will depend on the apples. Remove the spice bag and let the chutney stand for some hours to cool before bottling. This chutney improves with time.

RHUBARB-APPLE CHUTNEY

4 lbs. rhubarb	1½ tsps. mustard seeds, bruised
2 onions	2½ tsps. allspice berries
2 cups white sugar	2½ tsps. ground ginger
3 cups cider vinegar	1 lb. raisins, chopped fine
2 Tbs. salt	1 lb. tart apples, chopped fine

Peel the rhubarb if needed, and cut it into small pieces. Chop the onions fine and put with the sugar, vinegar, and salt in a heavy kettle. Add the spices, bring to a boil, and simmer for 5 minutes. Add the raisins, apples, and sliced rhubarb. Simmer for 2 hours, or till the chutney reaches the jam stage. Seal in hot sterilized jars and let stand for 2 weeks before using. Store in a cool place.

HAWAIIAN CANTALOUPE CHUTNEY

1 large unripe cantaloupe	½ tsp. ground cayenne pepper
5 light-green Italian peppers	2 Tbs. salt
1-inch piece of green gingerroot	1 Tb. mustard seeds
½ lb. dried apricots	3 dried hot red peppers
4 cups cider vinegar	1 Tb. allspice berries
1 lb. light-brown sugar	2 cups seeded raisins
2 garlic cloves, mashed	

Pare the cantaloupe and cut it into strips. Slice the Italian peppers fine. Soak the gingerroot in water for 30 minutes, then peel it. Chop it with the apricots. Heat the vinegar in a heavy kettle. Add the sugar, garlic, cayenne, and salt. Tie the mustard seeds, red peppers, and allspice berries in a muslin bag and drop it into the kettle. Simmer for 30 minutes. Add the green peppers, raisins, and apricot mixture. Simmer for another 30 minutes. Add cantaloupe strips and simmer for 45 minutes more. Remove spice bag. Seal the chutney in hot sterilized jars. Let stand for 6 weeks before using.

CRANBERRY CHUTNEY

2 cups fresh cranberries	¼ tsp. ground ginger
1 cup cold water	¼ tsp. garlic salt
1 cup white sugar	1 Tb. light-brown sugar
2 Tbs. vinegar	4 Tbs. seeded raisins
½ tsp. ground cayenne pepper	4 Tbs. slivered almonds

Wash and drain the fresh cranberries. Put water and white sugar in a heavy kettle and bring to a boil. Add all other ingredients at once. Boil over very low heat, stirring constantly, for 10 to 15 minutes, or till mixture becomes fairly thick. Cool, and serve with curries or meats. If chutney is to be bottled and kept for a longer period, longer cooking is required; in that case add more liquid. When the mixture is like jam, spoon into sterilized jars.

GOOSEBERRY CHUTNEY

16 lbs. full-grown but still green gooseberries
4 large garlic cloves, mashed
3 cups white-wine vinegar
3 cups sugar
4 Tbs. salt
8 lbs. seeded raisins
1 lb. almonds, slivered

Mix all ingredients in a heavy kettle and simmer to jam thickness. Let stand in the hot sun for 2 days before bottling. This method of sun cooking can be used only in equatorial regions. In more temperate zones the mixture must be cooked much longer, or baked in very slow oven heat for 24 hours before bottling.

KUMQUAT CHUTNEY

2 cups kumquats
½ cup honey
2½ cups dark-brown sugar
½ cup water
2 cups white-wine vinegar
1 large onion, minced
1 garlic clove, mashed
1 tsp. salt
¼ cup mixed candied fruits
2 cups sliced rhubarb
1 cup seeded raisins
1 cup chopped celery
1 tsp. ground ginger
1 tsp. ground cinnamon
1 tsp. ground allspice
Juice of 1 orange
1 Tb. Worcestershire sauce

Halve and seed the kumquats. Put them in a heavy kettle with the honey and simmer for 10 minutes. Simmer the sugar, water, and vinegar for 10 minutes to make a syrup. Add the syrup to the kumquats and add the other ingredients. Simmer for 30 minutes, or till fruits are clear and the mixture is like jam. Seal in hot sterilized jars.

HAWAIIAN PAPAYA CHUTNEY

2 medium-sized papayas
3 cups brown sugar
2 cups white-wine vinegar
4 Tbs. salt
2½ cups crushed pineapple
1 tsp. ground allspice
6 garlic cloves, mashed

6 firm bananas
1 lb. seeded raisins
2 whole cloves
4 Tbs. dried red chilies, ground
1 cup almonds or macadamia nuts, blanched

Pare the papayas and cut into pieces. Simmer sugar and vinegar together for about 20 minutes to form a syrup. Add the salt and all other ingredients. Simmer in a heavy kettle, stirring constantly, for about 1 hour, or till papaya is soft and the mixture is as thick as jam. Seal in hot sterilized jars. Let stand for some days before using.

PEACH CHUTNEY

4 lbs. ripe peaches
¾ cup crystallized gingerroot
1 onion, chopped fine
½ cup seeded raisins
1 garlic clove, mashed

2 Tbs. chili powder
2 Tbs. mustard seeds
1 Tb. salt
2½ cups brown sugar
4 cups malt vinegar

Peel and pit the peaches. Chop the gingerroot into large bits. Put onion, raisins, and garlic through a food chopper. Chop the peaches and put them in a heavy kettle. Add remaining ingredients and simmer for 1 hour, till mixture is thick and rich brown in color. Pour into hot sterilized jars and cover at once. Let stand for a few days before using.

FRESH PRUNE CHUTNEY

10 large fresh Italian prune-plums
1 cup white sugar
¾ cup cider vinegar
2 tsps. salt
1½ red chilies, crushed

2 tsps. mustard seeds, crushed
½ onion, minced
½ cup chopped preserved gingerroot
1 cup seeded raisins

Halve and pit the plums. Put all ingredients in a heavy kettle and let simmer for 45 to 60 minutes, or till a jam is formed. Seal in hot sterilized jars.

NOTE   Almost all fresh fruits can be made into chutneys following this recipe.

YOGA CHUTNEY (Sun-cooked)

12 ripe tomatoes, chopped
½ lb. dates, pitted and chopped
1 lb. tart apples, peeled and
   chopped
2 dried red chilies
2 small onions, chopped
1 small garlic clove, mashed

1 Tb. mustard seeds
5 cups white-wine vinegar
1 cup honey
½ cup chopped mint leaves,
   fresh or dried
½ tsp. salt

Mix all the ingredients and put in a deep stone jar. Cover with a muslin cloth and stand in the hot sun for 10 days. Then bottle the chutney and store in a dark room. In most parts of America this chutney would need cooking, as the climate does not permit the sun-cooking described here.

SIMPLE TOMATO CHUTNEY

2 lbs. fresh tomatoes
1 Tb. sliced green gingerroot
1 garlic clove, mashed

1 Tb. dried chilies
2 cups wine vinegar
1 Tb. salt

Warm the tomatoes in the oven and slip off their skins. Mash to a pulp. Grind the gingerroot, garlic, and chilies together and add to the tomatoes. Let this mixture steep for 1 hour. Add the vinegar and salt and simmer in a heavy kettle for about 45 minutes, till as thick as jam. Seal in hot sterilized jars.

HORSERADISH CHUTNEY

1 lb. green tomatoes
8 onions
12 fresh red chilies
2 Tbs. salt
1 cup grated fresh horseradish

2 cups dark-brown sugar
2 Tbs. ground cinnamon
2 Tbs. ground cloves
2 cups malt vinegar

Slice the unpeeled green tomatoes, onions, and the chilies. Arrange in a crock with the salt sprinkled between the layers. Let stand overnight under pressure and in the morning drain off all the liquid. Put the drained vegetables in a heavy kettle. Add the horseradish, sugar, and spices, and pour the vinegar over all. Simmer over extremely low heat for 12 hours, adding more vinegar if chutney thickens too fast. Cool before bottling. Let stand for 6 weeks before using.

HAWAIIAN BANANA PICKLE

1 dozen firm bananas, peeled
1 lb. dates, pitted and chopped
2 large sweet onions, chopped
½ tsp. ground ginger
1 tsp. ground allspice

2 cups cider vinegar
⅔ cup dark molasses
2 cups water
1 tsp. salt

Cut the bananas into 1-inch slices and add to the chopped dates and onions. Mix the spices with the vinegar and stir in molasses, water, and salt. Add to the fruit mixture. Put all in a stone jar and bake in a very low oven for 1 hour or more, till a rich brown jam is formed. Seal in hot sterilized jars and keep in a cool place.

PICKLED FIGS

8 lbs. fresh ripe figs
1 cup whole cloves
4 lbs. brown sugar
2 cups fine white vinegar

1 Tb. ground cinnamon
1 tsp. ground mace
1 tsp. ground allspice

Wash and peel the figs. Insert 1 clove into each. Simmer the sugar and vinegar with the ground spices till a thick syrup is formed. Pour this over the figs and let stand for 1 hour. Strain the syrup off the figs and return syrup to the kettle. Boil for another 10 minutes, then cover the fruit again. Repeat this process for 3 days running, then seal while hot in hot sterilized jars.

GUAVA PICKLE

3 qts. guavas, unpeeled	2 garlic cloves, mashed
3 cups cider vinegar	1 Tb. ground cinnamon
5 cups white sugar	1 Tb. ground cloves
5 onions, chopped fine	4 tsps. ground allspice
5 small red chilies	3 Tbs. salt

Put the unpeeled guavas through a food chopper. Add to the other ingredients in a heavy kettle and simmer for about 2 hours, till the mixture becomes like jam. Seal in hot sterilized jars. Store in a cool place for some weeks before using.

HOT PEACH PICKLE

2 lbs. nearly ripe firm peaches	1 tsp. chili powder
2 cups cider vinegar	1 tsp. ground ginger
2 cups brown sugar	½ cup sultana raisins
1 tsp. salt	

Blanch the peaches in boiling water and slip off the skins. Use a silver knife to halve the peaches and remove pits. In a heavy kettle boil half of the vinegar with the sugar and salt added, till it forms a syrup. While still boiling, dribble it over the peaches. Return all to the kettle and simmer till fruit is clear and soft. Add the rest of the vinegar, the chili powder, ginger, and raisins. Simmer for 30 minutes, or till the mixture becomes like jam. Remove from the heat, stir well, and let cool. Bottle in sterilized jars. Let stand for a month before using.

HAWAIIAN PINEAPPLE PICKLE

4 cups pineapple chunks, fresh or canned	1 cup brown sugar
1 cup cider vinegar	1 tsp. whole cloves

If fresh pineapple is used, prepare it first. Put vinegar, sugar, and cloves in a heavy kettle and simmer till a syrup is formed. Add the pineapple chunks and simmer for 45 minutes or longer, till the fruit is clear, stirring constantly. Arrange the fruit in hot sterilized jars and pour the hot syrup over it. Seal while hot. This is an excellent relish for curries.

PLUM PICKLE

6 Tbs. seeded raisins	2 lbs. ripe firm plums, pitted
2 garlic cloves, mashed	4 cups brown sugar
½ tsp. ground dried chilies	1 tsp. salt
2 tsps. mustard seeds, ground	4 Tbs. blanched almonds
3 cups cider vinegar	

Put the raisins, garlic, chilies, and mustard seeds in a bowl. Add enough of the vinegar to make a smooth paste. Put the plums, the rest of the vinegar, and the paste in a heavy kettle with the sugar. Mix well, then add the salt and almonds. Simmer over low heat for 2½ hours, keeping tightly covered but stirring occasionally. Cool before bottling. Seal in sterilized jars. Keep in a cool place for 6 months before using.

DRIED-FRUIT PICKLE

This is a favorite pickle for Europeans in India who often find it difficult to obtain fresh fruits. Any kind of dried fruits may be used but in equal proportions.

¼ lb. dried apricots	½ tsp. peppercorns
¼ lb. dried apples	1 cinnamon stick, 2 inches
¼ lb. dried dates	4 cups malt vinegar
¼ lb. seeded raisins	1 cup sugar
1-inch piece of green gingerroot	½ tsp. salt

Wash the dried fruit well and drain. Simmer the dates till tender. Pit and cut into rings. Cut the other dried fruits into small pieces. Arrange all neatly in a jar, putting paper-thin slices of the green ginger, a few of the peppercorns, and pieces of the cinnamon stick in between. Simmer the vinegar, sugar, and salt together till a rich syrup is formed. Pour this boiling over the fruits. Stand the jar in the hot sun for 2 weeks, or bake in a slow oven (250°F.) overnight. Let stand for 2 months before using.

PICKLED LEMONS

Jars of pickled lemons are found in every Indian storeroom. They are believed to have great medicinal value.

6 lemons, unpeeled
4 Tbs. peeled and shaved green gingerroot

4 Tbs. minced green chilies
1¼ lbs. rock salt
4 Tbs. chili powder

Wash and dry the lemons. Cut lengthwise into quarters part way down, leaving the lemons like petaled flowers. Mix the shaved gingerroot, chilies, rock salt, and chili powder well. Coat the outside of each lemon with the mixture, then arrange the lemons one at a time in a jar, rind side down. Put some of the salt mixture on the inside of each lemon and partially close the quarters. Pour what remains of the salt mixture over the top. A thick layer of salt should cover the lemons. Cover the jar and stand it in the sun for 3 weeks. Or, if that is not possible, put in a slow oven (250°F.) for 1½ days. Do not use for 6 weeks.

MINCED-LEMON PICKLE

8 lemons, unpeeled
2 Tbs. salt
1 garlic clove, mashed
2 cups seeded raisins

1 tsp. chili powder
2 tsps. ground ginger
3 cups cider vinegar
3 cups brown sugar

Quarter the lemons, remove the seeds, and put in a bowl. Sprinkle the salt over them. Let them stand for 4 days, turning often. Mix the garlic, raisins, chili powder, and ginger with a little of the vinegar and let stand for 24 hours. Mince the two mixtures together. Add the sugar and the rest of the vinegar and put all in a heavy kettle. Simmer till the mixture becomes very thick. Let stand till cold before bottling. Use after 5 days.

PICKLED LIMES

9 limes, unpeeled
1 small onion, minced
1 green chili, minced
1 cup sultana raisins, chopped
1 tsp. each of cardamom pods,

whole cloves, mustard seeds, allspice berries, peppercorns
¾ cup malt vinegar
1 Tb. salt

Cut the limes into halves, remove the seeds, and squeeze the juice into a bowl. Peel off the rinds and set aside the remainder of the lime halves in a bowl of cold water until ready to use. Mince the rinds of the limes with the onion, green chili, and raisins. Add this to the lime juice in the bowl. Tie the spices all together in a muslin bag and put it in the bowl with the lime juice. Add the vinegar. Let this mince stand in a cold place for 36 hours, then put it in a heavy kettle. Add the salt and the drained lime halves. Simmer for 1 hour, or till lime skins are tender and transparent. Seal while hot in sterilized jars. Let stand for 6 weeks before using.

PICKLED PATNA ONIONS I

Patna or Bombay onions are the small white ones used almost exclusively for pickling in India. They are simple to prepare. Drop the onions into a pan of boiling water; after a few minutes lift out. When cool enough to handle, slip off the skins. (No weeping this way.) Parboil in just enough vinegar to cover. Cool, then drain off the vinegar into a bowl and reserve it. Arrange the onions in sterilized jars, with alternate layers of thinly sliced green gingerroot, a very few dried red chilies, and sprinkles of salt. Cover with vinegar. Let the pickles stand in the hot sun for 3 weeks, or till ready to taste.

PICKLED PATNA ONIONS II

Drop the onions into boiling water; lift out, and when cool slip off the skins. Sprinkle generously with salt and let stand in a bowl overnight. Drain. For each pound of onions measure 6 broken dried chilies and 1 tablespoon peppercorns. Add enough vinegar to cover the onions and bring the pickling liquid to a fast boil. Pour it over the onions. Store them in a crock or jar.

MINCED-ONION PICKLE

1½ Tbs. chili powder	2 Tbs. ground ginger
4 large strong onions, minced	1 tsp. salt
2 Tbs. mustard seeds, ground	2 cups cider vinegar

Rub the chili powder well into the onions to form a paste. Add the spices and mix well. Let stand for 4 hours. Add the salt to the vinegar, bring to a boil, and pour over the onions. Store in sterilized jars.

STUFFED MANGO PICKLE

Mango stuffed is probably the most popular of all Indian pickles, but there are many other fruits and vegetables used in the same way—cucumbers, sweet green peppers, small green cantaloupes, the small Indian eggplants (*brinjals*), tomatoes, etc. In preparing these the fruits should not be soft, nor should the skin be removed, not even from tomatoes. And tops, when cut off to allow scooping out, should be reserved to be put on again. These stuffed pickles are kept in deep clay pots in every storehouse and the novice should be warned not to partake too liberally when they are served.

6 large firm green mangoes, unpeeled
8 cups water
½ cup salt
2 hot onions, minced
1-inch piece of green gingerroot, minced

6 green chilies, minced
2 garlic cloves, mashed
1 tsp. salt
4 cups vinegar
2 cups water
1 cup sugar

Put the mangoes to soak overnight in the brine made of 8 cups water and ½ cup salt. In the morning dry the mangoes, cut off the tops, and remove the pits. Scoop out most of the pulp, but leave a thick shell.

Make a chutney. Mix the mango pulp with the onions, gingerroot, chilies, garlic, and salt. (Add raisins and nuts if a fancier filling is desired.) Stuff the mango shells and fasten on the tops with food picks. Stand upright in a heavy kettle. Cover with the vinegar and 2 cups water, or more vinegar if desired. Let everything stand for 24 hours. Then add the sugar to the liquid. Simmer in the same solution for 30 minutes. Pack the mangoes, top up, in deep crocks or jars. Pour the pickling vinegar over them. Cover and store for several weeks before using.

STUFFED GREEN CHILI PICKLES

Cut off the tops of the chilies and reserve them. Scoop out the seeds. Make a mixture of equal parts of salt and fennel seeds. Stuff the chilies, put back the tops, and fasten with food picks. Stand the peppers upright in a crock or deep jar. Pour enough mustard oil to cover the peppers into a kettle. Bring to a boil and pour over the chilies in the crock. Cover and let stand in a cool place for 6 weeks before using.

FIERY VEGETABLE FILLING FOR PICKLES

Simmer together 2 cups cider vinegar, 4 garlic cloves mashed, ½ pound green gingerroot shaved thin, 1 pound mustard seeds, 1 pound brown sugar, and 1 tablespoon salt. Add 2 cups mixed diced hard vegetables such as turnips, carrots, pumpkin, etc. Simmer for 30 minutes, or till most of the liquid is absorbed and the vegetables are soft. This very fiery filling is used to stuff cucumbers, mangoes, tomatoes, etc., prepared according to the recipe for stuffed mango pickle (see p. 208).

NASTURTIUM-SEED PICKLE

1½ lbs. green nasturtium seeds
1 small onion, minced
½ tsp. sliced red chili
½ tsp. whole cloves
½ tsp. ground mace
1 tsp. salt
2 cups wine vinegar

Soak the seeds in cold water for 2 days, changing the water several times. Put onion, spices, and salt in the vinegar and boil for 20 minutes. Pour over the seeds in a hot sterilized jar. Seal. Let stand for 3 months before using.

NOTE These seeds can be used in place of capers for sauces. In England they are used commonly this way but they are prepared according to a simpler method. To 1 cup vinegar add 6 peppercorns and 1 teaspoon salt. Gather the seeds on a dry day, put them in a wide-necked bottle, and cover with the uncooked vinegar. Let stand for many weeks before using.

YOGA PINEAPPLE RELISH

1 ripe pineapple	2 garlic cloves, mashed
1 tsp. salt	2 tsps. sliced green gingerroot
½ cup seeded raisins	2 cups cider vinegar

Peel the pineapple and cut it into 1-inch cubes. Sprinkle lightly with the salt and let stand for 1 hour. Drain off the liquid but do not rinse the fruit. Mix the other ingredients with the pineapple in a heavy kettle and bring to a boil. Simmer for 30 minutes, or till mixture is like jam. Seal in hot sterilized jars. Let stand for 4 weeks before using.

DRIED PRUNE RELISH

1 lb. dried prunes	½ tsp. chili powder
6 Tbs. brown sugar	1 tsp. mustard seeds
⅔ cup chopped onion	1 tsp. salt
4 Tbs. chopped crystallized gingerroot	6 pimientos, minced
¼ cup cider vinegar	½ cup almonds, slivered

Soak the prunes till well plumped, then drain and pit. Combine all the ingredients except pimientos and almonds in a heavy kettle. Simmer gently for 30 minutes, or till the mixture forms a thick jam. Fold in the pimientos and almonds and cool. Serve fresh, or seal while hot in hot sterilized jars.

YELLOW TOMATO RELISH

1 lb. yellow tomatoes	1 Tb. minced preserved gingerroot
1½ cups sugar	
1 unpeeled lemon, sliced thin	

Drop the tomatoes into boiling water for a moment, then drain and cool and slip off their skins. Chop the tomatoes fine. Mix with the sugar and let stand overnight. Drain off the juice in the morning and boil it till it forms a thread when a little is dropped from a spoon into cold water. Add the lemon slices, gingerroot, and tomatoes and simmer for another 5 minutes.

Seal in hot sterilized jars. Let stand in a cool place for a few days before using.

PRESERVED GINGERROOT I

1 lb. green gingerroot
2 cups white sugar

1½ cups water

Soak the gingerroot in cold water overnight. In the morning scrape the skin from it and slice it quite thin. Cover with fresh cold water and let come to a boil. Drain off this water. Cover again with cold water and bring to a boil. This process is repeated three times to remove the excessive pungency from the root. Now mix the sugar and water and simmer for about 20 minutes to make a syrup. Drain the gingerroot well and add it to the simmering syrup. Bring to a fast boil. Remove the kettle from the heat and let the gingerroot stand in its syrup overnight. In the morning return kettle to heat and bring the mixture to a boil once more. Let simmer for 10 minutes, or till the root is transparent. Seal in hot sterilized jars and let stand for several weeks before using. This is excellent for use in puddings, drinks, curry dishes, fresh salads, chutneys.

PRESERVED GINGERROOT II

1 lb. gingerroot
2 cups sugar

1 cup water
½ tsp. cream of tartar

Soak the gingerroot in cold water overnight, then drain. Scrape off the skin and slice the root. Cover again with fresh cold water and bring to a boil. Drain off, cover again with water, and bring to a boil. Repeat once more. Boil the sugar and water together for 20 minutes or less, to make a syrup. Add the gingerroot and the cream of tartar and cook till the root is transparent. Seal in hot sterilized jars and let stand for some weeks before using.

CRYSTALLIZED GINGER

Preserved gingerroot is used for making crystallized ginger. Take pieces of preserved gingerroot from the syrup and spread out on a wire rack to dry for a day or two. Or place in the hot sun as the Indian housewife does. When dry, roll the pieces in fine granulated sugar and store in airtight jars.

GINGER FIG CONSERVE

Cut 1 pound fresh black figs into small pieces. Soak in cold water for several hours, then cook in a heavy kettle till soft. Add 1 cup ginger marmalade (any good commercial brand). Bring to a boil and seal at once in hot sterilized jars.

GINGER MANGO CHIPS

2 lbs. fresh ripe mangoes
1 lemon, sliced very thin
1 Tb. sliced gingerroot

1 cup sugar
2 cups water

Pare the mangoes, pit them, and cut the pulp into slices. Add the lemon and gingerroot. Simmer the sugar and water together for 20 minutes or less, till a thin syrup is formed. Add the mango mixture and simmer till the gingerroot is transparent. Drain the mixture through a sieve till it stops dripping. Spread the slices out on a rack over a shallow pan and let the chips dry completely in a low oven.

BLACK FIG PRESERVE

4 lbs. ripe black figs
1 cup water
1 cup honey
1 Tb. vinegar

¾ cup orange juice
Grated rind of 1 orange
1 Tb. whole cloves
1 cinnamon stick, 2 inches

Simmer the figs gently in the water for 30 minutes, till figs are soft and the liquid is all absorbed. In a separate pan put the honey, vinegar, orange juice, orange rind, and spices. Bring to a boil and let simmer gently till a thin syrup is formed. Remove the spices and add the figs. Simmer until the preserve is as thick as jam. Seal in hot sterilized jars.

Guava

This is a hard pearlike fruit, which tastes much like a quince. It puckers up the mouth when eaten raw, but it makes an excellent addition to many dishes. It is known to Westerners usually through guava jelly, but in the East it has other uses. Guava jelly melted down with orange marmalade makes an excellent glaze for basting hams or poultry. Indians often combine guavas with mangoes, but the most common use is for making preserves.

GUAVA MARMALADE

Choose overripe guavas. Without paring, slice them and place in cold water in a heavy kettle. Bring to a boil, then reduce heat and simmer for about 1 hour, till the pulp is soft. Force the pulp through a sieve or food mill and measure the pulp. Add the juice of ½ lemon and 1 cup sugar to 1 cup of sieved pulp. Simmer for 20 minutes longer, or till a jam is formed. Seal in hot sterilized jars.

GUAVA JELLY

Cut 3 quarts unpeeled red guavas into large slices. Cover with cold water, bring to a boil, and simmer for 1 hour or longer, till the fruit is very soft. Put in a jelly bag and let the liquid drip into a bowl without squeezing. Measure the juice; for each 1 cup juice add 1 cup sugar and the juice of ½ lemon. Simmer for about 45 minutes, till the juice jells when a little is dropped onto a cold plate. Pour into hot sterilized jars and seal while hot.

PAPAYA MARMALADE

Peel 10 firm ripe papayas. Dice the pulp and weigh it. Put in a heavy kettle with sugar equal in weight. Add 4 cups water, the shredded rind of 5 small oranges, and 1 tablespoon sliced gingerroot. Simmer for about 45 minutes, or till the mixture becomes a thick jam. Mash once during the cooking to make the jam smooth.

PAPAYA LIME MARMALADE

Force the pulp of 5 very ripe papayas through a sieve or food mill. Add the juice of 1 lime, 1 tablespoon pineapple juice, and 5 cups honey. Put in a heavy kettle and simmer for 1 hour, or till the mixture becomes a thick jam. Seal in hot sterilized jars.

TAMARIND MARMALADE

4 cups peeled tamarinds   4 cups sugar
4 cups water

Cover the fruit with the water, adding a little more if necessary. Simmer for about 1 hour, till fruit is soft and the pulp loosened; drain. Press the pulp through a sieve. Remove the seeds and any fibers. Mix the pulp with the sugar in a heavy kettle. Simmer carefully for about 30 minutes, till the mixture begins to coat a wooden spoon. Add a little water if needed and stir occasionally to keep the marmalade from sticking. This is a sweet-sour jam. Seal in hot sterilized jars. Store in a cool place.

ROSE-PETAL JAM

3 cups unsprayed rose petals   4 Tbs. honey
4 cups ice water   4 Tbs. lemon juice
6 cups white sugar   1 tsp. salt, or more

Gather fine large pink or red rose petals at dawn when the dew is still on them and during the season when aromatic oils are at their peak. Wash in several changes of ice water. Drain each time without bruising. Drain finally and cut into strips. Add to the 4 cups of ice water; bring to a boil and simmer for 10 minutes. Drain off the water into a heavy kettle. Add the white sugar and simmer till a light syrup is formed. Stir occasionally with a wooden spoon. In the meantime in another kettle mix the rose strips with the honey and lemon juice and simmer for

30 minutes at 220°F. on a candy thermometer. Combine the two syrups and add salt to taste. Simmer till the mixture forms a jam. Pour while hot into sterilized small dainty jars. Seal while hot. If the jam becomes sugary at any time during the next months, stand it, still sealed, in hot water; it will clear again.

Chapter 18

DESSERTS AND CONFECTIONS

NO COUNTRY has more fiery dishes than India and no cuisine offers sweeter sweets to offset them. In the native bazaar the road is lined with women squatting on the ground before their mats mounded high with colorful herbs and spices. The sweets vendors weave in and out among the buyers, trays on their heads, calling out their wares—*rusgullas, jalabis, halwas*—each district has its own special dessert. Most of them, like our own confections, are much too complicated to be made at home. The Indian housewife buys her supply in the bazaar.

A few standard ingredients go into these sweets such as jaggery (a molasseslike sweetening made usually from palm sap), coconut, semolina, rice flour, and honey; also rosewater which is by far the most popular flavoring in the land. It is used not only in the food and for tinting, but is also sprinkled lavishly over guests. It is bought in varying qualities and prices in the bazaar.

Nevertheless, in spite of all those desserts dripping with honey, the most usual dessert in India is fruit, either served by itself or made into ices or cooked into puddings or pies.

CALCUTTA FRUIT SWEETS   ❊   *6 servings*

6 apples	1 cup slivered almonds
Juice of 6 oranges	½ cup heavy cream
1 Tb. honey	Grated nutmeg
¼ cup pistachios	

Pare and slice the apples and arrange in a buttered baking dish. Mix the orange juice with the honey, nuts, and cream. Pour the mixture over the apples. Grate nutmeg lightly on top. Bake in a moderate oven (350°F.) for 30 minutes, or till apples are tender.

STUFFED FIGS

Allow 2 figs per person. Simmer large firm figs in water till soft but still firm; cool. Cut a slit in each fig. Mix cottage cheese with shredded pineapple and few drops of lemon juice. Stuff the figs with this mixture. Serve very cold.

KUMQUAT ADACHI   ❋   ❋   ❋   *6 servings*

2 cups unpeeled kumquats   3 cups sugar
1 cup water   Tiny pinch of salt
8 egg whites

Simmer the kumquats in the water for about 1 hour, till soft. Mash them by hand or in a blender till a thick smooth mixture is formed. Beat the egg whites until stiff, then add the sugar and salt. Fold this meringue carefully into the kumquat mash. Grease a 2-quart baking dish and sprinkle it lightly with sugar. Pour in the kumquat mixture. Bake in a hot oven (425°F.) for 25 minutes. Serve with whipped cream.

Mango

This fruit, fabled in the Far East as food for god and rajah, became a favorite with Westerners too. The trees are now being grown successfully in the southern parts of the United States and in nearby tropical islands. However, little advice is available to the shopper as to choosing and using the fruit. It is unfortunate indeed if the novice first samples one of those small hard green mangoes, often brown spotted, with a taste which resembles bitter turpentine.

Mangoes grow wild all through southeastern Asia just as many of our grapes, apples, and peaches grow wild in the West. Wild mangoes are bitter and distasteful and are used by the natives only for making hot chutneys. The cultivated mango is large, smooth-skinned, and oval shaped, ready for eating when the first blush begins to tint its greenish-gold coat. How is it eaten? It is admittedly the most awkward of fruits, and the old-timers in India say the only suitable place to tackle one is in the bathtub. The pulp is always firm and must be softened for eating by being pressed gently all over with the fingers, then a tiny slit is made with a fruit knife and the contents are spooned out; or, more vulgarly, sucked out. A more formal way is to cut the unpeeled fruit into sections and pull them away from the pit, and serve to be eaten from the peel with a spoon. We have used the method of paring the unsoftened fruit and slicing and serving it like a fresh peach, but the pulp of the mango clings so tenaciously to its huge pit, that the richest part of the pulp is wasted this way.

When choosing mangoes at the supermarket, avoid those that are very small or very hard. They will not ripen in a day or two like the avocado, as the salesman may tell you. If they are close to the proper stage, they may ripen if placed on a kitchen window ledge in the sun, but maybe they will never become luscious. It is better to choose those which feel somewhat tender but not mushy and when the first blush of rosy color has appeared.

When serving mangoes as a formal dinner dessert, fruit knives are in order, and even more important the finger bowl. The Hindu's little brass water bowl was no doubt the forerunner of our lovely crystal ones, but either kind adds to the beauty and appeal of a curry meal. Drop the petal of a flower or an almost invisible sliver of lemon into the water, to make the service truly correct.

SIMPLE MANGO DESSERT

Chill sieved fresh mango pulp. Spoon it into tall sherbet glasses and top with whipped cream. Serve as a dessert to a hot curry dinner.

MANGO FOOL

Choose fully grown but still green mangoes for this dish. Peel and slice them and barely cover with cold water in a heavy kettle. Simmer gently till the pulp is soft. Force through a sieve, removing all fibers. Sweeten the mash to taste with granulated sugar. Since mangoes vary greatly in flavor, do this carefully, tasting as you go. Chill in the refrigerator for several hours. Add cold milk or cream to bring the pulp to the consistency of ice cream; use equal portions of milk and mango pulp, or half as much heavy cream as mango pulp. Blend well. More sugar may be added to taste. Serve very cold.

MANGO ICE   ❀   ❀   ❀   ❀   *4 servings*

1 cup sugar   ¼ cup lemon juice
4 cups water   5 egg whites
4 cups sieved mango pulp

Boil the sugar and water together for 5 minutes. Add the mango pulp from well-ripened fruit. Add the lemon juice and mix well. Cool the mixture and freeze in refrigerator as for ice cream until mushy. Beat the egg whites until stiff. Turn out the mush into a bowl, beat until the mixture is smooth, and fold in the egg whites. Blend gently but thoroughly, then freeze again until firm.

MANGO ICE CREAM   ❀   ❀   *4 to 6 servings*

Ice cream has become a very popular sweet in India since the introduction of refrigeration. While the majority of homes in the villages do not yet have this luxury, the ice-cream vendor with a modern cold box is ever present.

½ cup sugar   Juice of 1 lime
⅛ tsp. cream of tartar   ½ tsp. salt
⅓ cup water   2 cups heavy cream
3 cups sieved mango pulp

Boil the sugar, cream of tartar, and water together till a syrup is formed thick enough to form threads. Add the mango pulp and lime juice and stir well. Simmer for 5 minutes and remove from the heat. Cool in refrigerator. Add salt to the cream and whip it till stiff; there should be 4 cups. Fold it carefully into the cold mango mixture. Freeze in the refrigerator for 2 hours or longer before serving.

Papaya

This amazing fruit serves as sweet, vegetable, spot remover, meat tenderizer, and sedative. It is rich in vitamins A and C and the sugar content is 4 to 10 per cent of its pulp weight according to the type. The papaya grows on an exotic palmlike shrub, often growing to 30 feet in height, which bears clusters of oblong fruits resembling melons. Fruits often weigh up to 5 pounds. The shrub is a native of the Americas, and it was first brought north to southern Florida by Portuguese sailors in the eighteenth century. It is now extensively cultivated in Florida, in the Far East and in almost all tropical parts of the world, for it will give fruit and shade within two years after planting.

Firm papayas can be purchased in many supermarkets, and usually they will ripen at room temperature in 3 or 4 days. They are ready to eat when slight pressure from a finger leaves a faint dent on the smooth skin. Inside the dark-green skin there is an orange-colored pulp and a myriad of small peppery black seeds which are scooped out like cantaloupe seeds. Unused portions can be wrapped in wax paper and stored in the refrigerator for another day. Europeans in India have concocted many fine desserts from this one fruit.

MANGO-PAPAYA PIE   ❋   ❋   *6 servings*

1½ cups sieved papaya pulp	5 Tbs. sugar
1½ cups sieved mango pulp	2 eggs, separated
2 cups water	¼ tsp. salt
¼ tsp. ground cinnamon	Baked pie shell, 8 inches

Choose fully ripe fruits to make the pulp and make sure all fibers are removed in sieving. Put both pulps in the top part of a double boiler and add the water, cinnamon, and 4 tablespoons of the sugar. Beat the egg yolks till creamy and add. Bring the mixture to a boil over boiling water and simmer for 20 minutes, or till the mixture is thick and smooth. Stir constantly. Pour into the baked pie shell and cool. Beat the egg whites with the salt till stiff. Fold in remaining sugar and beat again till the sugar is completely dissolved. Spoon the meringue on top of the pie, spreading it to meet the crust all around. Bake in a moderate oven (325°F.) for 15 minutes, until delicately browned.

PAPAYA SHERBET

Mix equal amounts of sieved papaya pulp, sugar, orange juice, and heavy cream. Freeze in the refrigerator for 4 hours.

HONEY PERSIMMON SWEET   ❋   *6 servings*

1 cup unsalted cashews, crushed
1 Tb. butter
½ cup plus 1 Tb. honey

2 tsps. orange juice
2 cups sieved persimmon pulp
½ cup heavy cream

Mix the crushed cashews with the butter and 1 tablespoon of the honey. Press into an 8-inch pie plate to make a crumb crust. Chill. Mix remaining honey, the orange juice, and the persimmon pulp. Chill. At serving time spoon the persimmon mixture into the cashew piecrust. Whip the cream until stiff and spread it over the top.

Coconut

Coconut is almost as necessary to curried dishes as rice, but in India it is also used as a sweet, a vegetable, and an appetizer. Fortunate indeed is the one who first savors this fruit or nut just as it is gathered fully ripened from the palm. The velvety soft pulp is as luscious as a peach and must be eaten with a spoon.

HAWAIIAN COCONUT
SHERBET   ❋   ❋   *4 servings*

2 coconuts
3½ cups boiling water

1½ cups sugar
1 or 2 drops of almond extract

Crack the coconuts, scrape out the pulp, and grate it. Pour the boiling water over the coconut and let it stand for 1 hour. Squeeze the liquid through a muslin cloth and add it to the sugar. Stir till the sugar is dissolved. Add the almond extract. Freeze until mushy, then fold in some of the grated meat and freeze until firm. Or freeze the sherbet till firm and serve garnished with the coconut shreds.

HAWAIIAN COCONUT MOUSSE ❋ ❋ *6 servings*

1 large coconut
2 cups milk, heated
¾ cup sugar

1 cup whipped cream
1 tsp. vanilla extract
1 envelope unflavored gelatin

Crack the coconut, scoop out the pulp, and grate it. Set aside 1 cup of the shreds. Pour the heated milk over the remainder of the coconut pulp and let it stand for 1 hour. Squeeze this through a muslin bag. Add the sugar to the liquid and stir till sugar is dissolved. Fold in the 1 cup grated coconut and the whipped cream. Add the vanilla. Soften the gelatin in a little cold water, then dissolve over hot water; add to the coconut mixture. Freeze in refrigerator trays for several hours.

COCONUT BALLS

1 cup sugar
1 cup water

½ lb. shredded coconut
Colored flavorings (optional)

Simmer the sugar and water together till a thick syrup is formed. Add the coconut and simmer for 1 minute longer, or till the coconut begins to cling together. Do not overcook the mixture. It should be quite sticky when taken from the heat, and the balls crisp up quickly. Take from the heat, let cool slightly, and roll the coconut into small balls with the fingers.

If you wish, the coconut may be presoaked in various tinted colorings to make pretty sweets.

COCONUT CUSTARD ❋ ❋ *4 servings*

1 cup grated fresh coconut
1 cup coconut milk (see p. 16)
4 eggs, beaten light

½ cup heavy cream
1 cup honey
Tiny pinch of salt

Mix the coconut, coconut milk, and eggs together first. Blend the cream, honey, and salt and fold in. Pour into a 4-cup baking dish. Bake in a moderate oven (325°F.) for 30 minutes, or till the custard is firm.

SESAME BALLS   ❊   ❊   ❊   ❊   *4 servings*

½ cup sesame seeds   ⅓ cup seeded raisins
½ lb. dried apricots   ½ cup honey
½ lb. dates, pitted

Toast the sesame seeds in a hot oven for 1 minute; remove from oven. Grind the apricots, dates, and raisins together, or chop fine in a mixing bowl. Bind the fruits with the honey. Roll into small balls and coat with the sesame seeds. Keep cold. Serve after the hot curry meal.

Puddings

Puddings (*halwa* or *hulwa*) are a favorite Indian dessert. They may be made very simply from the ever-present rice or *dal*, or they may be elaborately concocted with nuts, fruit pulps, and spices.

DAL HALWA   ❊   ❊   ❊   ❊   *4 servings*

This pudding is very popular among the villagers. It is made from the same hard cake of mashed legumes that the Indian cook uses to thicken curry.

1 lb. dal (see p. 26)   1 tsp. ground cardamom
2 cups water   ¼ cup sugar
2 Tbs. butter   ¼ tsp. ground saffron

Soak the *dal* in the water for 1 hour or more, till it softens to a thick paste. Heat the butter and fry the cardamom. Stir in the sugar and simmer gently till a thick syrup is formed. Add the soaked *dal* and the saffron. Simmer, stirring constantly, for 10 more minutes, or till the mixture forms a thick sauce. Pour into a greased shallow pan and let cool before cutting into squares.

CARROT PUDDING   ❊   ❊   ❊   *4 servings*

1 lb. carrots, grated
4 cups milk
4 cardamom pods
2 whole cloves
2 Tbs. butter
1 Tb. cornstarch

1 cup sugar
1 cup slivered almonds
¼ tsp. salt
½ tsp. ground saffron
Rosewater

Simmer the grated carrots in the milk for 10 minutes; keep the milk just under the boiling point. Strain off the carrots and set them aside; set aside the strained milk as well. Fry the cardamoms and cloves in the heated butter. Stir in the cornstarch and simmer for a minute, till a smooth paste is formed. Add this mixture to the strained milk. Add the sugar and simmer in the top part of a double boiler over boiling water for 20 minutes, or till the sauce is smooth and thick. Stir in the cooked carrots, the almonds, and salt. Pour into a greased shallow pan. Sprinkle with saffron and let cool. Raisins may be added if desired. Sprinkle rosewater over the pudding just before serving.

POTATO PUDDING   ❊   ❊   ❊   *6 servings*

2 cups cooked mashed potatoes
4 Tbs. sugar
1 Tb. buttermilk
1 tsp. vanilla extract or other flavoring

6 eggs
2 cups milk

Mix the potatoes with the sugar, buttermilk, and vanilla. Beat 4 eggs thoroughly and mix well with the potatoes. Spoon into a buttered deep pie plate. Make a light custard with the remaining 2 eggs and the milk. Pour it over the potato mixture. Bake in a very hot oven (450°F.) for 10 minutes; then reduce heat to moderate (325°F.) and bake for 30 minutes longer, or till a knife comes out of the custard clean.

SAFFRON RICE HULWA   ❈   ❈   *4 servings*

½ lb. butter
½ lb. sugar
½ lb. uncooked rice, ground to
powder

½ tsp. ground saffron
Rosewater (optional)

Melt the butter and stir in the sugar till it dissolves. Add the rice powder and cook in the top part of a double boiler, covered, over boiling water for 30 minutes. Stir often. When a thick paste is formed, add the saffron and rosewater. The mixture should be thick enough to stiffen when cool. Pour into a greased shallow pan and let cool before cutting.

SQUASH PUDDING   ❈   ❈   ❈   *4 servings*

2 lbs. zucchini or yellow squash
2 cups water
Pinch of salt
½ cup butter

½ cup sugar
½ tsp. ground saffron
¼ tsp. rosewater

Peel the squash and dice. Simmer in the water with a pinch of salt till squash is soft and most of the liquid is absorbed. Drain thoroughly. Melt the butter and add the sugar. Stir and simmer over low heat till sugar is melted and the mixture is syrupy. Stir in the squash and saffron. Add rosewater after taking from the heat. Mixture should be as thick as jello. Pour into a greased shallow pan and serve cold.

NOTE   In India and England the squash used would be vegetable marrows. Any kind of squash may be used.

CUSTARD PUDDING   ❈   ❈   *4 servings*

1 cup milk
½ cup butter
½ cup sugar
6 egg yolks, beaten

¼ cup almonds, ground
½ cup pistachios, ground
Rosewater

Heat the milk in the top part of a double boiler over simmering water. Add the butter and sugar and simmer till a thin syrup forms. Beat the egg yolks; add a little of the hot syrup to them, mix well, and then add the yolk mixture to the butter and sugar. Simmer gently, stirring often, till mixture is as thick as jam. Add the nuts last. Pour out the custard into a greased shallow pan. Sprinkle rosewater over the top. Let stand for several hours and serve cold.

GREEN-GINGER PUDDING ❋ *6 servings*

1 cup butter
1 cup sugar
½ tsp. ground cardamom
½ lb. green gingerroot, diced

½ cup mixed nuts, ground
½ tsp. ground saffron
Rosewater

Simmer the butter and sugar together till a thick syrup is formed. Add the cardamom and simmer for 1 minute longer. Stir in the diced gingerroot and ground nuts. Pour into a greased shallow pan. Sprinkle with saffron and let stand till cool. Cut into squares and sprinkle with rosewater before serving.

ALMOND PUDDING ❋ ❋ ❋ *4 servings*

4 Tbs. sugar
½ cup water
4 Tbs. butter

2 tsps. cornstarch
½ lb. almonds, ground
½ tsp. rosewater

Boil the sugar and water to make a thick syrup. Melt the butter and stir in the cornstarch. Simmer till a smooth paste is formed. Add the almonds and syrup and simmer till the mixture is very thick. Add rosewater last. Pour into a greased shallow pan and let cool before cutting into squares for serving.

BANANA PUDDING ❋ ❋ ❋ *6 servings*

6 ripe bananas
2 Tbs. butter
2 Tbs. water
6 Tbs. sugar
½ tsp. grated nutmeg
½ tsp. ground cardamom

1 Tb. ground pistachios
1 Tb. ground almonds
1 tsp. rosewater or vanilla extract
¼ tsp. salt

Peel the bananas and mash to a pulp. Fry lightly in the butter. Heat the water, sugar, and spices together for about 10 minutes, till a thin syrup is formed. Add the mashed bananas and simmer till the mixture is as thick as jam. Add nuts, flavoring, and salt last. Pour into a greased shallow pan and let cool before cutting into squares.

BREADFRUIT PUDDING ❋ ❋ *4 servings*

The breadfruit, or jackfruit as it is often called, is one of the ugliest-looking and most disagreeable-smelling fruits in the world. Yet this huge warty gourd has within it a delicious pulp. Few Westerners have ventured to use it, but those who have are loud in its praise.

1 coconut	½ cup sugar
1 ripe breadfruit	½ tsp. salt
1 cup boiling water	

Crack open the coconut, scrape out the pulp, and grate it. There should be about 3 cups. Split the breadfruit and scoop out the pulp; save the two pieces of breadfruit shell. Mix the pulp with the grated coconut. Make a syrup with the water, sugar, and salt. Add the syrup to the mixed pulp and put it in the breadfruit halves. Bake in hot ashes to a custardlike pudding.

Out in the *sahib*'s cookhouse the odorous shell is discarded. The breadfruit pulp is mixed with the coconut and syrup and baked in a buttered dish for 2 hours, or till the pudding is firm.

SEMOLINA HALWA ❋ ❋ ❋ *4 servings*

Semolina is a processed hard wheat which looks much like the American cereal Cream of Wheat. The grains are so refined that semolina is still a mainstay in English hospitals for invalid and baby diets. It is probably the best-remembered pudding of old British hill-schools for boys in India and the one which appeared monotonously on the *sahib*'s table. Semolina is cheap, easily and quickly cooked, and very digestible. Because of its rich glutinous content, it is a most desirable ingredient for thickening puddings in a humid climate.

1 cup sugar
2 cups water
1 cup butter
1½ cups semolina or Cream of
Wheat

1 cinnamon stick, 4 inches
3 cardamom pods
½ cup seeded raisins
½ tsp. rosewater

Boil the sugar and water together for about 10 minutes, till a syrup is formed. Melt the butter and brown the semolina. Add the syrup to the browned semolina, then add the whole spices and the raisins. Stir well and simmer for about 20 minutes, till the mixture becomes a very thick sauce. Pour into a wet mold and let set for some hours or overnight. Sprinkle the rosewater over the pudding after turning it out of the mold, just before taking it to the table.

NOTE   This is the basic semolina *halwa*. Nuts and spices of many other kinds may be added to it, only taking care that no juicy ingredient is used, for that would spoil the stiffness of the pudding. Syrups and fruit-juice sauces are often served with it.

FIRNI RICE (Pakistan)   ❋   ❋   ❋   *4 servings*

½ cup Cream of Wheat or semolina
4 cups milk
1 cup sugar

Pinch of salt
2 Tbs. pistachios
2 Tbs. silver dusting

Mix the Cream of Wheat with the milk in the top part of a double boiler and bring to a boil. Simmer over boiling water, stirring constantly, for 15 minutes. Add the sugar and the pinch of salt and stir till the mixture is very thick, taking care not to let it scorch. Add the pistachios and pour into a wet bowl. Let the pudding cool for 4 hours or longer. Turn out on a plate and cut it into slices. Dust with silver.

NOTE   Silver dusting can be obtained at a confectioner's.

GUNDAR PACK (East India)   ✻   ✻   *6 servings*

1 lb. white flour
½ lb. farina
1 lb. unsalted butter
4 cups milk
⅛ tsp. salt

2 cups sugar
Food coloring if desired
¼ cup slivered almonds
¼ cup pistachios
6 cardamom pods

Mix the flour and farina well and stir into the boiling butter. Add the milk, salt, and sugar and cook, stirring constantly, till the mixture is very thick. Add coloring if desired. Rinse out a bowl and press the pudding lightly into it. Sprinkle the nuts and cardamoms on top. Leave till cold and cut into squares to serve.

ALMOND CAKE   ✻   ✻   ✻   ✻   *8 servings*

9 eggs, separated
2 cups brown sugar
1 cup whole-wheat bread crumbs
1 cup blanched almonds, finely ground

Grated rind of 1 lemon
1 tsp. baking powder
Pinch of salt

Beat egg yolks light and add the brown sugar. Beat well. Mix the bread crumbs, ground almonds, and lemon rind with the baking powder and stir into the egg-yolk mixture. Beat the egg whites with the salt till stiff. Fold both mixtures together. Pour into a well-greased springform pan. Bake in a moderate oven (350°F.) for 1 hour. Whipped cream or honey may be served with this.

CHESTNUT CAKES   ✻   ✻   *about 12 cakes*

25 chestnuts
1 egg, separated
½ cup honey
3 Tbs. heavy cream

1 tsp. almond extract
1 tsp. orange extract
Pinch of salt
1 tsp. sesame oil

Cut a slit in each chestnut and bake or toast them for 20 minutes, till the shells begin to crack. Remove both the shells and inner skins and put the chestnuts in a pan with just enough water to cover. Simmer for about 45 minutes, till the nuts are very soft. Drain nuts and mash well. Beat the egg white until stiff and mix with the mashed chestnuts, honey, and cream. Fold in flavorings and salt. Oil a cookie sheet with sesame oil. Drop the batter by tablespoons onto the cookie sheet. Flatten the tops very gently with a wet knife. Beat the egg yolk lightly and brush a little on top of each cookie. Bake in a slow oven (300°F.) for 10 minutes.

HONEY COCONUT COOKIES ❋ ❋ *8 dozen cookies*

4 cups bran flakes
2 cups chopped nuts, any kind
3½ cups grated coconut (about 1 coconut)

1 tsp. vanilla or lemon extract
¼ tsp. salt
Scant ½ cup honey

Mix all ingredients, using only enough of the honey to bind the other ingredients together. Drop the mixture by tablespoons onto a greased cookie sheet. Bake in a moderate oven (350°F.) for 20 minutes. These will be gummy when done, but they will become crisp as they cool.

ALMOND MACAROONS ❋ ❋ *about 18*

6 Tbs. ground almonds
Grated rind of 1 lemon

7 Tbs. sugar
4 egg whites, beaten stiff

Mix all ingredients together. Drop by small spoonfuls onto cookie sheets lined with unglazed paper. Bake in a moderate oven (325°F.) for about 25 minutes, or till pale yellow.

COCONUT MACAROONS ❋ *about 2 dozen*

3 eggs, separated
1 cup ground nuts, any kind
½ cup shredded coconut
½ cup honey

Grated rind of 1 lemon
½ cup potato flour or instant potato

Beat the egg yolks till creamy and stir in the nuts and coconut; mix well. Stir in the honey, lemon rind, and flour; mix well. Beat egg whites till stiff and fold into the batter. Drop by small spoonfuls onto a greased baking sheet. Bake in moderate oven (350°F.) for 12 minutes.

CASHEW STICKS   ✳   ✳   ✳   *about 15*

2 cups brown sugar
4 eggs, lightly beaten
1 cup flour
1½ tsps. baking powder
¼ tsp. salt
2 tsps. ground cinnamon
¼ tsp. ground allspice
¼ tsp. ground cloves
2 cups ground unsalted cashews
4 Tbs. butter, or more
½ cup confectioners' sugar

Add the brown sugar to the beaten eggs. Sift in the mixed flour, baking powder, salt, and spices. Lastly fold in the cashews. Spread the butter thickly on a baking sheet with sides. Pour the batter evenly over the baking sheet in a thin layer. Bake in a moderate oven (350°F.) for 15 to 20 minutes. Watch carefully —if cooked too long the sticks will be brittle instead of gummy. Remove from the oven and while still hot cut into 3-inch squares. Roll the squares into little tubes which will at once become crisp. Sift confectioners' sugar heavily over them.

PEANUT-BUTTER CAKES   ✳   *5 dozen cookies*

1 cup butter or peanut oil
1 cup brown sugar
1 cup peanut butter
3 cups cake flour
2 tsps. baking soda
Pinch of salt
2 eggs, well beaten

Cream the butter and sugar together till creamy smooth. Beat in the peanut butter bit by bit. Sift in the mixed flour, baking soda, and salt. Add the beaten eggs last. Squeeze this soft mixture through a pastry tube and drop in tiny portions onto a greased baking sheet. Bake in a moderate (350°F.) for 12 minutes, or till done.

LEMON HERB CAKES   ❋   ❋   *2 dozen cookies*

1 Tb. grated lemon rind	¼ cup peanut oil or butter
Juice of 1 lemon	1 egg, beaten
1 tsp. caraway seeds	2 cups whole-wheat flour
1 tsp. sesame seeds	½ tsp. baking soda
1 cup brown sugar	½ tsp. salt

Mix the lemon rind, lemon juice, and spices well together. Cream the sugar and oil well. Add the beaten egg and mix again. Combine spice mixture with egg and sugar. Sift the flour with the soda and salt, and add it very slowly to the batter. Mixture should be just firm enough to handle. Shape into a long roll. Wrap in a towel and let stand in a cold place for 24 hours. Cut into 1-inch slices and put on an oiled baking sheet. Bake in a hot oven (400°F.) for 15 minutes.

Doughnuts and Fritters

Some of these tempting-looking sweets cooked in hot oil or boiling syrup are found on the tray carried on the head of a vendor at every railway station in India. *Rasgullas* are the delight of every Indian boy, no matter what his race.

RASGULLAS   ❋   ❋   ❋   ❋   *6 servings*

4 cups rich whole milk	12 cardamom pods
1 large juicy lemon	2 cups white sugar
2 Tbs. semolina	6 cups water

Boil the milk and add the lemon juice. As soon as the curd begins to form, in about 5 minutes, remove the milk from the heat. Pour the curd through a muslin cloth and let it drip all night. Do not squeeze the bag. In the morning remove the dry curd and mix it with the semolina. Knead till a smooth dough is formed. Divide into small portions about the size of a small lime. Flatten out each piece, drop 2 cardamom pods on it, and roll up into a ball. Continue till all the rounds are used.

Boil the sugar and water for 15 minutes, or till a thin syrup is formed. While the syrup is still boiling hard, drop a ball into it; if the ball does not break, you will know dough is ready. Boil the cakes slowly; they will puff up to twice their size as golden balls. The syrup must be kept thin at all times. Add a very little boiling water if it becomes too thick.

FLOUR RASGULLAS   *   *6 or more servings*

3 cups whole fresh milk
Juice of 1 lime
3 cups white flour
½ cup lump sugar

½ cup cardamom pods
2 cups white sugar
6 cups water

Bring milk to a boil and add the lime juice. When curd forms, put it in a muslin bag and let it drip overnight. Remove the dry curd next morning and knead with it the white flour till a smooth dough is formed. Shape into small balls. Insert 1 lump of sugar and 2 cardamoms in each; cover the filling well. Boil the white sugar and water till a thin syrup is formed. Drop in the balls of dough, a few at a time, and fry till puffed and golden.

BANANA PUFFS   *   *   *   *8 servings*

2 cups flour
¼ tsp. salt
8 Tbs. butter
¼ cup buttermilk

4 Tbs. shredded coconut
3 ripe but not too soft bananas
4 cups vegetable oil
Lemon wedges

Sift the flour and salt into a bowl. Cut in the butter. Add the buttermilk and mix well. Roll out on a floured board into a thin sheet. Cut into saucer-sized rounds. Mash the coconut and bananas together and drop a spoonful on each round. Fold over each round into a pasty and seal the edge with water. Bring the oil to a fast boil and drop the pasties in. Fry till golden brown. Serve hot or cold with wedges of lemon. Or bake the pasties in a hot oven (400°F.) for 20 minutes.

POMEGRANATE-BANANA FRITTERS �֍ *8 servings*

4 bananas
1 or 2 Tbs. pomegranate juice
    or grenadine syrup
1 egg, lightly beaten
½ cup milk

½ cup flour
2 Tbs. ground almonds
1 Tbs. minced crystallized gin-
    gerroot

Mash the bananas and add a little fresh pomegranate juice or grenadine syrup. Make a batter. Mix the egg, milk, and flour and beat until smooth. Stir in the almonds and gingerroot. Dip large scoops of the banana mash, about 2 tablespoons, round with 2 spoons, and dip into the batter. Quickly place on a buttered cookie sheet and bake in a moderate oven (350°F.), or fry in hot oil, until well puffed up and light brown.

JALABIS

Jullabees or *jelabis* or *jalabis* are puffed-up doughnuts or cakes. Like American doughnuts, they are simply made, but it takes the skilled hand of a native cook or housewife to produce them.

1 lb. flour (about 3 cups)
2 cups water
1 Tb. yogurt or curd (see p. 30)

4 cups vegetable oil

Make a batter of the flour and water as for thin pancakes. Let it stand, covered with a cloth, for 12 hours. Then add the yogurt or curd and mix well. In a heavy kettle bring the oil to a boil. Pour the batter mixture into a funnel or pastry bag and let small portions of it drip into the boiling oil. The cakes should swell up like doughnuts to the size of a teacup. Turn the cakes during the cooking to brown both sides. They may be eaten as they are, or they may be dipped into confectioners' sugar or into syrup before being served.

NOTE   The Hindu housewife puts her batter in a hollowed-out coconut shell which has had several small holes pierced in it.

The batter dribbling through this simple funnel into the boiling oil puffs up into all sorts of fantastic twists. Saffron mixed with the water is often added to tint the cakes for festive occasions.

APPOOS (Feast Day Pancakes)   ❋   ❋   *4 servings*

½ cup brown rice
3 eggs, well beaten
¼ cup honey
¼ cup butter
¼ tsp. ground cinnamon

¼ cup crystallized gingerroot, minced
1 Tb. chopped candied cherries
¼ tsp. salt
Oil for frying

Cook the rice until tender but still firm; cool. Mix with all other ingredients except oil. Cook the batter on an oiled griddle as you would cook pancakes.

Yoga Sweets

The yogis eat many sweets to pep up their plain diet, but they still adhere strictly to dietary rules in the use of ingredients. White sugar is never used; brown sugar, honey, or the raw unrefined sugar found in native bazaars is used instead. Lard is always banned, and saturated fats of any meat are tabooed in favor of oils from soybean, corn, peanut, mustard, sesame, etc., which take their place. White flour is seldom if ever used; instead, whole-wheat, oatmeal, barley, rice, potato, or soybean flour is used. These can all be bought in the native bazaar and in America in shops specializing in health foods. Juices of fruits and the boiled-down essences of vegetables are used largely even in sweets. Yogurt is used extensively, and the dried milk made from reduced whole milk (see p. 30).

YOGA OATMEAL CAKES   ❋   *6 dozen cookies*

2 cups brown sugar
½ cup sesame or peanut oil
4 cups quick-cooking oatmeal
2 eggs, well beaten

1 tsp. almond or orange extract
Pinch of salt
1 Tb. butter

Cream sugar and oil together and mix with the oatmeal. Add the eggs, flavoring, and salt. Use the butter to grease the cookie sheet liberally. Drop the thin batter in small spoonfuls onto the sheet. Bake in a moderate oven (350°F.) for 20 minutes.

YOGA FRUIT YAM SWEETS   ❋   *8 servings*

4 sweet potatoes
¾ tsp. salt
4 oranges, halved

1 cup shredded fresh pineapple
Grated rind of 2 extra oranges
1 cup dark-brown sugar

Bake the potatoes in their skins, cool, and scoop out the pulp. Mash the pulp with the salt. Scoop out the pulp of the 4 oranges and set the peels aside for use. Mix the potatoes, drained pineapple, and grated rind together. Pile the mixture into the empty orange shells. Mix the orange pulp with the brown sugar and pile on top. Bake in a moderate oven (350°F.) for 30 minutes.

YOGA CHEESECAKE   ❋   ❋   ❋   *4 servings*

2 cups milk
½ Tb. lemon juice
1 Tb. butter
2 egg yolks, well beaten

1½ Tbs. ground nuts
Crumb piecrust
¾ cup brown sugar

Bring the milk just to a boil, then add the lemon juice and remove from the heat. Put the mixture in a muslin bag and let it drip for 4 hours. Take out the dry cheese left in the bag and mix it with the butter, egg yolks, and nuts.

Make a crumb piecrust of graham-cracker or cornflake crumbs mixed with butter and sugar. Line a greased pie plate with the crust. Fill it with the cheese mixture. Sprinkle the brown sugar over the top. Bake in a moderate (350°F.) for 45 minutes, or till set. Serve cold.

YOGA BUTTERMILK PIE   ❋   4 to 6 servings

1 cup honey
3 Tbs. rice flour
½ tsp. salt
3 eggs, separated
2 cups buttermilk

6 Tbs. butter
¼ tsp. cream of tartar
1 cup ground unsalted cashews
½ cup brown sugar

Blend the honey, rice flour, and salt in a bowl. Beat the egg yolks till creamy and add the buttermilk and 2 tablespoons of the butter, melted. Then mix together. Mix remaining butter with the cashews and sugar until well blended. Press into an 8-inch pie plate to make a crumb crust. Add the cream of tartar to the egg whites and beat until stiff. Fold the egg whites into the buttermilk mixture and pour the buttermilk filling into the crust. Bake in a moderate oven (375°F.) for 45 minutes, or till the filling has set.

YOGA LOW-STARCH PIECRUST

2 cups soybean flour
¾ cup olive or nut oil
Juice of ½ lemon

1 egg, well beaten
⅛ tsp. salt

Blend the soybean flour and oil well. Add the lemon juice and beat again. Add the egg and salt and beat again. Mixture should then be thick enough to roll out on wax paper. Roll into a circle and use to line an oiled pie plate. Chill until ready to fill and bake. If making a baked pie shell line the dough with aluminum foil and fill with dried rice or beans to keep the bottom flat. Bake in a very hot oven (450°F.) for about 12 minutes, or until browned. Cool before filling.

NOTE   Soybean flour is available in health shops and specialty stores.

YOGA ICING

Beat just enough honey into cream cheese or thick sour cream to make a fluffy topping for cakes or puddings.

Confections

Indian desserts are so sweet that it is hard to distinguish them from candies. While the desserts are designed to be eaten at once, these confections will keep for some time if stored in airtight containers.

PISTACHIO BARFI

½ cup dried milk (see p. 30)   ½ cup sugar
½ cup pistachios   1½ cups water
½ cup butter

Prepare the dried milk. Put the pistachios in boiling water for 1 minute, then remove; let them cool and slip off the skins. Simmer the butter and dried milk together for 15 minutes, stirring constantly. Make a thick syrup by boiling the sugar and water together. Slowly add it to the butter-milk mixture and fold in the nuts. Let simmer for 5 minutes longer, then turn out on a slab and let the mixture cool. Top with fresh fruits. This confection is a sort of fudge mixture.

YOGURT PENOCHE

4½ cups brown sugar   ½ cup unsalted cashews,
2 cups yogurt   chopped
½ tsp. vanilla extract   ½ tsp. salt
½ cup seeded raisins

Stir the sugar into the yogurt in a heavy kettle. When well dissolved, turn on the heat and bring just to the boiling point. Turn heat low and simmer gently till a soft ball forms when a little is dropped into cold water. Let cool and add the vanilla, raisins, cashews, and salt. Pour into a shallow pan and when cold cut into pieces.

NOTE   Salted nuts are never used for sweets.

DRIED FRUIT BALLS

½ cup nuts, any kind
¾ cup dried apricots
1 tsp. each of grated orange and
lemon rinds

3 Tbs. dried milk (see p. 30)
1 Tb. lemon juice
½ cup toasted grated coconut

Put the nuts and apricots together through a food grinder. Stir in the grated rinds, dried milk, and lemon juice and mix well. Shape into small balls and chill briefly. Roll in the toasted coconut. Keep cool until serving time. The mixture may be pressed into a shallow pan and cut into squares. Dip the squares into toasted coconut.

TURKISH DELIGHT
(Turkish Paste)

2 cups granulated sugar
½ cup cold water
3 envelopes unflavored gelatin
¾ cup orange juice
3 Tbs. grated orange rind
4 Tbs. lemon juice

¼ lb. candied cherries
¼ lb. candied pineapple
1 cup almonds or cashews,
  chopped coarsely
1 cup confectioners' sugar

Boil the granulated sugar and water together till a thick syrup is formed. Soften the gelatin in the orange juice and stir it into the simmering syrup. Simmer for 15 minutes. Add the orange rind and the lemon juice. Cool for 5 minutes and add the candied fruits and the nuts. Rinse out a shallow pan (8 inches square) and pour in the mixture. Let stand in a cool place overnight. The mixture should then have a firm jellied texture. Cut into 1-inch squares and roll in the sifted confectioners' sugar. This will keep for many months if kept airtight.

ARABIAN DELIGHT

4 cups sugar
¾ cup water
1 Tb. lemon juice
5 Tbs. cornstarch

5 Tbs. almonds
5 Tbs. hazelnuts
5 Tbs. pistachios
1 cup confectioners' sugar

Boil the sugar and water till a thick syrup is formed. Mix the lemon juice with the cornstarch to a smooth paste and add to the syrup. Simmer, stirring constantly, for about 15 minutes, till the mixture thickens. Take from the heat and let cool for 5 minutes. Chop all the nuts and stir them into the syrup. Pour it into a rinsed shallow pan. Let stand in a cool place overnight. Cut into 1-inch squares and roll in the sifted confectioners' sugar.

MARZIPAN (Indian Method)

This is one of the most popular sweets throughout the East.

6 Tbs. almonds, ground fine   6 Tbs. confectioners' sugar
¼ cup rosewater

Mix the almonds with the rosewater to make a thick paste. Put in a saucepan and set the pan in a kettle of hot water. Cook over very low heat till a tiny amount spooned onto the hand no longer sticks. Make it as dry as possible without scorching. Coat a stone slab (marble) or pastry board with the sugar. Roll out the almond mixture on it and set aside till firm.

MARZIPAN (English Method)

2 cups granulated sugar   3 Tbs. confectioners' sugar
¾ cup water   ½ tsp. almond extract or rose-
4 Tbs. almonds, ground   water
2 egg whites, beaten well

Boil the granulated sugar and the water together to 240°F. on a candy thermometer. Remove from heat and let cool. Add the ground almonds and egg whites. Stir over a still warm but not lighted burner for a few moments. Turn out on a slab or flat china dish and work in the confectioners' sugar, stirring with a spatula till mixture is cool enough to handle. Then knead with the hands till sugar is incorporated and the mixture is smooth. Add flavoring and mold into shapes. Cool completely before using.

Fresh Flower-Petal Sweets

In India there is a delightful custom of sending friends a basket of fresh rose petals, gathered at dawn while the dew is still fresh on them. These may be used in preparing potpourri to go into ancient heirloom jars, but more likely will be crystallized for use as garnishes for festive dishes. The housewife can make her own supply, using either rose or violet petals.

CRYSTALLIZED ROSE OR VIOLET PETALS

Use 4 cups of fresh petals gathered preferably at dawn. Remove stems, bits of green, etc. Wash the petals and drain in a colander, but do not crush in any way. Stir 2 cups white sugar into 1 cup boiling water, using only a wooden spoon. Simmer till a light syrup forms, in about 15 minutes. Drop in the flower petals and simmer again till the syrup forms a soft ball when a small amount is dropped into cold water. Take from the heat. Stir constantly till the mixture reaches the coarse sugar stage. Turn out the petals on a fine-mesh wire rack where the extra sugar will shake off. Let cool. Pack very gently in small wide-mouthed jars. Petals will keep for months.

FROSTED FRUITS OR LEAVES

Wash and drain sprigs of fresh mint, bunches of grapes, clusters of fresh currants, or other individual leaves or fruits. Dip into a bowl of unbeaten egg white, then into another of finely granulated white sugar. Place in the refrigerator and let the sugar harden. These make fine table decorations or garnishes for desserts. Any small fruit may be used in this way.

Chapter 19

DRINKS

THE VAST HERDS of goats, cows, and milch buffaloes roaming along India's dusty roads are evidence that milk must be that country's main drink, and it is. There are many milk mixtures, as well as varieties of flavoring used to make this drink palatable in a land where refrigeration or ice is a luxury known only to the rich. There are yogurt drinks, for instance, which are now becoming known around the globe as health-giving. *Lassa* is one of these, a drink of the yogis. Another favorite milk drink is fresh buttermilk.

Another popular drink, mead, dates back to Old Testament days and is mentioned several times in the sacred Vedas of India. Mead is made of honey and each nation in the East has its own special recipe. Gandhi often added mead to his goat's-milk diet. In the West, the early Saxons used it for their libations, adding to it hazelnuts, almond milk, or mulberry juice. In Elizabethan times it was served in golden goblets to the revelers at royal banquets, but the commoners were content with their pewter mugs of mead to which they added flower petals of various kinds or raisins, spices, and herbs. Hungarians have always used mead for festive occasions, blending it with almond milk and honey from the acacia blossom. They claim it brings good luck. People all over the world have always believed this drink brings longevity. Honey is used for other drinks in India as well.

Lemon juice is popular everywhere as the basis for cooling drinks, but in the East much use is made of other fruit juices as well. Oranges, limes, pineapples, melon pulps, berries, currants, tamarind, pomegranate—all blend well in drinks. Other fruits un-

familiar to the West are also used. In India rosewater is most favored as a sweetening, but Westerners usually find this too cloy-
ing. Combinations of curd or yogurt with fruit pulps are popular
in India for cold drinks. As with curried dishes, so with drinks—
the presentation is always as attractive as possible. For instance,
sprigs of mint or pomegranate seeds are often added for beauty
and flavor.

LASSA ❋ ❋ ❋ ❋ ❋ ❋ *2 servings*

½ cup yogurt   Salt and pepper
2 cups ice water   Sugar

This is a favored cooling drink all over India and is reputed to
cool the blood. Beat the yogurt into the water till the mixture is
smooth. Add salt and pepper, or sugar, to taste.

MEAD ❋ ❋ ❋ ❋ ❋ ❋ *3 servings*

Combine 3 cups water and 1 cup strained honey. Boil the mixture until it is reduced by one third. Skim off any scum and
store the liquid in a wooden cask for 4 days. It is then ready to
serve as a drink.

MADHUPARKA

This is the sacred mead used especially for religious ceremonies.
It is made of honey and whey in equal parts. Whey is the
liquid part of milk which remains after the curds have been
separated for cheese making. On special days a bowl of this
mead is offered to the gods in the temple, or is placed before the
household god in that little niche made especially for it in the
mud wall of every courtyard.

YOGA HONEY VINEGAR

Another drink based on honey is this one, in which the liquid
is fermented before being used. It is being widely used today,
especially in health cocktails and salad dressings. Boil 5 cups

water with 1 cup honey for 10 minutes. Store the mixture in a cool place and allow it to ferment for 2 months before using.

In some parts of Africa this liquid is used to preserve meats. Also, slips of rare plants have been kept alive for days in this fermented honey during transportation to some other part of the world for grafting.

YOGA APRICOT MILK   ❊   ❊   *2 servings*

Mix 1 cup apricot pulp with 1 cup milk and ½ cup honey. Chill until very cold and serve immediately. This drink is especially high in calcium content.

POMEGRANATE JUICE

To extract the rich juice of the pomegranate, first press all around the ball of fruit till the pulp can be felt loosened inside. Slit the fruit open and squeeze the juice out into a bowl or press through a sieve. Use as an early-morning tonic, for it is high in potassium, iron, and iodine. Or add it to milk to make a flavored drink. Or combine with mead, or add to salad dressings and curries.

RHUBARB DRINK   ❊   ❊   ❊   *about 3 cups*

2 cups sliced fresh rhubarb   ¾ cup honey
6 Tbs. lemon juice   Mint sprigs

Make rhubarb juice; simmer the rhubarb in just enough water to cover till it is tender, then strain; there should be 2 cups liquid. Mix with the lemon juice and honey and chill. Dilute with cold water to taste, or serve small portions of the undiluted mixture. Decorate the glasses with fresh mint sprigs. This drink has great laxative properties and is also used as a spring tonic.

TAMARIND DRINK   ❊   ❊   ❊   *4 servings*

The pulp of this delightful tangy sweet-sour fruit is used for many drinks in the East. The flavor is somewhat like that of lemon. Soak the pulp of 6 to 10 tamarinds in 4 cups water over-night. In the morning drain off the juice and add sugar to taste. Chill before serving.

ALMOND DRINK

20 almonds	1 tsp. sugar
2 cups milk	Grated nutmeg

Blanch the almonds and pound into a paste. Mix the paste with the milk, sugar and grated nutmeg. Serve very cold.

NOTE For many years it has been known, not only in India, but all around the world, that nutmeg adds energy to the in-valid's eggnog or milk. Nutmeg is now being used widely in stronger drinks for musicians and other people who have to work for long hours under stress, for it has been discovered that it gives needed pep.

COCONUT JUICE

The juice of green or unripened coconuts is used as a drink in tropical lands where the coconut palm grows, but the juice of the ripe coconut is not of value to the Indian. In America the juice of the ripened nut is used for many party drinks. The coconut milk which is so essential to many curry recipes is an extract made from the pulp. This too is sometimes used for drinks in the West. For more about the coconut and for a recipe for coconut milk, see page 16.

INDIAN COFFEE

Add 4 tablespoons of very finely ground mocha to 4 cups freshly boiled water. Bring to a full boil again, then remove from the heat. The coffee is ready to pour. Often 1 tablespoon rosewater is added to the pot. Sugar is usually added by the Indian. Serve in tiny cups.

ROSE-PETAL TEA

To make this exotic tea, steep fresh rose petals, or other flower petals, in boiling water. Add leaves of fresh rosemary or lavender. Strain and serve as other tea is served.

PISTACHIO AND ROSE-PETAL DRINKS ❋ *about 4 cups*

1 cup pistachios
½ cup dried rose petals
3 cardamom pods
1 tsp. black peppercorns

1 tsp. aniseeds
¼ cup blanched almonds
4¼ cups milk

Soak the pistachios in cold water overnight, then drain and slip off the skins. Put the dried rose petals, spices, and nuts in a bowl and add ¼ cup milk. Blend until the mixture is pasty, then put it all through a food grinder or chop in a blender. Cover with a clean cloth and let it stand for 30 minutes. Add the 4 cups milk to the mixture, mix well, and turn into a jelly bag or cheesecloth-lined sieve. Let it drain completely. Chill the liquid and use for making fancy or, in India, feast-day drinks.

NOTE Dry the ball of rose pulp left in the cloth. Store it in the refrigerator. Use it to flavor puddings and other desserts.

INDEX

Sambals or Savories, 182; see also
  Appetizers
Chutney Ham, 187
Coconut Sambal Sauce, Hot, 188
Egg, 188
Fish, I and II, 185
Mango, 188
Miniature-Shrimp, 187
Shark, 186
Shrimp, American, 187
Shrimp, Curried, 186
Smoked-Fish, 186
Spicy Dip for Sambals, 189
Sauces; see also Salad Dressings
  Avocado Dressing, 164
  Banana Coconut Dressing, 164
  Carrot Sauce, Yoga, 164
  Chili Coconut Sauce, 188
  Coconut Sambal Sauce, Hot, 188
  Curried Sauce, Hawaiian, 20
  Curry Paste, Planter's, 19
  Curry Sauce I, 17; II, 18; III, 19
  Curry Sauce for Peppers, 148
  Darjeeling Relish, 191
  Korma, 20
  Peanut-Butter Dressing, 164
  Sauce (for Calcutta Meatballs),
    55
  Spicy Dip for Sambals, 189
  Tomato Sauce, Curried, 117
  White Sauce, Basic, 17
  Yogurt Mayonnaise, 31
Savories, 182; for recipes see Ap-
  petizers; Sambals or Savories
Scallops, Curried, 106
Semolina Halwa, 227
Sesame Balls, 223
Sesame seed, 12, 137
Shark Sambals, 186
Shellfish; see also names of Shell-
  fish
  Koftas, North Indian, 105
  Timbales, Hawaiian Curried, 105
Sherbet, see Ice Creams and Ices
Shikar (Hunter's) Curry, 76
Shrimp(s) and Prawn(s)

American Shrimp Sambals, 187
Bamboo Prawn Curry, Thailand,
  110
Bengal Shrimp Pulao, 131
Calcutta Gray Shrimps, Curried,
  111
Curried Shrimp Sambals, 186
Goa Shrimp Curry, 109
Hawaiian Curried Shrimps, 111
Madras Prawns, Curried, 113
Malay Curried Shrimps, 110
Miniature-Shrimp Sambals, 187
Nilgiri Curried Shrimps, 113
Prawn Soup, 41
Shrimps or Prawns, Curried, I,
  107; II and III, 108
Shrimps or Prawns, Pulao of, 130
Singapore Curried Shrimps, 112
Shub Deg (Mutton Curry), 60
Sikh Curries, 70
Sikh Kababs I and II, 71
Singapore Curried Lobster, 103
Singapore Curried Shrimps, 112
Singapore Dressing, 178
Sole, Fillets of, Curried, 102
Soufflé, Ham, Curried, 66
Soups, Cold
  Apple, Curried, 42
  Broccoli, Curried, 43
  Buttermilk Fruit, 43
  Coconut, Curried, 42
  Dal, 44
  Potato, Curried, 44
Soups, Hot
  Almond Lamb Mulligatawny, 40
  Chicken Mulligatawny I and II,
    37
  Curried Ginger, 38
  Lentil Mulligatawny, 39
  Mutton Mulligatawny, 39
  Prawn, 41
  Rice, Hawaiian, 41
South India Curried Eggplant, 69
South India Curried Pork (ham),
  65
South India Curry, 69

Village Curried Oxtail, 80
Vindaloos, 95
  Chicken, Portuguese (Goa), 95
  Duck, Portuguese (Goa), 95
Vinegar, Honey Vinegar, Yoga, 243
Violet Petals, Crystallized, 241

Watercress Chutney, 191
Western Style Standard Beef Curry, 48
Wheat-Free Orange Bread, 171
White Sauce, Basic, 17

Yams, see Sweet Potato(es) and Yam(s)
Yoga Dishes
  Apricot Milk, 244
  Avocado Dressing, 164
  Banana Coconut Dressing, 164
  Bean Curry (*Foogath*), 159
  Bean-Sprout Curry, 159
  Bread, 168
  Bread, Unleavened, 169
  Buttermilk Pie, 237
  Cabbage, 159
  Carrot Sauce, 164
  Cashews, Curried, 157
  Cheesecake, 236
  Chutney (Sun-cooked), 202
  Coconut Chutney, 189
  Coconut Curry, 157
  dietary practices, 155, 235
  Dressings, 164
  Eggplant, 160
  Fruit Yam Sweets, 236
  Gingered Cucumbers, 160
  Green Peppers, 161
  Honey Vinegar, 243
  Icing, 237
  Lentil Bread, 168
  Low-Starch Piecrust, 237
  Nut Roast, 156
  Oatmeal Cakes, 235
  Parsley Curry, 161
  Parsnip Pancakes, 158

Peanut-Butter Dressing, 164
Peanut Cakes, 157
Pea Pulao, 163
Pineapple Relish, 210
Pumpkin Bread, 169
Red Cabbage, 160
Rice and Cabbage, 162
Rice and Lentils, 163
Sauces, 164
Sweet Potatoes, 162
Sweets, 235
Tomato Curry, 162
Yogurt Pancakes, 158
Yogurt, 30
Yogurt-Flavored Dishes
  Acorn Squash with Yogurt, 31
  Bengal Shrimp Pulao, 131
  Chicken *Biriana*, 133
  Chicken *Korma*, 85
  Egg Yogurt Dressing, 179
  Korma, 20
  Lassi, 243
  Moslem Spiced Chicken, 84
  Mutton Curry (*Shub Deg*), 60
  Orange Yogurt Dressing, 179
  Pumpkin Salad, 177
  Vegetable Yogurt Mold, 33
  Yoga Cabbage, 159
  Yogurt Fish Bake, 34
  Yogurt Fruit-Juice Dressing, 178
  Yogurt Marinade, 131
  Yogurt Mayonnaise, 31
  Yogurt Omelet, 33
  Yogurt Onions, 32
  Yogurt Pancakes, 158
  Yogurt Penoche, 238
  Yogurt Potato Pancakes, 32
  Yogurt Soy Cakes, 33
  Yogurt Spiced Cabbage, 31
  Yogurt-Stuffed Potatoes, 32

Zucchini
  American Curried, see note, 151
  salad, see note, 177
  Spiced, 152